D1824646

Penguin Books
East Wind, West Wind

Fang Xiangshu was born in Shanghai in 1953. He
graduated as a teacher of English as a Foreign Language
from Nanjing Teachers University, studied at Shanghai
Foreign Languages Institute, and first came to Australia in
1984 as an International Teaching Fellow. After complet-
ing a Graduate Diploma of Education at the Institute of
Education, University of Melbourne, he is now doing a
PhD. He is a lecturer in Chinese Language and Culture at
Deakin University.

Trevor Hay was born in Adelaide in 1946. He taught
English and Asian studies in high schools in Adelaide and
Melbourne, and was the first International Teaching
Fellow (tertiary) in China (1981–82); he has also been a
consultant for UNICEF in China. He speaks Mandarin
Chinese fluently, and is a regular contributor to
Melbourne newspapers, magazines and radio programs.
His first book, *Tartar City Woman*, won the Braille Book
of the Year award in 1991. He is a senior lecturer in
education at the Institute of Education, University of
Melbourne.

East Wind, West Wind

Fang Xiangshu and Trevor Hay

To Mark Elvin,
Best wishes.
Trevor Hay
July 1996

PENGUIN BOOKS

Penguin Books Australia Ltd
487 Maroondah Highway, PO Box 257
Ringwood, Victoria 3134, Australia
Penguin Books Ltd
Harmondsworth, Middlesex, England
Viking Penguin, A Division of Penguin Books USA Inc.
375 Hudson Street, New York, New York 10014, USA
Penguin Books Canada Limited
10 Alcorn Avenue, Toronto, Ontario, Canada M4V 1E4
Penguin Books (N.Z.) Ltd
182–190 Wairau Road, Auckland 10, New Zealand

First published by Penguin Books Australia, 1992
10 9 8 7 6 5 4 3 2 1
Copyright © Fang Xiangshu and Trevor Hay, 1992

Typeset in 12/13 pt Berner by Midland Typesetters, Maryborough, Vic.
Made and printed in Australia by Griffin Press Pty Ltd, Adelaide

National Library of Australia
Cataloguing-in-Publication data:
Fang, Xiangshu, 1953–
East wind, west wind.
ISBN 0 14 015986 X.
1. Fang, Xiangshu, 1953–   . 2. Chinese – Australia – Biography.
3. China – History – 1949 – Biography. 4. China – Biography.
I. Hay, Trevor, 1946–   . II. Title.
951.05092

For Yang Xiaoping –
'Death will be but a pause'

For Bi Lijun and Jennifer Hay,
who endured so much

For Effie Ella Clara Hay (Sally)

Contents

Note from Authors

In general, the system of transcription (spelling of Chinese words) used in this book is *Hanyu pinyin* – the Chinese spelling system currently in use in the People's Republic of China, and in international media agencies. This applies to the names of people and places (for example, Fang Xiangshu, and Beijing) and other examples where Chinese (Mandarin) words are transcribed. However, for the convenience of the reader, some words have not been transcribed into *Hanyu pinyin* but retained in a more familiar form (for example, Hong Kong, Yangtze, I Ching, Peking Opera, Sun Yat-sen).

Chinese names consist of a family name (such as Fang), which comes before the given name (Xiangshu). In general, the given name is used by family members and, in some cases, by intimate friends. Among familiars outside this category the usual form of address between friends and colleagues consists of the family name preceded by *Lao* (literally 'old') for seniors, or *Xiao* (literally 'little' or 'young') for juniors. Contemporaries below middle age may address each other as *Xiao* (for example, Xiao Fang), and when above middle age may address each other as *Lao* (for example, Lao Song). On formal occasions, Chinese tend to use a title, such as an occupational category, followed by the family name, or the full name (such as Comrade Fang Xiangshu, Secretary Kong, President Gui Hong). It should be noted that these are not strict rules but a guide to Chinese usage. In this book the authors have used whole names (for example, Hu Dachuan) and family names (Hu) interchangeably to give the same varied effect as occurs in the use of proper names in English.

The word 'cadre', used throughout, is a standard translation of the Chinese word *ganbu*, which denotes any rank in the Communist government or party hierarchy.

The unit of Chinese currency is the yuan, which consists of 100 fen. This currency is used for domestic purposes in the People's Republic of China. An alternative form of currency, foreign exchange certificates (*wai hui juan*), is employed for transactions between foreigners and various Chinese agencies, or for the purchase of goods and services with a foreign component.

During the period described in this book, $A1 was equivalent to 2.4 yuan. Fang Xiangshu's wage, as a junior university lecturer, was approximately 70 yuan per month, comparable with that of the average factory or clerical worker.

The jin is a Chinese unit of weight (1 jin = 500 g).

Prologue

Fang Xiangshu and I first met in 1981 when I stepped out of a brittle, cramped and smoke-filled aircraft into the pulverising heat of a Nanjing summer. In the south, where the heat and humidity were already more than enough for me, I had been warned several times that I should stay right away from Nanjing in the summer, and that Nanjing was 'one of the three furnaces of China'. The words were heavy with menace and foreboding, as if I were being warned not to stray onto the moor at night. I was also told that I should get out of Nanjing before the winter.

Fang had been assigned to meet me at the airport, and he must have been taken aback by my appearance at that first meeting. I was a classic foreign devil, alarmingly large, 'yellow-haired' and red-bearded. More than that, I happened to be wearing a purple silk shirt – a fashion statement akin to wearing lipstick in the eyes of the average mainland Chinese, who is inclined to be very rigid about appropriate clothing for the sexes. What's more, I was carrying a guitar case about the size of a small coffin, and wearing fur-lined, calf-high flying boots. The boots were for winter and simply would not fit into a suitcase that had been crammed with indispensables for a year of teaching English in China: Chinese dictionaries, Bullfinch's *Complete Mythology*, a stack of Russian novels, and a sample of great Western music, including J. S. Bach, Cole Porter, and Slim Dusty.

In spite of this inauspicious beginning, Fang became my teacher, guide and friend during the following months. During that time also, it was announced that he had passed an important examination and had become eligible to go abroad for further study. I took a photograph of him in my room in Nanjing on the day he heard the news. He wanted a special picture of himself, sitting in my ancient armchair, 'glass in hand', as he put it. Over my dusty bottle of duty-free whisky, his acrid Chinese cigarettes, and a disgusting mound of crabs and eels, we dreamed of the future, of co-operation in translation and research. We even dreamed of writing a book together. But we never dreamed of this one.

Fang finally came to Australia in 1984, after years of frustration and delay. For reasons we document he stayed on, and in 1988 we began work on our book. In fact it was November 1988, and the air was charged with memories of 1968, of student unrest and people power, of the 'Year of Dreams' in Prague, Paris and Chicago. But 1968 was a year of rude awakenings too. In Beijing 1968 was the year of demobilisation and disgrace for the Red Guards, although fellow-students around the world continued to get high on the fumes of China's Cultural Revolution. Twenty years later, when Fang Xiangshu and I began writing, foreigners were still getting high on China, under the influence of the old 'capitalist roader', Deng Xiaoping. Economic pragmatism and the 'four modernisations' seemed to represent a new model of people-power in China. For a time it seemed our voices would be drowned out by the applause.

In 1990 Salman Rushdie, looking back on a year of amazing political changes, said 'those of us who were young in 1968 used to talk of that moment as some great shift in power toward the people. But actually nothing happened: a few kids ran down the street chased by the police.' Rushdie and others said that 1989 might well be the year when people-power really happened. But they were not talking about China. In June 1989 a few kids ran down the street in Beijing, chased by the People's Liberation Army. But those kids, whatever their aims, made it possible for foreigners to talk about human rights and democracy in China without being called naive or accused of being ignorant of Chinese culture or of China's 'stage of development'. Not that their murderers have run out of arguments, or apologists – they now claim that there is no such thing as 'abstract' human rights. But nowhere are they more abstract than in China.

Fang and I took a long time to make real progress with this book. For one thing, it was difficult to decide who should be the narrator, or how much of each person's story should be told. We talked for hours and hours about it. At one stage we decided that it was such a difficult matter that we needed to put the whole thing into the hands of a narrator, a kind of literary counsel, who would present the story on behalf of the two clients. But then we did not know the ending, especially since things kept on happening to both of us. As Somerset Maugham observed, fact is a poor story-teller when it comes to this business of a beginning and an ending. Of course, this story was always going to be about Fang and China, and might well have begun and ended there, but for an incident in a street in Melbourne in July 1986 – an incident which tangled our lives together in a way that neither of us could ever have imagined, for all our talk and all our dreaming.

About the time of the massacre in Beijing in June 1989, we resolved some of our difficulties about who was telling the story and so on, and we decided where we would start and where we would finish. But then 'fact' intervened and insisted on telling the story its own way, regardless of our wishes as human beings or our judgement as authors. It is still a story of China. It is still Fang Xiangshu's account of what it is like to be in trouble in a totalitarian society, and of great moments in his life during the astonishing period from Mao's Cultural Revolution to Deng's 'open-door policy'. But it is also a reminder that everywhere you look, including the Western 'democracies', people are being chased down the street by the agents of the state.

Some names and places have been changed in the telling of this story, for the usual reasons.

Trevor Hay

1   The Return of the Scholar

The day I had been dreading had finally come. 14 December 1986. Ted Moroney drove me and Bi Lijun, my wife of four months, to Tullamarine Airport. Ted's wife Jean and their daughter Linda came along to try somehow to ease the pain of the separation that was only hours away. Linda was my former student, and her parents had made us part of the family. Bi Lijun was crying softly, and Jean and Linda had given up any attempt at small talk, but Ted pressed on resolutely with a tourist spiel on the suburbs through which we were passing. At the airport I busied myself with boarding arrangements, and in paying $A221 excess luggage fee.

Suddenly I saw three Chinese men, two of whom I recognised. One was the former First Secretary of the Chinese Embassy in Australia, Li Shunxin, now Deputy Director of the National Education Department's Foreign Relations Bureau. The other was Li's successor in the Embassy, Ni Chuanrong. I decided I should make myself known, and asked Bi Lijun and the others to go on ahead while I paid the obligatory respects to these big shots.

'Lao Li, Lao Ni, how are you?' I said, addressing them as familiars.

'Oh, it's Xiao Fang', said Li Shunxin, reciprocating my friendly manner. 'How are you? What are you doing here?'

'I'm flying to Beijing today, and then back to university tomorrow.'

Ni Chuanrong seemed delighted at this and introduced me to the third official, Deputy Minister Zhang of the National Education Department.

'This is Xiao Fang, you know Fang Xiangshu, from Nanjing Teachers University.'

'Oh,' said Zhang, in apparent recognition, 'yes, of course, he's the one you mentioned last night.'

I thought this was a little odd, but decided that they must have discussed me in relation to Trevor's court case, since it was such an unusual business.

'Lao Ni and I have come to see Deputy Minister Zhang off,' explained Li Shunxin, 'he's going on the same plane as you, it seems.'

'Xiao Fang, it's terrific that you're on my plane', beamed Zhang. 'Now if I get into any bother through not understanding English, you can give me a hand.'

They all seemed very cordial towards me, as if we were old friends who had not seen each other for years.

'Is your wife going home with you?' asked Ni Chuanrong.

'No, she wants to see if she can study for a year or two in Australia, and if that doesn't come off, she'll look up some relatives in Hong Kong for a while, before she goes back – she already has permission from Nanjing Teachers University—'

'Yes, yes, of course', they chorused, apparently quite anxious to dispel any impression that they had any concerns about Bi Lijun's plans or movements.

After a few more pleasantries, I rejoined Bi Lijun and the others near the international departure point. It was almost time to go, and there was little point in prolonging the agony, so I said my goodbyes and walked briskly through the doors which separate one country from another. In a way I was grateful for the doors that marked the border for me and separated Australia from China. Now I could face up to what lay ahead.

A little later, in the transit lounge in Sydney, I saw Deputy Minister Zhang again. At first it seemed that he might be coming over for a chat, to kill time, but when he got within greeting distance he suddenly averted his gaze and walked past. He continued on to a newspaper stand, bought a *Sydney Morning Herald*, found himself a chair and began reading. Just a short while ago in Melbourne, Zhang had said he did not understand English, and might need help during the flight.

At 1.15 in the afternoon, I boarded the aircraft and found that there were many empty seats. I chose a window-seat, and, when the plane took off, looked down on white surf dividing blue sea and green shallows from red-brown earth. Australia was so close, and yet so remote, so familiar and yet so strange. It was no longer a question of distance, or time, but of being excluded. The flight attendant eventually intruded on these thoughts to ask if I'd like a drink.

'May I have a gin-and-tonic, please?'

I felt like a character in the television program *Follow Me*, so popular in China as a means of improving one's English.

'Certainly, sir.'

All the passengers had been given a small bottle of white wine before the meal, but I thought I'd better keep mine and give it to someone as a gift, since I'd had no time to buy many presents for people before I left Australia. I drank some red wine, and enjoyed a seafood cocktail. From the back of the plane I could see rows of my compatriots in front of me, all wearing blue suits big enough to leave room for at least two jumpers underneath. The flight attendant was having some minor difficulties with these passengers because she could not speak Mandarin. When she reached me, I said, in English, 'White coffee, no sugar, please.'

'You must be the only Chinese who doesn't have sugar in his tea or coffee!'

'We Chinese are really fond of sweet things', I explained, and then for some reason thought of the movie *Some Like It Hot*, and Jack Lemmon, chin cradled in his hands, leering

3

at Marilyn Monroe, 'Hello-o-ooh, sugar.' I could not help feeling just a little proud of my sophistication in matters of Western culture.

Someone I couldn't remember had said that when you set out on a journey you always begin by thinking of the place you have just left, but as you go on you think more and more of your destination. It seemed to be true. Although I had felt very sentimental about leaving Australia two hours before, this emotion was now almost competely replaced by the desire to find answers to the questions I would have to face. Why did the Foreign Languages Department suddenly seem unable to go on without me? Why was I being recalled? How upset would the administration be over my involvement in Trevor's court case, and the subsequent delay in my return? Nevertheless, my greatest anxiety, and the biggest question, was whether Bi Lijun's parents would approve of me. I had never even seen my parents-in-law, not even to ask for her hand.

The courtship, of necessity, had been a secret in China, because I was a teacher and she was a student in the same university. Not that I was *her* teacher, but it was still a matter of policy as well as convention, that we should not have such a relationship. In any case, students were not permitted to date at all during their studies, let alone with a staff member. In spite of that, our romance had continued for two years, during which we could do nothing more intimate than to write letters to each other. When she graduated, the secret could be revealed, but then I was overseas in Australia. Eventually she too had a chance to go to Australia; her parents gave their consent for her to go abroad by herself, and to be married to a person they had never seen. Now this mysterious son-in-law was returning, leaving 'the pearl of their palm' behind, alone in a strange land. What sort of reaction would they have to all that? Should I have taken her with me?

4

At nine o'clock in the evening the plane landed at Beijing airport. Everything went smoothly – entry formalities, customs, baggage collection. At ten o'clock I walked out of the airport carrying one large and one small suitcase, and with two smaller bags strung around me. A little swarm of taxi drivers buzzed about, attracted by the prospect of a fare from one so burdened; they were quickly repelled when I explained that I was going only a little more than a kilometre to the Capital Airport Guesthouse. Some said they might be able to manage it if I could pay in Hong Kong dollars or American dollars. I offered them Australian currency, but they had never heard of it and wanted to know the official exchange rate. I told them: '2.4 Chinese yuan per dollar, hard currency'; but they insisted on American or Hong Kong dollars, even Japanese yen or Deutschmarks. *Not* Australian dollars. I felt very disappointed, almost slighted, at their rejection of my Australian currency. After some time I found a driver who would accept *wai hui juan* (Chinese foreign exchange certificates), for which I traded some of my Australian currency at the airport exchange counter.

When I arrived at the guesthouse, I found the entrance door locked. I looked through a window, and saw one or two lights, and people moving around – and a reception office which appeared to be open for business. I knocked several times on the door, but no one took the slightest notice. Then two taxis pulled up and deposited six or seven more travellers. They observed the locked door; one of them knocked, but there was no answer – then several began knocking in unison, making a terrible din. Two white-clad attendants emerged from the office, but they made no move whatever to open up.

'What do you want to go knocking on the door for? There's no vacancy', one shouted.

The new arrivals were represented by a female comrade,

5

who protested that they had booked their rooms before they went overseas on the 28th of November.

'Who took the booking? Family name, and given name?' countered the attendants. This stymied the travellers.

'Well, this person was male, quite young, tall and dressed in a sort of white uniform.'

'Everyone here wears a white uniform, but we have no tall young men', said a voice from within. From my position I could see the owner of the voice, a tall young man.

Once again the delegation seemed lost for words, and they held a little conference to determine their next move. After a while the spokeswoman returned to the battle, with a touch of desperation in her voice this time. I thought of the fox in the fable, flattering the crow about his delightful voice and elegant gestures, and tricking him into a burst of song so that he dropped the piece of meat he held in his mouth. What means of persuasion would she employ to make these white crows open their beaks and drop the keys?

'Comrade, since you keep such precise records, and rely on such accuracy of detail, it must be possible to check the records to see if there was a booking made on the 28th of November.'

'What's the point of checking? If there's no vacancy, there's no vacancy. You can check as much as you like, but it won't create a vacancy.'

Both attack and defence grew louder and louder in their claims and rebuttals, and each development of the argument forced the contestants closer and closer against the pane of glass, like dogs barking ferociously at each other through a fence. By now, the insiders had summoned staff reinforcements, and quite a crowd had gathered to repulse the invaders with shouts and sneers.

After some considerable time, it appeared that some of the insiders might be taking a slightly more conciliatory stance. The register was produced, opened at the page for

28 November, and pressed up against the dirty window for the outsiders to view.

'There you are. See for yourselves!'

The spokeswoman replied to this gesture.

'How about turning on a few lights in there? I can't see a thing.'

I craned my neck to see over the grubbiest part of the glass, and peered inside to see what the reaction would be. I could not see a great deal beyond a large sign which proclaimed this guesthouse to be a 'Beijing Municipality Advanced Level Model of Courtesy and Civility'.

Meanwhile, things had reached a stalemate. No one wanted to back down, and there appeared to be little hope of any mutually satisfactory resolution to the problem. A man of about fifty or sixty made his way to the front of the exasperated travellers. He seemed to have an air of authority about him, as if he were not used to being trifled with. Everyone fell silent.

'All right, what's going on here? What seems to be the problem?'

'We made a booking long ago, and they won't let us in.'

The rather imposing figure surpassed all expectations.

'Right. I happen to know that the Capital Airport Guesthouse is run by the National Ministry of Transport. Open this door! I want to make a call to the Minister.'

At last the outsiders had a champion. A thrill of relief and excitement ran around the exhausted little band, which a moment ago had been resigned to total defeat and humiliation.

The two guesthouse staff who were manning the door exchanged glances. Not a word was spoken. Suddenly the door swung open, and in the melee I was able to dart into the foyer, a suitcase in each hand and two bags dangling around my neck, feeling rather like an ant buried under a large crust. I was determined that I would do *my* arguing from the inside. When the commotion subsided, negotiations were recommenced – largely on a first-come, first-served basis. Our collective identity as fellow-travellers had been lost somewhere in the dash across the threshold. I explained my situation to a young man.

'Look, I didn't book, but surely you can find something for me? I don't even mind if there's no bed. Just a place to sit overnight is OK. In any case I'm going on to Nanjing tomorrow, and it's already eleven o'clock now. It's freezing outside!'

The attendant saw that I was on my own, and nodded. He led me upstairs, and opened the door of one of the rooms. There was already someone inside.

'This is a double room. There are two beds. There's an empty one for you.'

The occupant of the other bed sat up as the attendant left, slamming the door behind him. I was very embarrassed, and apologised to my room-mate for waking him in the middle of the night. He didn't seem to mind at all, but threw on some clothes and got up to give me a hand with my luggage.

'When you are at home, you can rely on your parents, but when you leave home, you must rely on friends', he said reassuringly.

After a little conversation, in which he found that I was about six years older than himself, he began calling me *da ge* [big brother].

'*Da ge*, I'm sorry but I don't think I'll be able to go back to sleep now. I wonder if you'd mind if we had a cigarette and just chatted for a while?'

'Yes, of course. It's my fault for waking you. Have one of mine.'

My Peter Jackson packet led to curiosity about where I had bought such an unusual brand. 'Marlboro' or 'Three Fives' he knew, but Peter Jackson was a strange-looking packet to him.

'I bought them in Australia. I've been abroad, teaching and studying for two and a half years.'

'Really? That must have been wonderful! Tell me about it. Are there all kinds of strange ways and customs to get used to?'

In the course of answering a dozen questions and comparing foreign ways with Chinese, I discovered that this new friend was on a business trip, representing a fur factory in the town of Yanji, Jilin Province, not far from Huma, where I had done my own stint of 're-education' in the late 1960s and early 70s. Huma county, Heilongjiang Province, and the Yanji area, were not only close geographically, but very similar places – poor, backward and remote. People in these areas regarded someone who had ridden on a bus as a citizen of the world. Now here was a young man who flew planes to Beijing and negotiated contracts for his work unit! I reflected on the massive changes which had occurred in China since the 1960s. There was just no comparison, and life was unquestionably better now.

When I came to the part of my story concerning more recent difficulties, of paying for a taxi and so on, the younger man groaned in sympathy, and magnanimously declared, '*Da ge*, don't you worry about your luggage any more, or those damned taxi drivers. *I* will carry your luggage to the airport in the morning!'

'No, no, no, please – that's not at all necessary, but thank you, my friend.'

I was really moved, and comforted, to think that after so long away and after all these changes I could bump into such a good sort – and from my old village at that. I offered him the little bottle of Jacob's Creek riesling I had been given on the plane; the young man made the customary refusals, but finally accepted. After a little more discussion I suggested that since my friend had business in the morning and a very early flight to catch, he should try to get some sleep.

On the third night after my arrival in Nanjing, I wrote to my wife.

Dearest Lijun,

How are you?

Once again we are separated and once again the time has come when we have only letters to speak for our feelings. I don't know how much more of our lives we are going to spend apart. It is just a little more than four months since we were married, and here we are, separated again. I know that after you came to Australia I promised you we would not be split up again, and I can't begin to tell you how sorry I am that I have failed you. Tonight oceans divide us, but don't forget our wedding ceremony and Kahlil Gibran's words, in the poem that we chose –

'Love one another, but make not a bond of love.
Rather let it be a moving sea, between the shores of your souls.'

I had a good trip, despite a bit of fuss and bother getting a ticket to Nanjing at Beijing Airport. That reminds me, if you can't get an offer to study overseas with private sponsorship, and you have to return, don't get a connecting flight from Beijing. It's much more convenient to fly to Hong Kong and then on to Nanjing or Shanghai. I got in to Nanjing on the fifteenth, at about seven in the evening. Dean Rui, Secretary Kong, and my old classmate Jianhe, now working in the Personnel Department, were at the airport to meet me. They seemed excessively formal and polite I thought, and yet weren't in much of a hurry to answer any of my questions.

'Where will I be living?'

'Oh, never mind, we can discuss that later. For the time being you can stay at Wu Shen's place, he can live out for the moment.'

'What classes will I take, what level, which grades?'

'Later, later.'

Well, if everything could be discussed later why did they issue 'twelve gilded commands' to get me back from Australia, and away from you?

We all know each other pretty well, since I have been out with them on a number of occasions to various cities to conduct entrance exams for the university. They had always been very nice to me, and I couldn't see why two years abroad should make such a difference that they should put on bureaucratic airs. Jianhe told me, rather officiously, that the Dean and Secretary were extremely busy. He went on to say that since the reforms there are a lot of new regulations at the university, and one of them is that only cadres at department level or higher, or staff members of the rank of professor or associate professor, are entitled to the use of a vehicle. If it were not for the fact that it was the Dean and Secretary who had come to the airport, if it had been just some old ordinary staff member, then I would not have been able to avail myself of this privilege. In other words, 'Don't get the idea that this car is for you. Your status doesn't warrant use of the university mini-bus.'

Jianhe's hint was pretty broad, and I wasted no time in thanking these important cadres quite

11

profusely. But I didn't really understand. There isn't a direct bus between the airport and the university, and it would be almost an impossibility to get the airport bus to the city centre and then change to the public bus for the university. Since I had so much luggage, how would I manage without the college mini-bus, our 'little loaf'? It was not a matter of status but of necessity. Anyway, when the driver heard me thanking the big shots, he seemed to get quite annoyed with me and said, 'I hadn't even had my meal when they grabbed me for this job.' So I had to make my apologies to him and shower thanks on him too. Everything seemed to have been arranged at the last minute, and I couldn't see why. I asked Jianhe in a very low voice if the Foreign Languages Department had received my cable, and he said he had heard something about it a week or so ago.

I'm writing from Wu Shen's room at the moment, and pretty soon I'll have to let him have it back. He came around this morning, and asked me if I could possibly go back to my own place because he needs his room again. So these days I'm on the run a bit, looking for a place to settle. I've also been several times to see the bosses, to ask about my teaching duties, and my accommodation, but they either tell me they don't know, or like the other day at the airport they say, 'Later, later, we'll discuss all that later.' I don't mind, let them say what they like about the teaching duties, but I do need a place to stay. Anyway, no more complaints, what's the point? What can't be changed can't be changed, and that's that, and my complaints will never alter the pace of life here – perhaps my reaction is what is known as 'the second culture shock'. They say the shock of coming back is more severe than the first, when you arrive in a Western country for the first time. But believe me, it is always easier to adjust from a quick tempo to a slow one than vice versa. In fact, I suppose I'll soon be like every one else around here, oblivious to the characteristics of Chinese behaviour which seem so outlandish to foreigners – like the woman I saw the other day near the Drum Tower, blithely hawking at the foot of a large 'No Spitting' sign, and no one taking the slightest notice. I'm going to see your parents on Saturday, the twentieth. I'm a bit worried about it – what they'll think of me, etc. – but, as they say, 'The rice is cooked' and it's too late to change anything now even if they don't like me. Well, I'll close for now, and write again soon. Give my regards to Jean and Ted, and everyone.

All my love,
Xiao Fang

Nanjing Teachers University
1989, December 17

In fact, things became more and more difficult for me after I wrote the letter, but culture shock was the least of my worries. The first strange impressions I had recorded on my return were only a vague premonition, and the uneasy feelings I had over the issue of my accommodation were only a hint.

For days I traipsed around from department to department, office to office, in search of accommodation, and reflecting on the differences between cultures and systems. No doubt

13

socialism has some very fine points, and the expense of accommodation in the West was astronomical from what I could judge – maybe there was some truth in the claim that poor people in Melbourne slept in disused water pipes or garbage containers – but it is still a real drawback to depend on your work unit for the allocation of a place to live. 'From each according to his ability to each according to his needs.' Well, my ability was not insignificant, and my need was pressing enough, but then the Party had long ago edited Marx's words, and now it was 'to each according to his contribution'. Isn't that what happens in the West too? – you contribute enough money and you can have whatever you need. The odd thing was that I had had no difficulty obtaining a room to myself before I left for Australia, and my friends and colleagues, Wei He, Su Jin and Gao Yong, who were still in America and Australia, also had flats which were left vacant for some time while they were away. When the university's property and accom-modation allocation clerk heard my story he was also a little puzzled. How was it that a thirty-three-year-old university staff member, with ten years' service, was having difficulty finding a flat for himself and his wife? Especially when his wife was herself a staff member. The clerk said there must be some mistake, and that he would check it all out and let me know.

Next time I went to the accommodation office, the clerk had changed his tune.

'Yes, it's true that some people have their accommodation reserved for them while they are abroad, but that's because it was allocated under the old regulations. Since we are in a period of reform there are, of course, new regulations, and the old ones no longer apply.'

'Well, what are the new regulations?'

'The new regulation stipulates that these requests should go through the proper channels, more systematically than

14

in the past, and you should therefore go back to your own department and lodge a formal request for due consideration. You know, you really ought to appreciate the problem here. I would not have thought that you could forget, even after your two years in Australia, that there is an acute shortage of accommodation here in China.'

'Oh yes, of course, I understand completely, and I'm not asking for any preferential treatment. I'm perfectly happy to be treated just like any one else. China has an enormous population and scarce resources, and everything must be done according to the regulations – to be fair to every one. I have no disagreement whatsoever with any of that. I'm really only asking for my basic entitlement, just like every one else.'

'Well, be that as it may, requests for accommodation are not yet being processed. You must wait until the proper time, and then you should take your turn. Your request will be considered in due course, according to the proper procedures.'

'But I saw Zhao Yangqin ten minutes ago, on my way to this office, and she was right in the middle of shifting her things. She said everybody was busy arranging accommodation at the moment. Don't misunderstand me, but I would have thought that my needs were, if anything, more pressing than hers.'

'Oh, that's quite different. The flat she is moving to is in a separate category reserved for special cases. Only the president of the university has discretionary power to approve allocations from this category.'

'What's so special about Zhao Yangqin?'

'Comrade, we have not yet progressed to the stage of "to each according to his needs". We are at a transitional stage of "to each according to his contribution". Comrade Zhao and Comrade Shen Pangeng have made a great contribution to our university, and given us a great deal of prestige abroad

15

after their most successful musical tour of Australia. Perhaps you also have made such a mighty contribution and our president is unaware of it? Perhaps you had better go and see him right away and let him know of your accomplishments?'

I was really stung by this. Had I not myself been involved in the arrangements to bring the musicians to Melbourne, as a result of the sister-college relationship between the Melbourne College of Advanced Education and Nanjing Teachers University? Had I not also helped to ensure the success of President Gui's visit to Melbourne to sign an agreement between the institutions? President Gui himself had made a point of thanking me for my work and asking me if there was anything he could do for me. At the time, even a promotion seemed possible, but now I could not even manage a place to live, let alone promotion!

But there was not much point going on about all this to him.

'I haven't made such a great contribution, but still I think my need is quite urgent, and my case should also be regarded as one of those in the special category.'

'All right, all right, but don't tell me about it. If you think that way, go and see your department about it, or talk to President Gui.'

I was really steamed up, and rushed off to the Foreign Languages Department. The administrative officer of the department, Yun Man, a very helpful lady, listened patiently to my complaint, and then said, 'Xiao Fang, calm down, I don't know how to explain to you the complexity of this situation.'

'What complexity?'

'I believe you will understand later. But now, as your senior colleague, for your own benefit I must remind you that it won't do you any good to go on arguing the point in office after office about your accommodation. At the very

16

least, people will start to say that you have risen above yourself after two years abroad. Modesty is always the great virtue of us Chinese.'

'Director Yun, I have no wish to make myself out to be something special, and I'm not arguing about taking my turn for permanent accommodation, but I must at least have somewhere to stay right now.'

'Xiao Fang, we have arranged a place for you to stay, and we'll see what we can do about the problem in the future.' She took out a key from her desk drawer, and said, 'I have to tell you that this place is not all that satisfactory, but even so it was not easy for me to get it for you. You know, for some days I have been begging the university administration to provide a place for you. Once you move in, don't make any complaints. Just believe me – the mouth is the source of disaster.'

Director Yun's attitude was quite sincere, and I had no reason not to believe her. From what she had said, I could also gather that there were things that she could not say. The suggestion seemed to be that I had said something wrong, at least in the view of the leadership.

When I left her office there was still an hour and a half to kill before my appointment with the department heads. Originally an appointment had been made the night I arrived at Nanjing Airport, and I was to see them the following day. However, when I got to the office I was told that our Foreign Relations chief, who apparently had expressed a wish to be present, was busy with Japanese guests. I thought at the time that this business about the Foreign Relations chief seemed to suggest that they were paying rather special attention to Australia, and that struck me as rather unusual.

I wandered off through the campus gardens, bare now except for an occasional magnolia or winter plum blossom, but still beautiful, especially from certain points under the

17

carved and painted eaves of the great halls, or viewed while walking between the red wooden beams of the little sheltered corridors, dripping recent snow from their roofs. I began to think about what lay in store for me, and how I would go about explaining the differences between Chinese and Western culture if I were accused of any improper or 'bourgeois' influence as a result of my stay in Australia.

Usually, when a student or staff member returns from overseas, it is customary to give a talk to students and staff on the highlights of the visit. And usually that person meets with members of the university administration beforehand to ensure that the talk is properly 'balanced', and 'well-rounded'. As a result, the first two-thirds of the talk is devoted to the comparative affluence of Western society and its technological advancement, interspersed with humorous anecdotes about life and customs in strange lands, and fascinating tales of exotic landscapes and natural features. To achieve the required balance, the last third is devoted to shocking revelations about the evils and pathologies of Western life, such as AIDS – the inevitable consequence of decadent and immoral sexual behaviour and 'emancipation'. This charge is supported with an abundance of compelling evidence and mountains of statistics on prostitution, extra-marital sex, high divorce rate, teenage promiscuity, adultery, so-called 'de facto' relationships (to be pronounced with heavy irony), homosexuality, single mothers, etc. Overall, it would appear that Westerners simply refuse to treat sex with the appropriate gravity. Everyone is sleeping with someone they shouldn't. The last third of the talk is always conscientiously noted by a very attentive audience, and it seems to have twice the impact of the first two-thirds.

Of course, several people had enquired of me over the last few days as to when I would be presenting my talk, but now that I was due to see the administration, I was quite confident that they did not want to discuss the matter of

18

balance in my homecoming address. My own agenda was also much more serious than that, and I really wanted to see if I could get to the bottom of the strange treatment I had received. In China there are 'three big categories' of problems which can cause you very serious troubles – political, economic, and 'life style'. The most serious is the political category. But I couldn't see how I could be in trouble of this kind. After all, during 1985 and 1986 the Party and the Government were themselves discussing political reform and tolerant attitudes almost every day. They even used the phrase 'double hundred', referring to the old slogan 'Let a hundred flowers bloom, let a hundred schools of thought contend.'

The economic category refers to corruption, bribery and embezzlement. I hadn't done anything remotely like that. I had brought back all the money I was supposed to hand over to the Jiangsu Provincial Government, but then Bi Li-jun *had* mentioned some business about rumours – I was thought to have become a millionaire in Australia and to be the owner of a car, some even said a golden Mercedes Benz. I told Bi Lijun that, in a way, I could be regarded as a sort of 'millionaire' compared with our colleagues back in China.

When she first arrived in Australia, I was a part-time lecturer at Victoria College in Melbourne, and the head of the campus knew that I had to support not only myself but a wife, so she gave me more teaching to do. As it happened, at about that time a colleague went to Japan, and I also took over her responsibilities, with the result that for some weeks I could make almost $A500 a week – the equivalent of an entire annual salary for my colleagues in China. If the leaders were told only this without any other explanation, such as the high cost of living for two people, and the possibility of an overseas student fee of several thousand dollars for Bi Lijun, and that the opportunity for such a high income only lasted a very short time, then of course they might easily get the wrong idea. As for my 'golden Mercedes', it was in fact a 1962 yellow Volkswagen which my friend Trevor Hay had allowed me to use. So, given the opportunity, I could dispose of the most likely rumours or allegations of misconduct in these first two categories. That left only the third – 'life style'.

It is a bit difficult to translate this last category from Chinese to English. The phrase is *shenghuo wenti* or *shenghuo zuofeng wenti,* literally 'life problem' or 'life-style problem'. Whatever the dictionary says, everyone knows there is a much clearer translation – sleeping with someone you shouldn't. This is the least serious of the three, but the most sensational. The punishment is usually a term of 're-education'. The trouble is that, unlike the other two, it is rather difficult to produce convincing evidence to refute allegations against you. How can you prove that you have not been sleeping with someone you shouldn't? And you certainly can't get away with saying, as in the case of the yellow Volkswagen, that the claims have been exaggerated.

It is always difficult for people returning from abroad to China – you just can't explain the 'life style' in foreign countries. Most Chinese students are alone, separated from their families, and there is a tremendous sense of isolation, a sudden shock in realising that there seems to be no one around, compared to China, no one to talk to – in fact the whole place seems deserted. 'Culture shock', isolation, the vast living space, unsupervised and unobserved by any neighbours, tends to make you feel a little light-headed and lonely. 'Peach-coloured' incidents (that is, sexy, romantic 'affairs', rather than the content of Western 'blue' movies) often take place under these circumstances. Sometimes the affairs are not all that peachy, because one of the partners may take advantage of the other's language difficulty, or transport and employment problems, to impose unwanted attentions. The Chinese Embassy and its student unions have tried to take control of illicit sexual activity – solicited and unsolicited – but it is not easy to catch the culprits. I have only heard of one case where a couple, both married, but not to each other, were caught 'on the spot' indulging in 'random sexual relations'.

It has always puzzled me why people in this situation would so forget themselves as to fall upon each other in full view of Chinese student union officials. Indeed, these same union officials are so thoroughly considerate as to ring one's house from time to time, checking to see if there are any unregistered male or female voices lurking uninvited in your household, just in case you should be overpowered by some succubus or incubus, I suppose. Because of this kind of conscientious supervision, overseas Chinese tend to go out of their way to ostentatiously avoid all public forms of interest in the opposite sex. In fact, the men are so worried by the possibility of gossip that they overcompensate with public displays of affection for their male colleagues. In this way they dampen speculation on the part of fellow-Chinese, but unwittingly arouse it among their Western friends.

In my own case, I was very careful not to accept invitations to witness 'bare-bottomed dancing', in bars or clubs, even when my colleagues insisted and said, 'What harm is there in looking?' Sometimes they really gave me a difficult time over it – 'Xiao Fang, what's happened to that so-called broad mind of yours? You are always the first to insist that these sort of things are personal, and no one else has the right to make judgements or interfere. Don't try to tell us that you're not interested!'

'Okay, okay', I would protest. 'I still think it's a matter of your own individual business whether you go to those places or not, so it's also my business if I don't want to go – but you needn't worry, you know I won't inform on you. I don't even want to know where you're going.'

21

I remember one time when I really was in a difficult position because of a colleague, and I just didn't know how to go about things. He had said to me that the whole point of being overseas, in a different culture, was to sample foreign delicacies. Early one morning, at about two o'clock, I returned from a trip earlier than expected. I had told my colleague I would not be back that night, but my plans to stay elsewhere overnight had been changed. On my way along the corridor to my room I passed a Greek female teacher's bedroom, and was surprised to hear male laughter coming from her room. As I turned the key in the lock of my door, the laughter came to an abrupt halt. The next day my colleague came to me, all smiles.

'Heh, heh, strange business, strange business! Suddenly, in the middle of the night, she decides she wants to try my ginseng cigarettes – oh, that one has so many interesting stories to tell, heh, heh.'

'Well, no problem', I said cagily. 'You have plenty of ginseng cigarettes on hand, don't you?'

I was really thinking that he had been a damned fool to come and blurt it out to me, because I just didn't want to know any of his business, and would rather have been in a position to feign ignorance if anything developed out of it. I didn't care if his Greek goddess wanted ginseng cigarettes or a piece of his Chinese sausage, but what if he told some- body else that he had talked to me about it? These are the subtleties that all Chinese must live with!

As I wandered about the empty campus in the sleet and wind, I went over and over things in my mind, wondering where the attack might come from. 'The mouth is the source of disaster.' What had I said and to whom, and where? The time was now getting on for half past ten, time for my interview with the department authorities. There was little more I could do, so I steeled myself and went off to face the music.

2 The Beginning of True Knowledge

That evening I sat in the dimly lit room I had been allotted. The stink of chicken manure, quicklime and damp cement added to the general air of misery in the room, along with broken windows letting in the freezing wind. I had spent a whole afternoon making this place as habitable as possible. First I tried to find the owners of the chickens, and then I swept the quicklime into a corner. Obviously this had been used as a storeroom for building materials. I then went to the student dormitory and scrounged for a few sticks of abandoned or broken furniture – a table, chair and some wooden boards to use for a bed. Now that all the signals indicated that I could be in serious trouble, I knew that I had to remain calm and think my situation through very clearly. The morning's interview with department heads had not made the situation much clearer, but certainly I knew that something was wrong.

During my two years in Australia the university's leadership had changed dramatically, as a result of Chinese central government reforms and the replacement of older cadres with younger and more professionally qualified ones. Hao Zhenyi had been made Dean after his year's experience as an International Teaching Fellow in Australia. Then, because of hepatitis, he was replaced with a lecturer who had spent years in Moscow in the 1950s. But the English language section was so large that it had to be staffed by a couple of sub-deans, chosen for their years abroad studying English in India and Britain. Since these two were, like myself, 'worker peasant soldier students' of the 1970s, I had

23

always enjoyed very cordial relations with them. Yet when I met with everybody in the office they all appeared very stony-faced, and gave the distinct impression that they would rather be elsewhere. One or two tried to excuse themselves, saying they had sick relatives to attend to.

Then I was told that the head of Foreign Relations would not be able to attend, but would try to talk to me some other time. I tried to pre-empt the difficulties that I imagined might be emerging for me.

'Oh, that's a pity, I thought we might have an opportunity to discuss the money arrangements.'

'No, no, it doesn't matter,' someone said, 'there's plenty of time yet for you to hand over the money.'

Then it started. What I call the preliminary skirmish, probing for weaknesses – they encouraged me to ramble on about everything in general: work, recreation, social events, teaching experiences and study. I noticed that some of them were dozing off. Finally, when I got to the part about my academic interests – 'the suitability of selected Western literature as teaching material in the context of Chinese political and cultural background' – they all sat up and began to take a keen interest. I must say I did not expect my topic to engage their interest in such a dramatic fashion. I began to feel that this might be a subject of some sensitivity. I explained that I had only just finished collecting materials, but had not yet started research. At this point, the heads started to nod again. I was having a lot of trouble pitching my address to the needs of my audience. In the end I left the meeting not much wiser than I had entered, but with a distinctly uneasy feeling about it all.

After I had returned to my room, I began to go over things in my mind, again and again, searching for some clue to the mystery. The room grew so cold that I cast about for some bedding to wrap around me, but what little I could find was old, threadbare, damp and mouldy. I went to my suitcase and took out the beautiful lamb's fleece and the mohair blanket which friends had given us as a wedding present, and wrapped them both around me.

I thought of Liu Aihua. She must surely know what this was all about. She was so well-informed and well-connected. Not only that, she had always been very considerate and helpful to me. I decided that I had better find some way to ring her in the morning.

Next morning I rang her from a public telephone in a shop near the back gate of the university.

'Hello, could I speak to Liu Aihua, please?'

'Mummy is busy with visitors. Who's calling please?'

'This is Fang Xiangshu, tell your Mama it is Xiao Fang.'

After a while I was greeted by a pleasant and familiar voice.

'At last you're back! I told them not to worry, that you would be back eventually. How are you? How's your wife?'

'Oh, we're all right. But I'm a bit worried about how to handle things now that I'm back, about handing over money and so on.'

'Oh, Xiao Fang – let me tell you, you can make a little bit of money because of the change in the exchange rate since we left.'

I tried very hard to find something to say, to prolong the conversation as much as possible, in the hope of picking up some useful hint about what was going on. I thought of Chen Decai, another exchange scholar.

'Oh, by the way, have you seen Xiao Chen? I remember you promised us both a dinner when we all got back.'

'Xiao Fang, exactly when did you get back?'

'Just a few days ago.'

'Then you should be taking it easy, perhaps you should go and see your parents in Shanghai. Do I have to play big sister to you all the time and remind you of your duties? There's plenty of time to be talking about parties and dinners later.'

'Yes, of course, of course, you've caught me out again – as always. OK. I'll get in touch with you later.'

After talking to Liu Aihua I felt greatly relieved. First, she didn't seem to have heard anything unpleasant, or she would at least have given me a hint. If there was something, it must be relatively minor. Second, and most importantly, there was absolutely no suggestion of any change in her attitude towards me.

So much had happened since Liu and I first met in 1984. At that time I was in very low spirits, because my dream of going abroad seemed further away than ever, despite the wonderful promise of recent years. In 1982 the Jiangsu Provincial Government held the first examination to select potential overseas scholars. My university sent eight candidates to compete with hundreds from other institutions. Although these were mainly middle-aged lecturers, there were a few candidates who had been sent along to the exams to gain a bit of experience for next time. They were not really expected to succeed. I was one of these.

The examination consisted of written and oral sections. The written part was itself divided into three sections: translation from Chinese to English of Lu Xun's 'The Story of a Kite', translation from English to Chinese of an article in *Time* magazine about American foreign policy, and some critical evaluation in English of a quotation from Francis Bacon.

As nearly as I can remember, the quotation from Bacon was 'To spend too much time in studies is sloth . . . to judge wholly by the rule of books is the humour of the scholar.' I really addressed myself to this challenge and began by paraphrasing it like this: 'To devote oneself excessively to academic pursuits is a kind of indolence, and it is part of the academic mentality to assess every situation by means of textbook knowledge.' Then, rather delighted with myself, and feeling very smug because I had recently come across this medieval usage of 'humour', which I felt certain my fellow-candidates would misunderstand, I went on, making a conscious attempt to fashion some clever epigram of my own to echo Francis Bacon in his exposure of scholarly arrogance – 'To know one's own ignorance is the beginning of true knowledge.' What I was really thinking, of course, was that to know the true meaning of the word 'humour' was the beginning of a trip abroad.

After the exam, when we were all conducting our post-mortems, I looked on gravely as my colleagues debated the meaning of Francis Bacon's words. I tried earnestly to act as if there was some confusion in my mind about the precise significance of the word 'humour', but inside I was secretly congratulating myself that I had pulled off a master stroke.

In fact, I took even greater pleasure in the way things had gone in the oral exam. The examiner turned out to be an associate professor in British and American literature. First, as a matter of routine, we talked about Jack London, Charles Dickens and George Bernard Shaw, but when we turned to those authors who were not discussed at school, like Joseph Conrad and Ernest Hemingway, I noticed a slight thaw in his impervious examiner's manner. Emboldened by these signs, I pushed on a little further, into the dangerous territory of D. H. Lawrence and George Orwell. He showed positive signs of illicit excitement at the mention of D. H. Lawrence, and, like a naughty boy who thinks he has found a partner to share the thrill of looking at dirty pictures, I pushed on to a discussion of *Sons and Lovers*.

Naturally, all this was discussed in a thoroughly detached way, but I noticed that he seemed a little more enthusiasic about this topic than he had been about Charles Dickens. I went further, thinking we were almost at the stage where I would curse myself if I did not make my move.

'Lady Chatterly deserves some praise in my view for her

spirit, if we judge the work from the standpoint of Marxist Leninist literary theory. After all, she eloped with a member of the proletariat, in defiance of bourgeois capitalist morality. If she betrayed anyone it was not her husband but the exploiting and oppressing feudal ruling class.'

'Exactly,' he said, rather breathlessly, 'you have hit the nail on the nose.'

Then he began to complain bitterly about the difficulties he faced, trying to obtain copies of literary works for scholarly analysis.

'How on earth did you manage to get your hands upon these rare literary gems?'

'Oh, it's quite easy – from my friends, you know, the Australian and American teachers, Trevor Hay and Adrian Frazier who worked in our department—'

'Really? What kind of collection do they have? Do you think I—'

'Well, let's see – Oscar Wilde—' I paused for effect and to judge his reaction. Yes, it was worth going on.

'Henry Miller—'

I stopped short of explaining that the library provided by the foreigners contained a number of even more fascinating magazines and books which had been employed in the interests of introducing us to the pitfalls of decadent Western society.

I left the room in a triumphant mood. I know that I am sometimes inclined to be carried away with myself, and it was not the first time my spirits had soared after an examination, but at this moment I was convinced that I had won an incomparable victory. Two weeks later my department was informed of the results of the examination. I had come top! But the exam was never intended to select young people like me, and a great argument ensued among the leaders about the relative merits of examinations as a form of selection, until finally the principle, 'Marks are the great leveller, everyone is equal before the examination', was upheld.

After that I became something of a 'big man on campus' (as I read once in an American article). I was often stopped by strangers who plied me with questions about what I would be studying, how long I would be abroad, who would sponsor me, and, most importantly, where I would be going. At first I enjoyed these conversations, and went away from them feeling very proud of myself, but then I began to get embarrassed because I could not provide the very information which I myself most wanted to know. I grew so tired of the repetition that I began to think about wearing some flash-cards around my neck, which I could rapidly turn over in response to each question:

Q. *'Which country are you going to?'*
A. 'America or Britain, but the possibility of Australia or New Zealand should not be excluded.'

Q. *'How long?'*
A. 'One year or possibly two, or even longer.'

Q. *'Are you going to do a degree? If yes, then what kind of degree?'*
A. 'Personally, I would like to do a degree, realistically an MA, or perhaps even a PhD, but of course it all depends on the leaders to decide.'

Q. *'Who is going to sponsor your study?'*
A. 'Most likely the Jiangsu Provincial Government, but to my understanding, people like me are encouraged to try to obtain foreign scholarships.'

Q. *'How are you preparing for the trip and when do you think you will leave?'*
A. 'The provincial Higher Education Bureau has asked me to stand by. It could be any time – tomorrow, next week or next year.'

I waited and waited, and still nothing happened. Finally people began to assume that I had returned from somewhere and asked me 'How was the trip?' When they discovered that I was still waiting, they enquired if the Party had changed its 'open-door' policy of sending people abroad. My stance on this was absolutely unequivocal: 'I can assure you, the Party will never change its position on this matter!' Privately, I was much less confident, and in fact I had heard on the grapevine that some cadres were manoeuvring to get their own relatives abroad, and that my position might be reviewed.

In August 1983 Shi Jiajun, head of Foreign Relations in the Higher Education Bureau, instructed me to provide six passport photos. I rushed to the Bureau with the photos, which I had obtained ages ago. Shi Jiajun was furious when he saw the photos, and said, 'Look at you, long hair and sloppy old jacket! Do you imagine that you are going to represent the People's Republic of China looking like that? Go back and get into something decent, a proper Sun Yat-sen jacket – and get your hair cut while you're at it. Then you can have your photograph taken. But hurry up, or it will be too late to worry about it!'

I came out cursing and swearing under my breath about bureaucrats – of course I only dared to be furious inside, certainly not on the outside. This behaviour was typical of Jiangsu bureaucrats and their arrogant, officious manner. I rushed back home and put on my *Zhongshan zhuang*, my Sun Yat-sen style jacket, usually called a 'Mao suit' by the foreigners I had met. I ran down the hill from my room to the university barber. She – many barbers in our area are rather pretty young girls from Yangzhou – asked me what style I would like.

'Short', I said, rather tersely.

'Oh, what a pity! Why do you want it cut short? It looks great just as it is, and so fashionable, just like a detective in one of those Japanese movies.'

'Just cut it', I said, even more tersely. 'And make it short and spiky enough to prick your finger.'

Then I ran down to the photographer's in Ninghai Road. I explained that I needed photographs urgently for my passport. He was quite obliging.

'Oh, of course, of course, you must be going overseas. How wonderful. Sit down, sit down. I'll do it right away. Now then, smile please – you'll have to try and look a little more cheerful than that, you are scowling at me. Come on now, smile—'

I glared at him, and pulled the corners of my mouth into a tortured grin. Next day I rode my bike back to Shi Jiajun's office with the photos. He stared contemptuously at them for some seconds, while I held my breath, and then tossed them into a file.

After that everything was quiet for months, until January 1984, when I was summoned to have a physical checkup at the Workers Hospital. In the hospital a clerk from Shi Jiajun's office handed me an envelope. I took out a form, which was headed 'Commonwealth of Australia, Department of Immigration and Ethnic Affairs'.

'Does this mean I am going to Australia?' I asked innocently.

'Who says so?'

'Well, it says here on this form "Commonwealth of Australia", both in Chinese and in English.'

'Really? So what anyway? I don't care if it says Australia or Albania, just have your physical.'

Once again, all was silence, but at last I could tell people where I was going. The response was disappointing.

'Australia? That's an agricultural country, isn't it? Lots of sheep. And kangaroos. But why did you have to go through all this just to go to a developing country?'

People knew almost nothing about Australia, but then neither did I, apart from what Trevor Hay had told me.

31

I decided to read all I could about the place, to make Australian friends whenever possible, and to seek the advice of anyone who had been there. I went to see Hao Zhenyi, who had spent a year in Australia as an International Teaching Fellow.

'The food is awful.' He pulled a face as if he were about to vomit. 'I became very sick there, you know.'

That was the extent of his advice, along with something about a vicious substance called cheese, the mere smell of which was enough to shake the resolve of even the boldest of cultural pioneers.

In the spring of that year Hao Zhenyi and another former exchange teacher in Australia, Chen Wenshen, were invited to a meeting with some of their old Australian friends at a nearby guesthouse. After the meeting they came to see me and told me that they had been introduced to a certain Liu Aihua from Jinling Education Institute. She, too, was going to Australia, it seemed. They were quite upset, because the whole thing had been arranged by some 'big shots' in order to smooth Liu's path when she went overseas.

'It's not fair, you are also a son of the motherland, and you also need some contacts to help you.'

'Oh, don't worry, I'm used to it. Some of us are not quite as legitimate as others, you know. There are sons of the first lady of the house, and then there are sons of the concubine.'

'Yes, but this Liu calls Fang Fei, "Auntie Fang".'

Fang Fei was the boss of the Jiangsu Province Association for Friendly Ties with Foreign Countries and the former head of Jiangsu Education Department. As fluent English speakers, she and 'Bishop' Ding Guangxun were placed in charge of United Nations document translation work, during the 1970s after United Nations' recognition of China. These two were the most hated people in Nanjing Teachers University, particularly because of the harsh treatment they meted out to some old intellectuals in the UN translation

32

group. In 1977 during my own short stint in this group I was quite puzzled as to why a bishop excited so much fear and hatred, but then I was told that Ding was formerly under the direct command of Premier Zhou Enlai, founder of the Chinese Secret Police.

After the visit of Hao and Chen, my opportunity to go abroad seemed as remote as ever, and I began to worry that someone would take my place. Two years of standing by, as if on alert, with no result. 'Plenty of lightning and thunder, but never any rain' as my grandfather used to say. Eventually I became quite ill with it all. One night in July 1984, as it was getting on for midnight, I suffered sudden and severe pains in my stomach. I struggled onto my bike and rode down to the Workers' Hospital Casualty Section. I fainted while waiting in the corridor, and came to, some time later, to find myself lying on a bench in the corridor, with an intravenous drip in my arm. I asked the nurse to contact the university so they could make arrangements to cover my teaching.

Next day, the head of the department came to see me, and informed me officially, for the first time, that I was going to Australia in August under the sister-state exchange program between the State of Victoria and Jiangsu Province. He instructed me to make my recovery as soon as possible so as not to interfere with these arrangements. I was now at the point, for the first time in almost three years, when I really did not *want* to go. I was sick in hospital, too weak to walk or stand. My girlfriend, Bi Lijun, was going to graduate in a week or so, and it would at last be possible for us to declare ourselves. But, if they wanted me to go I did not have much choice in the matter.

Ten days later I was discharged from hospital. I went to the Foreign Relations office for my regulation briefing on discipline and funding arrangements. There was a new chief, Lao Zhu, a very officious and self-important character. I had been on quite good terms with the old one, for whom I had acted as interpreter on a number of occasions. Things would be different around here from now on, it seemed.

'Comrade Fang Xiangshu, I have heard you are a very experienced interpreter, and I assume there is no point in wasting your valuable time and mine repeating things you already know perfectly well concerning disciplinary matters. *But*—', he said, pointing dramatically at me with one finger.

'Here we go again', I thought to myself.

'—but,' he said again for emphasis, producing a second finger, 'there are *two* things I must stress. The first is that there are no minor matters in foreign relations. Every little thing is crucial. The second is that there is a great difference between internal and external dissension. Whatever little difficulty breaks out among us Chinese, it should be kept in the family, and not spread around among the foreigners. These two points have a great deal to do with not only your personal dignity, but more importantly, that of the motherland.'

He went on and on for about half an hour, gesturing and emphasising all over the place, and I nodded gravely all through it, and mumbled reverently 'Of course, of course.' I was thinking of Bi Lijun, and meeting her later for a thoroughly bourgeois cup of coffee in the notorious Victory Café, where all sorts of foreign Bohemians and Chinese layabouts congregate to exchange 'internal' secrets. I don't know if Lao Zhu began to suspect that I was not paying attention, but he suddenly startled me with a very loud exclamation, and thrust something under my nose.

'This is the funding arrangement.'

I took a quick look. It was headed 'Jiangsu Province Government Document'. The idea was that while we were in Australia Liu Aihua and I would receive free accommodation, breakfast and evening meals. As well, we would receive, via Victorian Education Department sources, $A100

34

a week in spending money, amounting to $A5200 for the whole year. But this money did not belong to us. We were permitted to use 50 Chinese yuan ($A22) each month for our own purposes. For lunch, Liu was allocated $A4.50 daily, while I was allocated $A3.50. For all other necessary expenses we should keep receipts, and on our return should hand all other moneys back to the Jiangsu Provincial Government. When I read the bit about the lunches, I could not help protesting a little, especially since by now I was not really all that keen to go.

'Why does she get more lunch money than me? Does she eat more than me?'

'Comrade Fang Xiangshu, where you are going is a Western capitalist society. In such societies they pay particular attention to one's status. Liu is going as a lecturer, and you are going primarily as a scholar of English literature. While these things are not important in our socialist motherland, they can make a great deal of difference abroad. It is not that she needs to eat more, but she must eat food of a higher quality, for the sake of the international standing of the People's Republic of China.'

'Oh, I see. Yes, of course. But then there is another problem. Males need to get their hair cut more often than females, and I have heard that it is very expensive in foreign countries. What about the image of China in this case?'

'That is included in your spending money. Male comrades have their necessities and female comrades also have theirs. It is all taken into account. Besides, male comrades at least have some choice in the matter. Female comrades – as I was saying, you need not get your hair cut so often in Western societies. People overseas grow their hair quite long – just look at our countrymen in Hong Kong and Macao.'

'But Director Shi Jiajun told me I would be letting down the image of the motherland.'

'Forget about Shi Jiajun,' he said angrily, 'he is nothing.

No one takes any notice of him these days. He was in the Revolutionary Rebel faction during the Cultural Revolution, and has just been removed from his position because of his record as an anarchist.'

'What about transport?' I persisted. 'Should I keep all my tickets to show you on return? If I—'

He cut in, quite nettled by now, 'Comrade Fang Xiangshu, don't go on about the money. You will be perfectly all right. Every one is looked after more than adequately. Look at Chen Wenshen and Hao Zhenyi. They had enough left over to buy the "Four big items and the four little items".'

By this he meant the standard purchases of Chinese returning from abroad – fridge, washing machine, television and video ('big items'), and camera, watch, sewing machine and cassette recorder ('little items').

'Oh, I hope so', I said, with a note of scepticism.

'Of course, of course', he said, relaxing a little. 'For example, I have heard that in the place where you are going to stay, you can help yourself to as much as you like for breakfast, and there are bread rolls on the table. Just put some in your bag and save them for lunch. Also, when you get to the college, open the fridge and help yourself to some milk. Western fridges are always full of milk, just sitting around for anyone to use. Have some nice cold milk with your rolls.'

'But cold milk makes me feel sick! Do they have somewhere to warm the milk?'

He picked up another document, and brandished it at me with some menace. Then he composed himself, and said deliberately, 'The government is very considerate, and you really don't need to buy anything abroad. You can take washing powder, soap, razor blades, all that kind of stuff with you. I can even tell you where to get the family-size tube of "Beauty plus Cleanliness" toothpaste.'

36

He stretched out both hands to demonstrate the size of the tube, as if it were a torpedo.

I realised by now that I was going too far, but I just couldn't help myself. 'Can I get a giant roll of toilet paper at this place?'

He did not answer my question, but simply handed me the document he had been holding. It was yet another provincial government document. I scanned the paper: 'In order to assist overseas-bound personnel with their financial arrangements, the relevant work units should take responsibility for the provision of adequate funding.' Then I came across a scale of funds, which set out the amount to be allotted to each person, according to his rank. From what I could make out, I was entitled to 550 yuan, about eight months' salary! I had never in my life received so much money all at once. Looking down the list I noticed that lecturers got 900 yuan, but all capacity for resentment had been driven out of me by the astounding windfall. A smile must have found its way onto my face without my knowledge, because Lao Zhu remarked, 'Yes, that's better. Sooner or later, you all learn to appreciate just how much we have your welfare at heart in this office.'

After a considerable speech along these lines, during which I refrained from any further comment, not so much out of self-restraint as out of absorption in my plans for spending 550 yuan, he produced yet another document. This one was entitled 'Essential information for overseas-bound personnel'. It contained the facts of life pertaining to hygiene, grooming and etiquette in Western countries. Among the dos and don'ts were: when eating chicken or fish never spit the bones on to the table or floor; when eating soup, move your spoon from inside to out, do not shovel the soup from the bowl into your mouth; do not peel and eat lemons, but squeeze the juice on to your food, and do not drink from a bowl in which there are slices of lemon, this is for rinsing

your fingers; regularly trim the hairs in your nostrils . . .'
I felt rather complacent about all of this, but suddenly I
was shocked to read 'Never pluck your whiskers with your
fingernails in public.' I realised that I often did this,
particularly during political study classes. I resolved never
to commit the offence while abroad.

Finally, Lao Zhu gave me Liu Aihua's telephone number.
He told me that she wanted to talk to me about the travel
arrangements. I asked if I could use his office telephone, and
he seemed most obliging. This Liu really had some influence
it seemed. I rang her, and she asked to see me; so I rode
off immediately on my bike to see what it was all about.

I rode out through the back gate of the university and down
into Xikang Road. Ten minutes later, I stopped in front of
a very grand-looking house. I checked the address Liu Aihua
had given me, and found that this was the right place – a
two-storeyed, European-style building, probably built in
the 1930s for rich foreigners. I knocked at the door, but
there was no reply. I knocked louder, and finally the door
opened and a sort of *a-yi*, or maidservant-looking woman,
answered. Although China no longer had *yongren*, or ser-
vants, some high-ranking cadres were still entitled to
domestic staff, but they called them *a-yi* ['Auntie'] in the
interests of egalitarianism.

I announced myself, and was shown the way upstairs. A
slim and agreeable-looking woman, whom I took to be
about thirty, the same age as me, came to meet me at the
top of the stairs.

'Oh, so you are Xiao Fang? You haven't been well, have
you? I've been quite concerned about you.' Her manner
suggested she had known me for years.

'And you must be Liu Aihua? Glad to know you.'

'Please, call me Aihua.'

'OK, thanks', I said, although I did not feel comfortable

with this intimacy, normally reserved for family members or very close friends.

She showed me into a room, and after I was comfortably seated in an armchair, and provided with some Longjing tea, she asked me if I had friends in Australia. I explained that I only knew some ordinary teachers and lecturers, like myself. She went on to say that, to her understanding, everybody who went abroad tried to get an extension of their stay, after the completion of their work or study. She said that, if only one of us could stay on after the fellowship, and it turned out to be me, she would do nothing to jeopardise my opportunity. I responded immediately along the same lines. She smiled, and went on to say that she would try to find a way for both of us. I told her that I really appreciated her kindness, but I was not all that anxious to stay on in Australia, for personal reasons.

'Xiao Fang, let me tell you something that you don't know. One of the two positions in this exchange scheme was long ago decided in my favour, but the other one was between you and Jing Wenxun of Yangzhou Teachers College. I asked around, with people who knew both of you, and decided that you seem much easier to get along with. I'm not trying to take the credit, but you must know that is how it came about.'

'Oh, really? Thank you very much for your confidence in me. But I'm afraid you might have been a little too generous. I can be a bit difficult sometimes.'

'No, no, not at all.' She laughed. 'Anyway, I'm not worried. If you give me any trouble, I'll soon bring you to heel, just like a big sister.'

I also laughed. I rather liked her candour.

She seemed to read my thoughts, and said, 'Xiao Fang, I quite like your frank manner.' Then she became rather serious. 'You know, we are going to be overseas for at least one year. We ought to trust and be frank with each other.

The last group to go to Australia had terrible problems with each other. For example, at Hong Kong airport – before they had even arrived in Australia – they had a fierce argument. Shen Fengjia insisted on going out of the airport to have a look around, but Ye Shengnian would not hear of it, because of the Hong Kong airport tax of a hundred dollars. Chen Shen didn't want to take sides. We two must have a united front on such matters.'

'Well yes, I don't know much about the last group, but I wouldn't blame Ye Shengnian for being a bit worried. After all, we only have fifty American dollars for travel requirements, and we might need this for taxis, or phone calls – that kind of thing.'

'Well, actually, I can arrange for us to take the return fare money with us, so as to give us a bit of flexibility. We can always top it up later. If you would like to see some of Hong Kong, I have already arranged a transit visa from the British Embassy.'

'Of course. In that case, why not?'

Then we discussed the travel arrangements. Liu told me that we were flying Qantas. This was the first time I had heard the word but, according to her, this Australian national airline had the best safety record in the world. The negative side of this was that they were very strict about excess luggage. As for the departure date, she suggested mid-August, if we could manage it.

'Well,' I ventured, 'since you want me to be frank with you, I'd better let you know that I'd like to see my parents in Shanghai, and my grandfather in Yixing, before I leave. Also, I haven't done any shopping or general preparation yet, because I have been ill as you know, so—'

'Yes, of course, no problem. What about late August? Would that suit you better?'

Then we made an appointment to meet at the Provincial Foreign Relations Office next day, in order to get travel

40

documents and authorisation for our money. I left her house feeling well pleased with my travelling companion. I felt certain we would get along very well together. She obviously had influence, and yet seemed very considerate and reasonable.

Next day we met at the Foreign Relations Bureau, and Liu took me to meet Fang Fei, whose office was in the same compound.

'Oh, so you are Fang Xiangshu,' she said, 'of the Foreign Language Department of Nanjing Teachers University?' She then began to speak in a mixture of Chinese and English, to demonstrate her familiarity with things Western, I suppose.

'Are you flying Qantas or Cathay Pacific? Are you stopping in Hong Kong? Are you going to Melbourne University, or Victoria College to teach some Chinese? Last time I was in Victoria, I went to the old goldfields at Ballarat, and I remember they had a kind of nineteenth-century historical re-enactment going on. I was introduced to a fellow in a period costume. I said, "Mr Pickwick, I presume?" ' She giggled with delight at the memory of her merry quip, and Liu Aihua and I joined in heartily.

After this introduction, she resumed her Chinese language and Chinese manner.

'You two are the pick of Jiangsu Province, the best and brightest of our Province. On your shoulders rests the heavy responsibility for promoting friendship and understanding between our two nations. I know that you will not let us down.'

Then she asked me to go and see if the travel documents were ready, and then to wait in the corridor for a moment while she had a chat with Liu. It didn't take more than ten minutes for the documents, but then I commenced a long vigil for Liu. Half an hour went by. Then another half hour, and another. I began to think of a movie I had seen, in which

Lenin, Stalin, Trotsky and Bukharin were arguing about the necessity for the October Revolution. Lenin's bodyguard, Vasily, was waiting outside in the corridor, pacing up and down and looking at his watch. The captions at the bottom of the film read 'Half an hour went by'; 'Another half an hour went by'; 'Another half hour'. After a few such captions Vasily's hair began to look very unkempt, his face appeared unshaven and a small pile of cigarette butts built up in the corridor. In my case I only had to wait five captions, before Liu re-appeared.

'Oh, she is such a caring cadre, that Comrade Fang Fei! If only they were all like her, there would be nothing for anyone to complain about.'

I decided that Liu Aihua was probably a bit naive.

Shortly after that I rushed to Yixing to see my grandfather. I had just received word that he was dying. But there was no train, and the journey took a whole day by bus, and I arrived too late. He was a little over ninety-six when he died. I was very sad about this. I had always felt a great affinity with him, and he in turn regarded me as his pride and joy. He had been enormously proud to hear that I had been selected to go abroad, and told everyone in the village about it.

I spent another day travelling to Shanghai to see my parents, and to do some shopping. My mother helped me with my packing: she seemed to think of everything I could possibly ever need, but I had to tell her about Qantas and the strict rules about luggage weight. She insisted that I weigh my suitcase, and so we dragged it to a nearby coal merchant. It was over the weight, of course; and then we began the search for things to discard. First to go were two family-size tubes of toothpaste and a family-size box of washing powder. Then I decided that I would carry my overcoat, and that in any case it would be quite handy to do this as it would be winter in Australia when I arrived.

It was a mistake to mention this, because it caused the coal merchant considerable alarm to think of a place where it could be winter in August.

By now I had US$1200 in my possession. I showed this wad to several neighbours, who marvelled at it, but could not help but remark upon the fact that those crazy Americans had created $5, $10, $20, $50 and $100 notes that looked all alike. Same size, colour, and almost the same design. Of course there were different heads on them, but all foreigners look alike anyway. My mother decided that I should divide it up into very small bundles and stash it all over my body, so that if I lost any I would only lose a small amount at a time.

On 20 August 1984 Liu Aihua and I went through Customs at White Cloud Airport, Canton. The Customs official looked at my declaration, and asked me to show my authorisation for taking foreign exchange out of the country. I produced the letter, but then he wanted to see the money. I began fumbling around all through my clothing for the little packets that my mother had insisted on secreting on my person. I even had some packets fastened to my underclothing with safety pins.

We arrived at Hong Kong airport at about one o'clock in the afternoon. There was no dispute between us as to whether we should go out of the airport. I wanted to buy a camera, to record my year in Australia, and she wanted to see a friend. She said her friend would wait at the airport exit, but we had some difficulty finding it. We went up and down the escalators several times until I said that I felt certain I knew which was the main exit. Liu was still not convinced, so she told me to look out for a man holding a dark-brown umbrella in his left hand, waiting near the exit. I was amazed.

'This sounds like a movie about the Communist underground during the Civil War. Do you know this person?'

'He is a friend of a friend. Hong Kong is a very complicated place. We need to take precautions.'

Sure enough there he was, standing near the exit sign, carrying a dark-brown umbrella in his left hand.

After we met, and we had explained what we wanted to do, he took us in a taxi to the Harbour City Shopping Centre. He bargained with the shop assistant for the price of my camera; I was given 7 per cent discount on a Fujica, a free film, and a business card for next time

Eventually, we returned to the airport, passed through Customs again, and then found ourselves sitting comfortably in a Qantas Jumbo, watching *Romancing the Stone*, on our way to Australia. After the movie, I said to Liu, 'Your friend in Hong Kong speaks fluent Cantonese and Mandarin.'

'Oh yes, he is a Chinese Government official stationed in Hong Kong.'

Despite our promising beginnings, conflict with Liu Aihua seemed inevitable not long after our arrival in Australia. She seemed naive, and at times ignorant, as if she were living in another world. Listening to her was much the same as reading the *People's Daily*, the official newspaper of the Communist Party of China. The first incident happened after we returned from a dinner to which we were invited by Australian friends. Our friends had been asking us about recent criticism of Chairman Mao's policy during the Cultural Revolution. I explained that while the criticism was aimed at the Cultural Revolution, in my view it had been Mao's policy since the anti-rightist campaign in 1957. Liu immediately corrected me.

'The *People's Daily* only mentions criticism of the Cultural Revolution. Xiao Fang, we cannot go beyond that point.'

'But I am just saying that this is my personal view.'

When we returned to Frank Tate House, our official

residence, she told me, in quite a grave tone, 'There is a great difference between internal and external dissension.'

'Well, in the first place it was not me who revealed dissension, because you interrupted me to voice a strong objection. In the second place, if you had taken a softer line, even if only on the surface, we could have demonstrated how open and reasonable Chinese society is, instead of creating the impression of internal conflict.'

In those days we had some problems of adjustment, but we decided as a matter of policy not to air our differences in front of foreigners. It never really occurred to either of us that *we* were the foreigners. This policy worked reasonably well, and Liu proved to be quite ingenious at providing diplomatic answers to even the most sensitive questions about China. Unfortunately, however, there came a time when I broke the rules myself. On this occasion, a couple of Australian friends asked us about premarital sex and arranged marriages in China.

'Is it true that most marriages in China are arranged by parents?'

'I wouldn't say most marriages, but certainly many marriages are arranged in this way', said Liu. 'This demonstrates the tradition of the Chinese people of respecting their elders.'

I found myself once again admiring her skill at handling a tricky area. She went on, 'At the same time this is also a very good way of finding a partner. Take my own case, for example. I was born in 1949 – the foundation year of the People's Republic of China, and so my given name is Aihua – "Love China"! My husband was also born in that year, and his parents called him Weiguo – "Defend the nation". My parents knew his parents long before we were born, and during our childhood Weiguo and I played together. We had no thought of marriage to each other, but when we reached marriageable age our parents made arrangements for us. I married him in order to please my mother, but then we found we were a very happy couple anyway.'

I began to feel uncomfortable with this. She had gone a little too far. It was beginning to sound like the network of nepotism that entrenched the privileges of the elite and made life so difficult for ordinary Chinese people. Suddenly one of our guests asked me, 'Xiao Fang, what do you think of arranged marriages?'

'Well, sometimes it can work quite well, but in the majority of cases I think the bad effects outweigh the good. There is no way I could accept a marriage arranged by my parents, although I love them and respect them. Actually, in the urban areas at least, most of the courtship and marriage arrangements are negotiated by a go-between. After the introductions and initial dating, to see if the couple suit each other, the go-between leaves the rest to the couple themselves. In a way, he or she acts as a kind of introduction agency, like you have here. A small minority of people handle the whole thing for themselves.'

In order to stress the diversity of arrangements, I countered Liu's example with my own. I told the group about Bi Lijun and me, and our secret liaison, suggesting by implication that Chinese people, like Western people, are not easy to stereotype.

By now our guests were less clear on the subject than before, but more interested.

'Is it true that in China people don't have premarital sex, or extra-marital affairs?'

Liu took this up with vigour. 'In China husbands love wives and wives love husbands, and very seldom do we hear about "affairs".'

I must have betrayed some dissatisfaction with her answer, by the look on my face or perhaps a gentle groan, because she raised her voice and looked sharply in my

46

direction. 'As for premarital sex, it is regarded as wrong and immoral in China. No one has the right to sex before marriage and it is very, very rare that it happens. Anyone caught is severely criticised.'

Although I was then thirty-one, I was not married and therefore it seemed I could not possibly know anything about sex, according to her. If I indicated any further expertise or interest in this matter, I might well be heading for criticism myself. In fact, however, I was not really threatened by her remark, but I did take the hint that I should not go any further. Liu continued, 'Recently a new Marriage Law has been passed, which stipulates that every one should have a physical examination prior to marriage. Any woman who is found to have lost her virginity will be seriously reprimanded by the doctor—'

I could not help but cut in: 'Just a minute – one thing I should make clear – the physical examination required by the new law is not meant to be for the purpose of checking women's virginity, it is supposed to be for checking on infectious diseases or genetic disorders or blood-type problems—'

Liu now forgot herself and took up the debate in Chinese, to the exclusion of our rather bewildered friends: 'Look, I know what I'm talking about. I have seen, with my own eyes, cases where the doctor has given women a terrible scolding—'

I also spoke, or rather shouted, in Chinese: 'I'm not saying that this does not happen. I can tell you that some hospitals in remote areas even impose a fine on women who have lost their virginity. What I am saying is that it is wrong, illegal and feudal. First of all, why should women bear the blame for this? In any case there is more than one reason for women to fail this test, like rape – maybe this explains why so many victims of rape commit suicide.'

'To stop immoral behaviour and to educate young people is the sacred duty of all citizens, including doctors!'

Although they did not know exactly what was going on, our guests were quite alarmed by now, and after a little while they made their apologies and left. Liu and I resumed the battle in private for at least an hour.

I was very upset, but not just because of the principles involved in this argument. I knew of a case myself, which had had tragic consequences. Wen Ming, a woman of twenty-four, a student-friend of Bi Lijun, became pregnant after seeing a lot of her fiancé during the university vacation. Signs of pregnancy were noted by cadres of the Communist Youth League. The political staff of the university found some pretext for admitting her to hospital, on suspicion of some illness or other, and then took a urine sample from her. When Bi Lijun visited her in hospital, Wen Ming told her what had happened and asked for help. Bi Lijun rushed over to see me, to see what I could do, but it was too late, because of the urine sample. If she had asked earlier, before she was admitted to hospital, I might have been able to contact her political instructor, who happencd to be my old classmate at university, and he might have been able to arrange an extended leave for her – but it was too late.

After the positive result of the pregnancy test was made known, Wen Ming escaped from the hospital and managed to get on a train to Fujian Province, where her fiancé came from. On the way, she had a miscarriage, as a result of exhaustion and anxiety. She was close to committing suicide. The university sent staff to find her, and when they finally did they promised they would keep her secret, if only she would just agree to come back. When she did return, she found that she had been condemned by the university administration in front of the entire teaching staff and student body, and her crime had been categorised as one deserving of shame for 'ten thousand years'. A severe official reprimand had been recorded in her file. Her fiancé had been expelled from Fujian University.

So it was that during the continuation of our argument, I became more and more agitated. Liu repeated her view that medical personnel had a duty to educate moral offenders, and I replied that I considered that such doctors themselves needed education in professional ethics, if not humanity. We could not reconcile our differences, and could only agree to take the matter up with a Chinese doctor of our acquaintance who was then working at Prince Henry's Hospital.

A few days later we went to see Dr Bai, a prominent surgeon from Capital Hospital, Beijing. To my relief, Bai agreed unreservedly that doctors had no business meddling in the moral affairs of patients, but should confine themselves to diagnosing illness. 'We are not police or political instructors', he said, finally.

Whatever Liu's private feelings on the matter, she took this set-back with grace and good humour. I felt this indicated that she was sincere about being a kind of 'big sister' to me, and would be tolerant of the disagreements which must inevitably rise between us. As for her conservative attitudes, I felt confident that we would see eye to eye as the time in Australia wore on, and she was exposed to all kinds of new things.

In fact, Liu Aihua and I did develop quite a close friendship. Although I still could not bring myself to call her 'Aihua', I was at least comfortable about addressing her as 'Xiao Liu', like a friend or colleague. One Saturday morning we Chinese students and teachers went to the home of the Party Branch Secretary, Li Gengxin, for political study. During this session Li made fun of my long hair, which had not been cut since the incident in Nanjing: 'Just look at you Xiao Fang, your hair is almost down to your shoulders. Maybe if you are lucky you might be mistaken for a Japanese, or more likely for a Vietnamese refugee—'. He dissolved into laughter at his own joke. When we returned Liu offered to help me out by cutting my hair. She

49

even offered to write to her husband and ask him to arrange for the next Chinese arrival in Australia to bring some electric clippers. I was very grateful to her, and expressed my thanks. She replied as she always did on such occasions, 'No, no, don't be silly. I am your big sister, remember? If your big sister won't look after you, who will?'

Liu was also very helpful to me in the matter of table manners and etiquette. I thought I was already quite a polished and sophisticated fellow, but she certainly taught me a thing or two. Bearing in mind the advice I had gleaned from the 'dos and don'ts' manual, I always avoided placing a knife in my mouth, but I had never paid attention to the precise way I used a fork. According to her, one should never place a fork in one's mouth concave side uppermost. She also pointed out on a number of occasions that my elbows were raised at too high an angle for polite society. At first I was a little embarrassed, although I did genuinely appreciate her advice, and she was always extremely tactful and sensitive in the way she handled the situation. My embarrassment melted away after a while, when I saw her struggling to make an impression on colleagues who were very resistant to her methods. For one thing, I was able to eat Western food without causing an uproar, unlike some, who always seemed to think they were being poisoned. Then there was Chen Decai, who was a foreign trade official studying marketing at Chisholm Institute of Technology.

Chen was well aware that he lacked training in Western cutlery drill. From Monday to Friday he got by, because we had Chinese-style food, with chopsticks. We had all kinds of Chinese delicacies that I, for one, had never seen in China. But when the weekend came around, and our own chef left us to the mercy of the general kitchen staff, Chen began to suffer anxiety. It was not the food that concerned him. In fact, if no one was watching him he would thoroughly enjoy it. The trouble was the knife and fork – and the constant reproach in Liu's eyes as she supervised his table manners to ensure that he was not doing irreparable harm to China's standing in the international community. The performance at mealtime was almost more than I could bear to watch, and I often asked Liu to forget about him; but she was 'indefatigable', as they used to say in our English textbooks, and persevered, like the foolish old man who tried to remove the mountains. One night, after watching Chen wielding his knife and fork like a dagger-thrower in the circus, and Liu smiling through gritted teeth, like a patient nanny with a disabled child, I could stand no more and stamped off to my room. Shortly after there was a knock on my door. It was Liu.

'Xiao Fang. You saw all that, didn't you? I was extremely patient, wasn't I? He just doesn't want to learn. It is his attitude, that's all. Every time I tell him something he says the same thing – "Yes, quite right, you are doing the right thing. Keep it up, and I will do the same for you when I notice you doing anything wrong." Me doing the wrong thing! To hell with him!'

I had never seen Liu lose her composure like this, even when we were having one of our ideological disputes. I felt it my duty as a brother to calm her down.

'Xiao Liu, take it easy! Of course I saw it all. He's impossible, I know. If I can help in any way, just let me know.'

'Well, he seems to listen to you more than to me. Perhaps you could have a word with him. I just can't stand it any longer!'

After she left I took out a packet of Double Happiness cigarettes that I kept for emergencies, and steeled myself for the ordeal of going up to his room to broach the topic of knives and forks and soup-slurping. If I could begin by tossing him a cigarette, in Chinese style, we could at least get off on a good footing.

I knocked at the door, and when he let me in I took out my packet. He was already smoking, but he was glad to give up the foreign brand for my Chinese cigarettes. He stubbed his own smoke out, and carefully placed the butt back in his pocket, cursing about tasteless foreign cigarettes. I told him to keep the whole packet. He made one or two ritual protestations, and then took it. I thought this was a suitable time to begin my missionary work.

'Xiao Chen, I don't want to talk about the image of China, as some people do, but I think you must realise yourself, that when you return to China, you will certainly succeed your father-in-law as head of all foreign trade for the province. I wouldn't be surprised if you were very soon to find yourself frequenting important state banquets for foreigners or invited overseas for important trade negotiations. So, it is in your own interests for you to polish your technique a little in handling a knife and fork.'

'I couldn't agree more, Xiao Fang. I can understand what you are trying to tell me. You know, I really am making an effort, but all this "image of China" rubbish makes me want to throw up. Anyway, who is really doing the damage to China's image? Is it me who goes scrounging through the weekend "trash and treasure" markets, like some miserable beggar from Anhui? What a disgrace! You and I, Xiao Fang, we may be poor – but we still have our dignity!'

'Well, I know what you mean, Xiao Chen, but to be fair, you know we all have to find some way to put a little money aside, and we can't very well do it with our savings, can we?'

'Since you mention this, I've been meaning to ask you if you might be interested in working one night a week in a factory?'

'What factory? What are they paying?'

'It's called Visyboard. They make cardboard containers, and they want a joint venture with Jiangsu. They want me to make some contacts for them. As for the money, I'm not sure, but I think it will be OK.'

'You know we'll have to be a little bit careful about this. We'll have to invite Liu Aihua, or there could be trouble about it.'

'To hell with her!'

He was evidently preparing to go out, because he began fumbling with a tie. He handled this with about as much despatch as his knife and fork, and after a while I offered to help him.

'Now look what that blasted Liu has done to me, with her bullshit about the image of China. I can't even tie my tie properly, and I know perfectly well how it is done.'

I took the tie off him and made a respectable knot, then I suggested that he just loosen it each time and slip it over his head, in order to 'save time'. He was so anxious to save his valuable time that he asked me to tie another five or six while I was at it. This gave me an opportunity to raise a few points about our 'internal' difficulties.

'You know, Xiao Liu is really quite well-meaning. She is only trying to help and we should give her a go.'

'Are you sure she's not just making fun of me, because she thinks even her farts are fragrant?'

I realised that I had a bit of work to do to defuse a potential crisis in our ranks. I went back to Liu.

This issue of employment, and earning a little extra money had already been a topic of some importance between Liu and me. I genuinely appreciated her difficulty about clothing. She was always being invited to some function or other, private or official, and this created some problems for her limited wardrobe. The 'trash and treasure' expeditions were her way of trying to build up a wardrobe as inexpensively as possible. Obviously she could not afford to spend the kind of money that fashionable new Western-style clothing entailed. She had brought quite a few pairs of slacks, but she just did not have enough skirts and dresses. I did not blame her at all, and in fact I rather admired her way of dealing with the problem, but it did not seem to be the solution, so I raised the issue of part-time work with her.

'I have talked to Xiao Chen, but things are a bit complicated. He thinks you are also damaging our image and he mentioned the "trash and treasure" business.'

'What's wrong with it? I have asked some close Australian friends, and they say there is absolutely no disgrace about it if you are in financial difficulty.'

'Yes, but that's the point, isn't it? We are not *supposed* to be in financial difficulty. No one is supposed to know that we have to turn most of our money over to the government. What I am saying is that your method looks very funny, as if you are just being a kind of Chinese "Scrooge". Besides, it could be a little dangerous. There is a Central Government document warning about buying foreign second-hand clothing.'

'Yes, but they only mean to discourage people from buying up boxes and boxes to take back to China.'

'No, not entirely. They also suggest that there is a danger of contracting AIDS. I know that's crazy, but what I mean is politically—'

'AIDS? What rubbish! They can go—'

'Yes, I know, but that's not the point, I'm just trying to say that this "trash and treasure" thing is not the answer to your problem – or mine. You know I also have a bit of difficulty about this money business.'

'All right then, if that's not the answer, what do you suggest?'

'Well, as I have been trying to say these last weeks, I think we should find part-time jobs.'

'But maybe that is not allowed by the Government.'

'But the basic aim is to protect the image of China, isn't

it? And you should bear in mind the old saying "When the general is cut off from headquarters, he must use his own discretion." '

'OK. That's fair enough, but just think about the situation if I were to get a job as a waitress in a restaurant, as you suggested the other day. What if someone I knew saw me? That could be very embarrassing, not only for me, but for Jiangsu, or the Victorian Education Department.'

'Yes, I know, I've been thinking about that, and I think the best thing for us is to try to get some private Chinese tutoring. You know quite a few people in the Education Department. Why not ask them to help us to find a job?'

'Xiao Fang, you don't understand. It's true that I know some very important people, but they are useless from our point of view. They are *too* important, and I would not even want to raise the subject with them. It would be better to try close friends who are academics, but not important officials. I think you have those sort of contacts.'

'Naturally I will try. But if I can't manage it, would you be prepared to work in a factory?'

After a little hesitation, she nodded.

Then I returned to the matter of Chen Decai: 'Actually, just a moment ago, Xiao Chen mentioned the possibility of working in a factory, so if you want to keep this option open, I would recommend that you watch your step a little bit with him.'

'I never would have thought he had any influence.' She smiled charmingly, 'OK, I'll go easy on him.'

A week later Chen and I had arranged to work one night a week in the factory, and Liu had commenced some tutoring work, which Trevor Hay had originally offered to me. I had passed this work on to her, and harmony prevailed in our little group for the time being. Liu seemed to have acquired an exemplary tolerance for imperfect table manners, and in any case Chen moved out soon afterwards.

55

The relationship between Liu and me entered a new phase. There were no more political disputes and, in fact, she even started to confide in me about the really 'internal' aspects of high cadres' 'life styles'.

Once I borrowed Fox Butterfield's *Alive in a Bitter Sea* from an Australian friend. I passed it on to her, to watch her reaction, expecting that she would attack it, because of its revelations about life in China, but to my surprise, she said, in hushed tones, 'Actually Fox Butterfield doesn't know the worst of it. No one could imagine what really goes on.'

She began to tell me a story about Ye Jianying. Marshal Ye Jianying was a military strongman who in 1976 played a very important part in toppling Chairman Mao's widow, Jiang Qing, and her followers. Without his crucial help, Hua Guofeng would never have succeeded in the power struggle after Mao's death. Ye Jianying became Chairman of the National People's Congress. According to Liu, when Marshal Ye Jianying visited Nanjing some years ago, Jiangsu Provincial Government arranged some special dancing girls to visit his residence every night. At that time dancing between the sexes was strictly forbidden for ordinary people. 'Old Ye was particularly fond of young girls of about eighteen to twenty, although he could not even walk without the aid of two bodyguards. They went to unbelievable lengths to find the right girls.'

I must have looked a bit shocked, because she became quite emphatic. 'You haven't heard anything yet. Another of Old Ye's hobbies was fishing. When he went fishing in Xuanwu Lake, the Government went to enormous trouble to clear the area. The Nanjing Military Region provided troops to cordon off the whole lake and surrounding district. They also dispatched People's Liberation Army divers into the lake to place huge fish on the end of his hook.'

'Jesus Christ!' – by now even my Chinese was beginning to be enriched with swearing I had picked up from Australians – 'It's like something out of the Qing dynasty.' There was a tale that the ingenious eunuch Li Lianyin once spread live insect-bait around the edges of Kunming Lake in the Summer Palace, and then invited the Empress Dowager to watch the Buddhist practice of *fang-shen* – releasing trapped goldfish into the water, in order to improve one's karma. The liberated goldfish darted off into the lake as expected, but suddenly stopped and turned to nibble at the bonus of insects floating in a trail along the surface of the lake. Li told the Dowager that the fish had turned back to kowtow to her, as a mark of their respect and gratitude.

After Liu's revelations about top cadres, I found it rather difficult to stomach her speeches to our Australian friends about the beauties of socialist government. But on the other hand, she did not go on in this way to me in private, and I supposed she was simply doing her job as an official representative of the People's Republic. We were getting along very well, and she promised to arrange for Bi Lijun to meet members of her family in China. An ideal opportunity arose when an Australian couple visited Nanjing. They were invited to meet Liu's husband, daughter, parents and in-laws. Bi Lijun was asked to come along to meet everyone, and to lend a hand with interpreting. When the couple returned, they invited Liu and me to their house, and told us of their adventures.

'Xiao Fang, guess what? We were picked up from our hotel by a black limousine with curtains.'

'Yes,' I thought to myself, 'and next you'll be telling me there was a chicken feather-duster in the back.'

Then they went on and on about the food, and the conversation they had, and so forth. They praised Bi Lijun for her wonderful interpreting skills, and then they began apologising profusely to me for making her work so hard that she did not have time to enjoy her own meal.

'Well, don't worry too much about that,' I said. 'Bi Lijun eats very little, perhaps she did have more than enough to satisfy her.'

'Yes,' added Liu, 'the main thing is that you had a good time.' Then she turned to me and said in Chinese, 'Xiao Fang, Bi Lijun must have been greatly honoured to interpret for the head of the National Water and Power Commission. Just imagine her pride at being able to say that she had interpreted for such a person, and to have it on her record!'

I was stunned, and stared at her for some seconds. Then I said, also in Chinese, 'Xiao Liu, I can assure you it's true that Bi Lijun doesn't enjoy food all that much, but I can also assure you that she would rather eat than have such an honour!'

I realised after this that some of the differences between us could not easily be overcome, at least in the short term. On the other hand, we were reasonably compatible most of the time, and we did stick to our bargain not to frustrate each other's opportunities or clash in public on important issues. We generally worked things out in private, and reconciled the major differences in a satisfactory – and cordial – working relationship. She worked hard and took on a lot of responsibility in dealing with Victorian government officials – things which I was not in a position to do, and anyway I had no taste for it. After two extensions of our stay in Australia, readily approved by both sides, we were both suddenly instructed to return to China by the end of August 1986.

My return was delayed a few months because of my involvement in Trevor Hay's court case. I realised that Jiangsu authorities might be unhappy about this, but I did not worry unduly because Trevor had initiated an exchange agreement between Nanjing Teachers University and the

Melbourne College of Advanced Education, and was regarded as an 'old friend'. I felt that they would not criticise me too harshly for trying to help him. Liu Aihua returned to Nanjing in August as instructed, and had been back nearly four months when I rang her. She must have known if there were any problems concerning me, and, whatever our differences in the past, she had always been frank with me. When she began her big-sister routine about visiting my parents and so on, I assumed there was nothing too serious to worry about.

3   *Twelve Gilded Commands*

For the time being, I resolved not to worry too much about my accommodation and my teaching duties. I would do as my 'big sister' said, and go to see friends and relatives, to pay my respects after my long absence in Australia. Surely, after a while, things would sort themselves out. Perhaps I had even misread the situation because I had been away from home so long. I decided that first I would go to see a friend, a lecturer in the Chinese department, who was now in hospital with kidney trouble.

I had not been so long away that I had forgotten the Chinese habit of taking all manner of fruits to a patient, so I went off to the free market in Ning Hai Road. The market stretched along both sides of the road for about 200 metres. The area seemed to bubble and boil with masses of noisy people. I walked slowly down the middle, taking in the sights and sounds. Pickled and roast duck and goose, pork, lamb, beef, rabbit and shellfish. Live chickens, ducks, geese, eels, fish, shrimps and crabs. Live tortoises on string leads, to prevent them making a dash for it, I suppose. Green and white cabbage, Nanjing radish, sweet potato, peanuts, dried mussels and pickled chillies. Plants and birds – cactus, coxcomb, orchids, larks, and even budgerigars, which I now knew, after all these years, to be Australian natives.

Then I was attracted to some noisy bargaining at the fish section. A woman was quarrelling bitterly with the fishmonger over the price of some great bewhiskered carp flapping about in a shallow basin. One of these poor creatures was dangling over the scales, and the woman was trying to wrestle it from the scales and into her shopping basket. The fishmonger was shouting and pointing at the scales, 'You have to pay another 10 fen.'

'5 yuan is already more than enough.'

'All right, I'll give you back your 5 yuan and keep my fish. There are plenty of other customers more reasonable than you!'

'I know what you are up to! You put the fish in the water to soak them and make them weigh more.'

At this there was a burst of laughter from the onlookers.

'How am I supposed to keep the fish alive if I don't put them in water?'

'Well, just take something off for the weight of the water then. 10 fen will do nicely.'

Then I heard another quarrel going on at the next stall. A shrimp-seller was locked in verbal combat with a man who had a large red armband, which declared him to be a taxation official. The official was apparently estimating the quantity of shrimps and making out a receipt.

'Let's see now, 50 jin of shrimps, so total tax is—'

'50 jin! You've got to be joking! I weighed them before I left.' He pointed to a big canvas bag, and said, 'I packed some river weeds around them to keep them moist. You've obviously mistaken the weeds for shrimps.'

'If I say 50 jin, then 50 jin it is!'

The shrimp-seller grabbed at the official's pen, and a little group of fellow-traders gathered around, urging the tax man to lower his estimate. One slipped a packet of cigarettes into his pocket. I walked on to the fruit stalls. The fruiterer was watching the battle with obvious interest.

'Fuck these tax-gathering blood-suckers! Cheating people comes as naturally to them as farting!'

'All right, all right,' I said, 'take it easy, you've got a customer.'

His whole countenance was transformed as I asked for

large quantities of his best apples and oranges, specially gift-packed in a little bamboo basket. Basket in hand, I wandered down to the snack stalls.

Roast sweet potatoes, fried dough twists in wafers, steamed and fried dumplings, duck intestine soup, chicken and duck blood soup, pork buns and red bean buns – my mouth watered, and in spite of my proud boast that I had sampled all kinds of exotic dishes in Australia, including even the most disgusting things, like rare lamb, I could not help thinking that I had missed a great deal these last few years. I sat down at a table and ordered a bowl of deep-fried 'stinking' bean curd, but then I couldn't make up my mind about a second dish – jellied bean curd with chilli, usually called 'bean curd brains', or wonton soup? All my past students knew that Teacher Fang was often to be seen here with a bowl of jellied bean curd, and I was extremely partial to it, but I decided against a second bean curd dish, and compromised with wontons in chilli sauce. The price had almost doubled while I had been away, but it was still only 80 fen (about 30 cents) altogether.

As I looked around I noticed a strange sign across the road, some distance down. I read the characters *Bai Lao Hui. Xican Kafei* – a Western food restaurant and coffee shop. But what did *Bai Lao Hui* mean? I began experimenting with sounds to see if there was some foreign word for which this was a Chinese phonetic approximation. Yes, of course, 'Broadway'. I decided to have a look at this Broadway Restaurant and Coffee House.

After I finished my bean curd and wontons, I ambled down to the 'Broadway'. A waitress came, and I started to order.

'A cup of coffee, please.'

'Do you want "Bird's Nest" brand imported coffee?'

After decoding 'Broadway' my mind was tuned in to the little tricks of Chinese translators of Western place names and brand names so I immediately realised that 'Bird's Nest' probably referred to 'Nestlés'. This time it was not a translation according to sound, but a translation according to meaning.

'OK. "Bird's Nest" coffee, will be fine', I said, with a patronising smile.

'And would you like a companion?'

I was shocked out of my complacency.

'Pardon? Did you say a companion?'

I could hardly believe my ears. If I was to be offered such services with a simple cup of coffee, it would seem that 'spiritual pollution' was indeed undermining the foundations of Chinese morality.

'Yes, a companion', she said impatiently.

'Er, no, I don't think so, if you don't mind—'

Anyway, I thought, if the companions are anything like you, who needs it? She stalked off, muttering, 'Country bumpkin, fancy ordering "Bird's Nest" and no companion! I've never known anyone yet to come in here and order "Bird's Nest" without a companion!'

I tried to think what else she could possibly have meant. Coffee – companion. Yes, of course, 'Coffee Mate'! What an idiot I had been! Where were my 'Clever Dick' translations when I needed them most?

After my coffee, I rode my bike along Ninghai Road to the Workers Hospital, to see my friend Mu Yi. When I walked into the ward, I got a terrible shock. I saw his name above the bed, but I just could not believe it was really him. He looked so old and wrinkled. I had already heard his story from other colleagues, and I knew he had had a very bad time in these last two years or so.

He was a very artistic type, and he loved calligraphy. In fact, he wanted nothing more than to devote his whole life to it, but the university authorities would not give their approval. That is the way of China. The 'authorities' are in every corner of your life. From eating to sleeping, from working to having children, you can feel their breath on your neck – in the office, in the classroom, and in the bedroom. They are so thorough, so all-pervasive, and their network controls everything, from political indoctrination to the distribution of contraceptives. A woman cannot even have her period without them knowing. Under these circumstances, people like my friend have no say in what they want or don't want to do.

Mu Yi must have sensed my presence, and he opened his eyes. He spoke in a very feeble, tired voice, and as he did I saw tears in the corners of his eyes.

'You've come back.'

There was a long pause, and then, just when I thought he had gone into a deep sleep, he said, 'Blue skies. Magnificent rolling seas. Thank you for the wonderful photos you sent from Australia. I can almost taste and smell them.'

I knew what he meant. These days even I sometimes thought that Australia had been a dream. At night when I woke up in total darkness in my miserable cold room, I wondered what was real and what was not. Like the ancient sage, I may have been a man who had dreamt he was a butterfly, or I may have been a butterfly who dreamt – for such a short time – that he was a man. But I clung to a vision of powdery sand, red iron rocks, deep-green sea, white caps, silver gulls against that strange and dazzling blue Australian sky, and Bi Lijun's black hair tumbling as she bends to pick up a piece of cuttlefish for Trevor's parrots. After a while my vision would fade. First the colour, then the shape, until only Bi Lijun remained.

I took some photos out of my bag to show Mu Yi. I had taken quite a few of the beaches at Wilsons Promontory, the most beautiful and strange beaches – I could never have imagined them. I handed them to Mu Yi.

'Would you like to keep them? I have copies.'
'Are you sure? I do really like them.'
'Of course.'
Suddenly I remembered a fragment of a modern poem I liked very much – 'I don't believe the sky is blue', by Bei Dao. I could not remember how it went, but I tried to capture its spirit in some words of my own that I wrote on the back of one of the photos:

> I don't believe the sky is blue,
> I don't believe the sea is salt,
> I don't believe the earth was ice,
> I don't believe – I don't believe.

A doctor came in and Mu Yi introduced him as Dr Wang. When he discovered that I had just returned from Australia, he was extremely interested and began asking me about short-term English courses. I also wanted to talk to him about Mu Yi's condition, so I asked if there was somewhere we could talk. He said we could go to his office. I told Mu Yi I had to go out for a while, and then followed Dr Wang out of the ward. I tried to be helpful by talking about all kinds of things to do with English classes. However, all he really wanted to know was where he could borrow about $A5000, and how he could find a part-time job to pay the money back and support himself at the same time. I am afraid I was not much help to him.

At last I managed to get in a word about my friend's condition. I asked him if there were any drugs, unavailable in China, that might help his situation. I thought I might be able to ask some friends to get them for me. The doctor told me that I should not worry about that, in fact, physically he was not in much danger. The problem was his state of mind. He asked me if I knew why he was so terribly depressed. I actually knew quite a bit about this, but I was not sure Mu Yi would want me to reveal it, so I said I didn't know.

Then the doctor began a long lecture about cause, symptoms, diagnosis, prognosis, and so on. Most of this went over my head, but one thing I understood very well – he might need a kidney transplant.

'Where would you get a new kidney?' I asked.

'Well, people can survive with one kidney, under some circumstances, so we can occasionally get a donor kidney from a family member—'

Again he lapsed into a lecture, and my head began to swim. When he had finished I returned to the problem.

'But my friend is not married and has only an old mother, whose health is poor. I don't imagine her kidney would be of any use. Is it possible that in some case where a person has died in a car accident, that the family might agree to a transplant?'

'No, Chinese people are very feudal about this. They want to be intact when they go to another world, so we can't get people to donate organs.'

'In that case, it is almost impossible for people in my friend's situation?'

'I'm afraid so. But if they have rich relatives or overseas contacts with hard currency, they might be able to buy one.'

I began to wonder if Dr Wang might himself be trying to do a deal with his own kidney in exchange for $A5000.

'Do you mean to tell me that some people will actually sell their own organs for hard currency?'

'No, no, of course not. Hard currency is very valuable and all that, but no one is going to sell his organs for it.'

'You said that if you are rich enough you can buy organs. So somebody must be selling organs.'

'Yes, but no one is selling their own. These are from the bodies of those who have been executed. The major organs are kidneys and corneas.'

'And the money goes to the families?'

'No, the government makes a good bit of foreign currency out of this. Except for a few that are reserved for high-ranking cadres, the organs are sold to patients who come specially from Hong Kong and Macao, and pay foreign currency for their hospital treatment and convalescence.'

The conversation had taken a ghastly turn, but I found myself fascinated by his matter-of-fact attitude.

'Are you saying that these organs are taken without the consent of the executed, and without even the knowledge of their family members?'

'Yes. And sometimes they are taken for experiments in liver and heart transplants. But of course recently this has become more widely known, and family members have begun to demand money.'

'What does the medical profession have to say about this?'

'It has nothing to do with us. We don't ask for it, and we don't contribute to it. The condemned are taken to an execution ground. They are handcuffed behind their backs, and a rope is tied around their necks and joined to their wrists, high up their backs, so that the pressure on their throats prevents them from calling out. The executioners kick at the backs of their knees to force them into a kneeling position, and then they fire a bullet into the top part of the nape of the neck. A police surgeon plunges a long steel needle into the hole left by the bullet, and stirs it around. After this he pronounces the person dead. Then a small piece of paper is placed near the point of entry of the bullet. On the paper is an arrow pointing to the bullet-hole, and underneath the arrow are the words "bullet entry point". A photograph is taken of this piece of paper. It is only after this that we become involved. Surgeons come out from a waiting ambulance, and dissect the bodies on the spot in their mobile operating theatre. The organs are rushed away to hospital in the ambulance. The remains are left for relatives.'

I pressed on with my next thought.

'What happens if there is an emergency? Does the patient have to wait for an execution?'

'As a rule, yes.'

'And what if the patient is not a Hong Kong customer, but some very high-ranking cadre?'

'Well, there are always people waiting to be executed. It is simply a matter of ordering an execution as required.'

I stood staring at him, not so much because I was shocked, but because I wondered how much further this would go.

'Look,' he said, 'I know what you're thinking, but what do you expect me to do about it?'

'Well, it's just – I know perhaps some of these people are criminals, but what if – I mean, you know – basic rights—'

'Yes, you mean human rights. I know you've just come back from overseas, but remember you are back in China now. You are concerned about prisoners' rights? Very commendable – but you tell me something. I am a doctor and you are a lecturer, both highly respected. But what rights do we have? What is the point of talking about prisoners? Whether we take the organs from their bodies or we don't, they are still dead. Maybe it would be more civilised if we had to obtain consent, but the issue is not what to do with their bodies but how to change the system so that they won't be executed in the first place – or even be prisoners in the first place.'

Then Dr Wang told me a little about the recent student demonstrations in Hefei and Wuhan. It seems he had been listening to 'Voice of America' broadcasts. I knew that he was telling me something of great importance, but I just could not get my mind off our conversation, so I said goodbye to him and went back to see Mu Yi. Back in the ward, Mu Yi was surrounded by a number of his students and they all appeared very excited, so I just said my farewells and left.

The first I heard about the 'student tide' was in the hospital that day. Two days later, on campus, everyone was talking about the student demonstrations and demands for democracy and political reform. Even more interesting, the official organ of the government-controlled media, which did not report the demonstrations at all, were discussing ways of achieving 'socialist democracy' and a legal system reflecting 'Chinese characteristics'. I noticed that, while the students were apparently raising the issue of political reform, and reform of the 'political system', the newspapers discussed reform of the 'administrative structure'. Nevertheless, there was an unmistakable implication of support from somewhere on high for political reforms, in keeping with the economic reforms which had begun seven years ago. I remember back in Australia I had read a magazine called *Asia Week*. On the front cover was a picture of a smiling and benign Deng Xiaoping. The headline was 'People Power in China?' and underneath were the words: 'Old Deng has quietly begun the biggest freedom feast in history. He wants the Communist Party to give up some of its power and give it back to the people. Get ready for the action.'

Maybe the demonstrations were 'the action'. Even if not, there was certainly something in the wind. I thought of a line from a Tang poem: '*Shan yu yu lai feng man lou*' [When rain is gathering in the hills, the pavilion fills with wind]. Now I understood why the students in Mu Yi's ward were so excited – I too became excited.

On 21 December 1986 I received a letter from my parents in Shanghai. I had written to them when I first returned to Nanjing. My mother had had a heart attack, and was now in hospital. I rushed over to the departmental office. The party secretary was there. I showed her the letter and asked if I could have leave to go to Shanghai. She seemed much more sympathetic to me than she had been a few days before, when I was trying to get accommodation.

'Yes, I've been thinking, maybe you should go back to see your parents, since you don't have teaching responsibilities at the moment. Actually, I also want to let you know that the leaders in our department have always trusted you and tried to protect you when necessary. As for the matter of writing to you and asking you to come back from Australia, you know that it had nothing to do with this department. We were instructed to do it by the Higher Education Bureau. In fact, they said if we didn't do it, no one from this department would ever again be selected to go overseas.'

She sighed and looked a little uncomfortable, as I made no response.

'They never explained to us why they had to have you back. We did arrange your teaching duties at that time, but things changed because you were delayed by your involvement in that court case in Australia. That kind of complication was simply beyond us. Perhaps there was even some misunderstanding, I don't know – but I think now it's time you knew something about the whole business.'

I was not at all reassured by her remarks, because during our recent telephone conversation, Liu Aihua had led me to believe that there was no problem. On the other hand, in view of the volatile political situation, it was just possible that a problem of some days ago was now no longer a problem. Perhaps the secretary's speech was the first movement visible on the political barometer, and she was preparing to defend herself against any departmental recriminations over the decision to get me back from Australia. I began to suspect that the student demonstrations were not simply a matter of interest, they might well be a matter of my political salvation.

On 23 December I went to Shanghai. As I came out of the railway station everyone was talking about the public transport restrictions which had occurred as a result of the student demonstrations. I went to the taxi rank.

'Where do you want to go?'

'Yongjia Road.'

'Can't go there, the city centre is blocked.'

Another train passenger standing near me cut in, 'Damn the students! They've fouled everything up with their demonstrations, the stupid mongrels!'

The cabbie called out to him, 'Hey, you! Watch your mouth! Who do you think the students are demonstrating for, if not for poor bastards like us?'

I turned round and gave my fellow-passenger a filthy look, to let the taxi driver know that I supported his stance completely. I walked away from the rank, but the driver called out to me, 'Hang on. Maybe we could go through the Jingan Temple intersection. It may not work and it will cost a bit more, but if you like we could try it? At least, even if you have to walk from there, it's a lot closer.'

'Terrific! Let's go.'

The other passenger came over to us.

'As a matter of fact, I could go that way too.'

'I don't care,' said the driver, 'it's up to him. He's paying the fare.'

The passenger turned to me, and said, 'Look, no offence about what I said just now. You don't mind, do you? I'll pay half to you, of course.'

'All right, that's fine. Come on, let's get going.'

At Jingan Temple my companion got out. As it happened we were in luck because the intersection was not blocked off. After a few more minutes I was home. There was no one to meet me. In fact the door was locked, so I searched for the key in the usual hiding-place, and found it. Inside there was a note on the table to the effect that my father had gone to hospital to see my mother. The hospital's address was included in the note. I took my brother's bike, which had been left standing in the corridor, and cycled off to Putuo District Number Three Textile Workers Hospital.

The regulations in this hospital were much stricter than the one in Nanjing. Patients were permitted a maximum of three visitors at a time, and all visitors had to identify themselves on arrival. The receptionist checked a big board full of bamboo strips, hung on nails next to each patient's name. There were two strips hung next to my mother's name, indicating that she already had a visitor. The bed number was 738, in Building 5. It was a very high building, much higher than anything in the Workers Hospital in Nanjing, and I had to take a lift to the seventh floor. There was one other person in the lift, just standing there waiting. I moved to press the button for the seventh floor, but a sign said, 'Do not press buttons. Wait for operator.' After two or three more people gathered, the operator appeared and used a key to start the lift. As we ascended, people motioned to her to stop at this floor or that, and she stopped the lift somehow without using the buttons. Not a word was spoken.

I went into the ward, and the first familiar thing I saw was my father's silver hair. He sat beside my mother, as she sat half-upright, supported by her pillow. She didn't look too bad, and in fact she greeted me with delight. I started talking about Australia, but to my surprise she seemed to know all there was to know. She not only knew about the oppositeness of seasons, unlike our old coal merchant, and about kangaroos, but also about Captain Cook's discovery of Australia, the Sydney Opera House, platypuses, and Ayers Rock. Suddenly she asked me why I had come back in such a hurry, and what I had done with my new wife.

'I know you can look after yourself. You left home when you were sixteen, and you have had a lot of experience, but what about Bi Lijun? Surely she must find it difficult being left all by herself?'

'Yes, I know, but she's trying to get an opportunity to study. If she can't, she'll be back soon.'

72

'But why couldn't you have stayed a bit longer and helped her sort things out?'

'Well, I was summoned to return – "twelve gilded commands" from the Emperor.'

As soon as I said this I realised I had said a great deal. Unfortunately for my parents, who knew their Chinese history, the words suggested an alarming parallel. I was alluding to the story of the great general and patriot Yue Fei, of the Southern Song period, who was recalled from the front by the Emperor Gao Zong, despite the critical stage of the battle against the Jin Tartars. Yue Fei could not bring himself to leave the battle, but after twelve commands from the Emperor himself, written in gold characters, he had no choice. When he returned to the capital, Hangzhou, he found that Minister Qin Gui had levelled trumped-up charges of treason against him. Yue Fei was sentenced to death, but before the sentence was carried out Qin Gui was asked what evidence he had for his accusations. '*Mo xu you!*' [No need for that!], said Qin Gui. Yue Fei was secretly put to death at the West Lake. Years later when Emperor Gao Zong died, the new emperor posthumously honoured the general for his loyalty and patriotism. A temple was built to the memory of Yue Fei, and iron figures of Qin Gui and his wife, who was considered the instigator of the plot, were erected near the entrance. For centuries small boys urinated upon the kneeling statues and visitors spat upon them, and when people prepared the dough sticks known as *youzha gui*, and twisted two strands together to throw into the frying oil, they remembered the treacherous Qin Gui and his wife.

My father looked terribly apprehensive. To use an expression he often used himself, he was 'a sparrow afraid of even the twang of a bowstring'. After enduring so much suffering in the late 1960s and early 70s, even a hint of impending danger was sufficient to cause him alarm. Now my own metaphor had suggested some serious political difficulty, a plot of some kind against me. Perhaps I had become a little tactless after my two years abroad and forgotten the subtleties of Chinese life.

'Oh, come on, Dad,' I said, 'it's 1986 now, not 1966. Look, I wouldn't be surprised if some promotion is waiting for me, after my experience in Australia. I haven't seen anyone yet who hasn't got promotion after their return from overseas.'

Although this made my parents feel a little better, my mother said, as she had on a thousand occasions in the past, 'As your father's mother used to say, "You cannot harbour malice against others in your heart, but you must prepare to shield your heart against the malice of others, this is the family motto." ' She went on, solemnly, 'You spoke of Yue Fei. Remember that your father's mother was of the Yue line, of Yixing.'

How could I forget? I had heard this not only from my mother, but from my grandfather, who died just before I went to Australia. Now it was my mother's turn to strike fear into my heart. Did she mean that history was going to repeat itself? What a tragedy, I thought, if the descendants of Yue Fei still have to live in fear of treachery. I resolved that I would not go obediently to my execution at the hands of liars and cheats, in order to be posthumously rehabilitated.

My mother went on, 'Your father and I are old. There isn't much left for us to fear. You kids are our pride, and you have all filled the last part of our lives with great happiness. If anything were to happen to you, I don't know how we could bear it. Please be careful.'

'Oh, don't worry, Mum, we can look after ourselves—'

'Yes, I know that very well. But I am particularly worried about your brother. He suffered so much in the Cultural Revolution. I'm not sure his health is up to it, the way he's working in America.'

My elder brother, Yang Xiaoping, had only been in America for four months. He had been among the best in the nation-wide examination for a scholarship to study at Columbia University Law School. He left China the day after Bi Lijun and I were married in Australia, and my parents had a feast for this occasion of double happiness.

'Mum, you really mustn't worry so much. I'm sure he'll be careful.'

In fact I was also worried that he might be overdoing the study. I told myself that I must write to him soon, and remind him that he had to watch himself.

4   *A Small Pond Cannot Contain a Dragon*

Back home that evening, over a long and rather disorganised meal and plenty of Qingdao beer, Dad and I chatted about Australia and about our relatives in Yixing. After some time, he went off to watch Peking Opera on the television, and I stood outside the back door, smoking. I lit one cigarette after another, in a way I had not done for many years. I kept hearing my mother's words about her children, and I wondered how I would feel as a parent. I would not want my children to repeat my experience or that of my own parents. I looked up at the clear winter sky and thought of the current government slogan '*Xiang qian kan*' [Look to the future].' What future? The past seemed much more in evidence than the future.

My earliest memories are of hunger. My father was away somewhere in Nanhui County, doing 'thought reform through labour'. I heard my mother whispering to my sister, who was three years older than me, that this was because of my father's 'rightist tendencies'. She said it would only be for a few years, and after that everything would be all right. I remember one day Mum opened a can of meat she had been keeping for a long time. She was going to make some dumplings for my father, who had been permitted a day visit. We had not seen him for six months. We three children helped enthusiastically with the dumplings, and then began an impatient wait for Dad. We waited and waited. He was expected around 12.30, but by two o'clock he still had not come. I remember feeling hungrier and hungrier. Finally, Mum steamed some dumplings for us but

Dad never came. Some weeks later, when he did turn up, he brought his own rice bowl with him – the one that Mum always called the 'great ocean bowl'. We children were fascinated by the size of it, but Mum explained that on Dad's farm everyone was allowed two 'bowls' of food – no matter how big or small the bowls. I said that I didn't believe anyone could eat two such bowls' worth of food, but Dad demonstrated his skill with two huge loads of rice gruel. Not only that, he polished off two ducks' heads, to go with his sweet potato liquor.

Somehow my mother always managed to conjure up banquets out of nothing for those special occasions when my father visited, and we all waited eagerly for the next one. All kinds of food were scarce in the early 1960s. My brother and sister and I had seen more apples and bananas in our primary school textbooks than in the flesh. Such things had more to do with mathematics than with meals. 'Three apples plus two apples equals how many apples?' Our teachers explained that apples had been stolen from the north by the Soviet revisionists, and sugarcane and bananas had been stolen from Taiwan by American imperialist invaders. Only the skins had been left by the American 'devils'. This fired our determination to liberate Taiwan, and we often sang at the tops of our voices:

> To fight the wolf you must have a club,
> To fight the tiger you must have a gun,
> To fight the invaders – Hey! – the people must
>   be armed.

In 1964, during one of his home visits, Dad broke his leg, and was allowed to stay at home for a few months, but his health seemed to get worse. He contracted hepatitis, and Mum always kept his bowl and chopsticks well away from ours, to avoid contagion. Just when we thought he

77

was recovering, he broke a couple of ribs, after fainting and falling downstairs. He was reasonably mobile again by late 1965, and I remember going out for walks with him along Huaihai Road and into Baoqing Road, with the great yellow leaves floating down from the plane trees. In the distance there was a loudspeaker, and a strange high-pitched voice was reciting Yao Wenyuan's article on 'Hai Rui Dismissed from Office'.

I tried to discuss this with Dad.

'In school they have been making us write criticisms of "Hai Rui Dismissed from Office", but I don't really understand. What's it all about?'

'Hai Rui was a Ming dynasty official, who was honest and worked very hard for the good of the common people. Because of his honesty, he punished wrongdoers, no matter how many important connections they had. Finally he upset some big shots, who made a false report to the Emperor about him, and he was dismissed from his job.'

'You mean he was a good guy, not a villain?'

Dad suddenly became rather nervous, and momentarily seemed lost for words: 'Mmm, first, the *real* Hai Rui was different from the one in Peking Opera. Second, there is some academic debate about whether Hai Rui was a good guy or not—'

'What does "academic debate" mean?'

'It means it has nothing to do with us.'

'But, if it has nothing to do with us, why do they ask us to write criticisms and essays?'

'What do the other kids do?'

'They just copy the newspaper.'

'Terrific. Why don't you just do the same?'

I was not very satisfied with my father's response, and I suppose he must have guessed that I was a bit unhappy with him, because he suddenly said, 'Come on, let me give you a test. Which dynasty came after the Ming?'

78

'The Qing.'

'Good. Which dynasty came before the Ming?'

'The Yuan.'

'Correct.'

Then he suddenly sprang his old motto on me, one he never tired of telling my brother and sister and me.

'No matter which dynasty is in power, you will always prosper if you have a special skill. Try to study hard at school and learn something which will be useful to you in later life. When you grow up you will know what I mean, and you will be very glad to have useful skills.'

In 1966 the voices on radio became more and more strident and inhuman, the music became more and more martial, and my parents grew more and more nervous. I often heard Dad whispering to Mum in the kitchen, saying that there was no need to worry, and all this fuss had nothing to do with us. The *People's Daily* editorials insisted that there was not going to be a political campaign, but merely a debate in the academic sphere. At eight in the evening, people in the neighbourhood listened intently to the radio news, and kept saying there was nothing to worry about – but they certainly didn't look as if there was nothing to worry about. But for me and my friends, who would normally be preparing for high school entrance exams, it *was* a carefree time. School suddenly broke up, without even the dreaded final exam, and we started summer vacation a month early. We were not even given the usual tedious homework to do during the holidays. All we had to think about was making model aeroplanes and going fishing in the streams near Longhua military airport.

On 23 August 1966 a little group of us were walking home, carrying buckets of small fish, and poles and gear from the day's outing. When we reached Pushkin Square in Yueyang Road, we suddenly encountered a very strange sight. A group of handsome young men and women in faded military uniforms, without cap badges or collar patches, but with thick red armbands and leather belts and straps, were plastering the statue of Pushkin with 'big-character posters'. We went over to see what was going on. Their armbands said, 'Shanghai Institute of Music Red Guard', and the posters said that Pushkin was a bourgeois poet who spread lots of 'poisonous weeds'. A very pretty girl recited quotations from Chairman Mao in a loud and dramatic style, rather like some Italian opera I had heard on the radio.

'A revolution is not a dinner party, or writing an essay, or painting a picture, or doing embroidery; it cannot be so refined, so leisurely and gentle, so temperate, kind, courteous, restrained and magnanimous. A revolution is an insurrection, an act of violence by which one class overthrows another!'

Then they all went mad, trying to smash the statue with hammers. Since the statue was bronze it resisted pretty well, but then they tried pouring ink all over it, all the time cursing and swearing like maniacs, even those slim and pretty, genteel-looking young girls. My heart was pounding furiously now. What if they found out that we had one of Pushkin's books in the house? Or that my Mum often read us 'The Tale of a Goldfish?' I felt certain that even one hammer blow would be more than enough to finish off my poor old mother. At last, I realised that this business *did* have something to do with us. This was, for me, the real beginning of the Cultural Revolution, which they said would 'touch everyone's soul'.

I ran home to find Mum and Dad frantically burning things in the little coal stove. The stove was already full of ashes, and Mum was scooping them up in a dustpan, and rushing back and forth to the toilet to flush them away. Among a pile of documents and letters and Mum's old diaries, was Pushkin, waiting to be cremated together with his Chinese colleagues Du Fu and Bai Juyi. In between burnings, Dad was writing quotations from Chairman Mao on pieces of paper and sticking them up all over the house. I noticed, in particular, 'If we have shortcomings, we are not afraid to have them pointed out and criticised, because we serve the people.'

Whether because of my parents' quick thinking or not, I don't know, but we didn't suffer as badly as others at first. Before the Red Guards reached our house, Dad posted up some big-character posters of self-criticism, declaring that Chairman Mao and the Communist Party had made him realise the error of his ways just in the nick of time. Less fortunate ones had their houses raided by Red Guards and were made to stand on stools outside their houses, exclaiming, 'I have committed the crime of exploiting the labouring class. I am a blood-sucking monster!' Gangs of kids roamed happily from house to house watching the unexpected entertainment of grown-ups being humiliated for a change. Even better, they soon discovered that these formerly all-powerful adults could be made to stand up, sit down, nod their heads or shake them, in accordance with one's merest whim, provided there were Red Guards in the vicinity. I must admit that, for a time, I was myself so diverted by these goings on, in which I participated enthusiastically, that I forgot my own family's troubles.

I took to wearing a phoncy People's Liberation Army cap and followed another boy around from lane to lane. He had a *real* PLA cap, and considered himself vastly superior to me, because, although the same age as me, he was much bigger. He even had a Red Guard armband that he must have filched from his cousin or some older friend. He wore it, not around his arm, but inside his cap, and would stand idly whistling in a corner of the lane, dangling the cap in front of him, waiting for a member of the exploiting class to appear. Just as the bourgeois reactionary was about to pass, the proletarian hero would step out and rakishly brandish his cap at him. If this did not stop the traveller in his tracks, he would call out, 'Hey you! Where do you think you're going? Hold it right there.'

'What? Oh, yes, of course. Sorry, I didn't notice—'

'Really? I see. You seem not to have noticed quite a few things. Let's see if you noticed yourself committing any crimes against the people.'

'Of course. Yes, I committed many crimes – ah, I – I exploited my landless farm labourers – but I didn't beat them—'

'Yes, but did you give them enough to eat?'

'But I didn't have enough to eat myself, no one did—'

'Rubbish. Don't give me that! You rich landlords had banquets of meat and fish every day, even for breakfast!'

This performance went on for some time, and I was spellbound and full of admiration at my friend's skill in extracting every last bit of power out of the magic cap. Finally, he would make his victim perform several bows, and he would say, magnanimously, 'All right then, off you go!'

After a while, however, things became more serious, and there were fewer and fewer of our old neighbourhood adversaries left to torment. The homes of people who were accused of being reactionaries were raided, and their things thrown out into the street. Reactionaries were driven out, and proletarians moved in. As far as I could tell, you knew a proletarian by the huge jars of pickled vegetables he always carried about with him, but my mother took us kids aside one day and tried to explain the situation.

'Look at our neighbour, Teacher Zhang, in No. 53. One day he was one of us, and the next he was a secret agent, and he and his family were driven out of their house. Anything might happen to any one of us – at any moment. Your Dad and I have been thinking that, rather than waiting to be thrown out, it might be a good idea to volunteer to

82

move. What do you say? At least we would have somewhere to go.'

We all thought that was a good idea, and for my part I didn't really mind moving, but I was alarmed at my mother's words, because I now began to realise how serious things were. And how could I face my old gang if they found out that I was from a 'bad background' family?

In September 1966 my family volunteered to move a few kilometres south-east to Dapu Bridge, to reclaimed industrial land which had been an open sewer before 1949. Now we all lived in one room, instead of two, and we shared a big kitchen and bathroom and toilet with twenty other families, instead of four.

This time my parents' quick thinking didn't keep us out of trouble for very long. In February 1967 my father was suddenly detained by the Shanghai Security Bureau. He was supposed to be a secret Nationalist agent who had committed crimes against landless farm labourers in the past. It was many years before I knew what this was all about.

About 1939 my father had been a primary school teacher. He had learnt to read and write from my grandfather, who could recite the 'Three Character Classic', the 'Hundred Surnames' and the 'Thousand Character Essay'.* This gave him special status and responsibilities as an 'educated gentleman', at a time when hardly any of the villagers could even write their names.

In order to do his bit to stop the Japanese advance, Dad joined the Nationalists, and risked his life in organising the local people's resistance movement. During the war he was

---

* These are classic texts which were used for over a thousand years as elementary readers for Chinese children. They were not widely used after the turn of the century.

involved in the capture of two farmhands who had been collaborating with the Japanese. These two men were executed. During the Cultural Revolution, the relatives of the men claimed that a bourgeois intellectual and former Nationalist agent owed two 'blood debts' to the poor peasants.

After Dad's arrest, my family suffered the fate of others, and I was now no longer a spectator, idly wondering at the piles of furniture in the street, or the crossed banners sealing the doors of my former neighbours' houses. All our things were smashed to pieces. Slogans were crudely daubed on the walls and ceiling of our room: 'Smash the clandestine Nationalist Yang Yun!', 'Blood debts must be paid in blood!', 'For you only humility and obedience are fitting. You have no right to freedom of movement and speech', 'The imperialist running dog's stinking daughter Fang Wen has only to make an honest confession to set foot at last on the right path', 'Long live the dictatorship of the proletariat!'

The slogans about Fang Wen referred to my mother, who gave me her family name. In 1941, before the outbreak of the Pacific War, her father was a police sergeant in the British Concession in Shanghai. In fact my mother had had to dissociate herself from her father after 1949, when he was expelled from Shanghai and forcibly relocated in Shandong Province, in a village of Rongchen County, called 'Little White' Village. He never returned to Shanghai, and died of an illness in 1959. My sister Yang Xinhan, my brother Yang Xiaoping (both of whom had been given my father's family name) and I never saw our maternal grandparents, but right up until their deaths my mother sent them 10 yuan a month to help them survive.

Early every morning my mother went to work in Shanghai Number One Woollen Sweater Knitting Mill, and reported to the Revolutionary Rebels concerning the crime of her

84

background, and did not return home until late at night after long criticism sessions. My sister was obliged to make a public announcement about her background to her school, Shanghai Number Two Girls Secondary. As a result she was put in the 'Children of bad background study group'. My brother made a similar confession in his school, Number Fifty-one Secondary, as I did in mine, Fenyang Secondary, and we were all assigned to 'study groups'.

We started the study sessions early in the morning, and returned home late at night. We were engaged in endless writing of forced confessions and denunciations of others close to us. We had to denounce our parents for the customary 'spreading poison', that is, talking sedition and counter-revolution in the household. They were supposed to have fostered talk of opposition to the Communist Party, socialism, and Mao Zedong thought. We were often forced to denounce our parents, and each of us took part in 'study groups' of a month's duration for this purpose.

In July 1967 the revolutionary committee of Number Two Girls Secondary School told my sister that because her family background was so bad, she would have to undergo re-education at Chongming Island, reclaimed land in the month of the Yangtze, near Shanghai. After our sister's departure, Yang Xiaoping and I were made to report to a study group organised by the Shanghai Public Security Bureau.

In this group they tried to persuade us to write a so-called 'open letter' calling on our father, Yang Yun, to bow to the will of the people. We did not co-operate at first, so they locked us in a basement for a long time, perhaps fifteen or sixteen hours, with no food or rest, while they screamed and ranted at us, until finally Yang Xiaoping fainted. At this time he was fifteen and I was thirteen. The next day they came again. This time we were taken out of the basement and led upstairs to a sort of auditorium. Hundreds of people were gathered, bellowing military songs at the tops of their voices. My brother and I were made to sit in the front row, with others very obviously in the same predicament. After a few songs, someone yelled 'March them out!', and about a dozen people, both men and women, all wearing dunce's hats, were pushed and shoved out into the centre of the stage. Each had a wooden board around his neck; on it was a painted slogan, denouncing their crimes – 'Down with counter-revolutionaries', 'Smash the traitors', 'Ten thousand deaths to the enemy agents', and 'Boil the rightists in oil'. The revolutionaries all around us seemed to have gone completely insane, shouting 'Long live the dictatorship of the proletariat', and 'Carry the class struggle through to the end'.

Dad's wooden board proclaimed him to be an enemy agent. A great big man in army boots kicked him in the hip and he dropped to the floor. We were afraid to betray the slightest emotion at this, and mechanically raised our arms, waving aloft the 'Little Red Book' of Chairman Mao which everyone was required to carry at all times. It seemed that if there were any hint of reluctance on our part we might have been torn to pieces by a frenzied mob. I don't remember how the meeting ended.

After they released us from the study group, my brother became extremely ill, and his blood pressure soared. He was sent to a medical research institute. He was terrified that he might be deliberately infected with disease in some experiment, and for a time was simply mad with fear. My own state of mind was also seriously affected. Just Mum and I remained at home. I could not sleep. I thought and thought, a thousand times, until my head swam, but still I could find no meaning for what was going on around me. I thought constantly of my father, and so it went on for weeks – no sleep, my head in a whirl, dizzy with exhaustion and anxiety, but still no meaning or reason crystallising out of the turmoil. As if overwhelmed by the struggle inside my head, my hair began to fall out, until finally only one strand was left at the back of my head, rather like a pathetic queue, a kind of stigma that would signal to others that I was a disgraced remnant of the feudal past, a fit target for their abuse and insults. My fake PLA cap now came in handy for disguising my shame, and I always wore it jammed down over my ears on the rare occasions when I ventured out of the house.

The time came when I could no longer avoid going out of the house. In answer to Chairman Mao's direction that students should return to school in order to wage revolution ('*Fu ke nao geming*'), my school, Fenyang Secondary, reopened, and I had to go back to join in 'revolutionary activities'. It was half an hour's walk from our new address to the school, and on the way there were plenty of hazards in the form of boys who would snatch my cap and throw it to the ground.

'Aha! An undercover baldy, eh? What you need is not only a false PLA cap but some false hair to go with it!'

My tormentors seemed to be everywhere, and no matter how careful I was to avoid any confrontation, I suffered this humiliation, almost every day.

There was one particularly nasty gang, led by a lout I dubbed 'Fathead'. They often hung around outside our place just about the time I was returning from school. After some very unpleasant experiences I adopted the tactic of hiding in a corner of the lane for hours, until it grew dark and they went on their way. Mum used to worry about me getting home so late, but I always lied to her about it, and told her that we had all been kept back for a criticism meeting. I couldn't bear to tell her what was really happening. There were times in 1967 when I was so low that I sometimes thought about suicide.

One afternoon, as I approached home, I was relieved to

see that there was no sign of the gang, and I quickened my step to get home before they turned up. Suddenly Fathead leapt out in front of me, from some hiding-place of his own.

'Ah, there you are! Haven't seen you for ages. Where have you been? We've been worried about you. Let's see now, how's that hair problem of yours?'

He snatched the cap from my head and threw it over a wall and into a plum tree. His followers all roared with delight at this.

'Well now. Look at you! I think you look terrific without a cap. What do you say, men?'

I tried to cover my head with my hands and make my way past the gang.

'Halt! Hands at your sides! Take everything out of your pockets.'

I emptied my pockets – a few cents, a few rice coupons.

'Anything in your shirt pocket?'

There was a cricket in a little ivory cage that I had put in my shirt pocket so that it would be warm. I had found the cage, which belonged to my grandfather, among the 'remnants of feudalism' that my parents had collected for burning. I clutched protectively at my pocket.

'OK. Take it easy. No one's going to steal anything from you. Just let's have a look.'

I took out the cage.

'Aha! A fake ivory cricket cage.' He signalled to his henchmen. 'Hey, come and have a look at this.'

I knew that once it had been passed on, the cage would disappear and each kid would ostentatiously deny that he had it, so I moved to take it from Fathead's grimy paw. He retaliated by punching me in the left eye.

'Keep your mitts off me, scab-head!'

I picked myself up from the ground, and went on my way. I knew I had no hope of retrieving the cricket.

Some days later, my eye had turned blue and yellow. I

was stopped in the corridor at school by Hu Dachuan, an old friend of my brother. He had been away somewhere and I had not seen him for some years. After a while I told him what had happened to my eye.

'All right, this afternoon I'll go with you.'

That afternoon, when we got to the place, the gang was there, waiting for me. I saw them in the distance and I said, 'Dachuan, let's go back and wait till they've gone.'

'Don't worry. I'm here', he said, with astonishing calmness. 'Just do what I tell you.'

So I followed him, right up to them. They seemed a little tense, I thought. I stopped about five or six metres short of them; I was afraid to go any further. Hu Dachuan just kept walking casually on. When he reached them he said, 'Shall we talk business first? Or just get started? One at a time? Or all together? It's all the same to me.'

Not a sound in reply. I stood enraptured. Already he had unnerved them terribly with his supernatural self-confidence.

'What's the matter? Don't you want to have a go?'

Still no reply.

'OK. Then we'll talk business.'

He jerked a thumb over his shoulder at me, still waiting tentatively in the background for my instructions.

'Which one of you was it who was disrespectful to my little brother? You?'

'No, not me. Nothing to do with me.'

He went one by one through this routine until he got to Fathead.

'OK. So it was me. So what? What are you gonna do about it?'

'Bravo! I admire your nerve. I can't stand fighting with chicken-hearted weaklings. Now I have a real hero to deal with! OK, you make the first move.'

'No. You go first.'

89

'All right, but just to be fair, I'll only use one hand and one foot. All right?'

He had both hands in his pockets, and languidly removed one hand in order to tweak Fathead's nose.

'That's the official start', said Hu.

Fathead was beside himself with rage. He lunged ferociously at his enemy's throat. Hu swayed gracefully backward, one hand still in his pocket, and tripped Fathead as he flew past, helping him on his way with his free hand, all in one magically fast and elegant motion. Fathead lay stricken and gasping, about four metres from where he had started out. He seemed unable or unwilling to move.

'This movement', said Hu, in a helpfully instructive tone, 'is a combination of "leading the goat in the direction it wants to go" and "phantom footwork".'

He turned to the others, who looked most apprehensive now, to see their champion so easily routed.

'If you are not fully satisfied with this demonstration, and you'd like to mount another challenge, I am more than happy to accommodate you. My name, by the way, is Hu Dachuan, and I will be glad to see any of you any time.'

Then his tone changed and his whole body seemed charged with a terrible menace. 'But, if any one of you lays a finger on my little friend here, I swear I will put a skylight in his skull!'

I floated home, thrilled and tingling under the spell of his wizardry. I would savour every moment of this encounter for the rest of my life. Next day, as I wandered home from school, still glowing with satisfaction, I was brought up short by the figure of Fathead, who had materialised in front of me. Of course, it had all been too good to be true. I was really in for it now.

'Little Brother, have a cigarette.'

He took out a packet of Flying Horse cigarettes. I puffed

away on one – it was actually my first cigarette and it made me feel quite sick, but of course I managed it with some aplomb, as if it were as palatable as icecream.

'Little Brother, you know it is natural for friends to squabble among themselves a bit. That's how you get to know people. Now about your genuine ivory cricket cage. It was all Rat Eyes's fault, the silly little bastard! He sold it for a few bucks and bought these cigarettes we're smoking right now.'

Rat Eyes looked very sullen, as Fathead swatted at him with his great ham-fist and then plucked the PLA cap from his head.

'Here you are, Little Brother, here's a real cap to replace your old pretend one. Let bygones be bygones, eh?'

'Yes, of course. Forget the past, I always say.'

At last I had a *real* PLA cap.

I was increasingly drawn into the company of outcasts, pariahs and ne'er-do-wells, the flotsam and jetsam of the Cultural Revolution, a diverse enough bunch, but all sharing the stigma of a counter-revolutionary pedigree. We often holed up in Li Dangang's place – me, Hu Dachuan, Zhu Zhongyi, Luo Shijing and Li Qiming, all of us about fourteen or fifteen. I encouraged the use of romantic nicknames, as if we were members of some fabulous secret society – 'Wild Sparrow', 'The Beggar', 'Giraffe', 'Old Bear', 'Perfumed Lady', and even the exotic 'Captain Browning', named after a dashing military figure in a Western novel. We all practised martial arts enthusiasticaly under the expert guidance of Hu Dachuan. Unfortunately, I was not much good at it, but I became indispensable to the gang in other ways. In particular, I was something of a tactician and strategist, and was soon styled 'Little Zhuge Liang', after the legendary military genius of *The Romance of the Three Kingdoms*, a famous story of ancient China. I earned my reputation by advising the others how to stay out of the clutches of the Public Security Bureau.

On one occasion, Luo Shijing's grandmother was attacked and savagely beaten while emptying the lavatory pits, a task assigned to her as labour reform, since she was a former landowner. After the beating she was thrown into the pit. Hu Dachuan could not wait to go in search of the thug 'activists' who had done this and give them a thorough beating, but I argued that we must be much more subtle unless we wanted to wind up in jail. I devised a plan. Wild Sparrow contacted Fathead and his gang and supplied them with a few packets of Flying Horse cigarettes. They awaited our signal, and then one evening, while we were all sitting conspicuously in the front row of a 'speak bitterness' meeting, in which an old peasant recounted the woes of life before Liberation, Fathead and his boys went to work. While we were shouting at the tops of our voices, 'Down with the bloodsucking landlord tyrants', our accomplices were using catapults to fire stones into the windows of all those who had taken part in the beating of the old woman. Glass was very hard to replace in those days. From the second floor of a distant building a light flashed on and off, twice. The mission had succeeded, and Hu Dachuan and I exchanged a glance, while screaming our revolutionary slogans. I felt great pleasure as I remembered the expression, 'The most satisfying victory is the one planned in a command tent, a thousand miles from the action.'

We often went to Hu Dachuan's place, which was empty, because his parents had been put in prison. We listened to some Western records he had been given by a friend. Hu Dachuan did not understand the words, but he was an excellent mimic, and after listening repeatedly to the records he could reproduce the sound, to our satisfaction anyway.

At night we often went up onto the roof and he would sing and accompany himself on an old guitar while we smoked and smoked. Years later I finally found out what he was singing – 'Old Black Joe'.

In March 1969 Hu Dachuan was labelled a 'ringleader' and a 'counter-revolutionary' and arrested by the Xuhui branch of the Shanghai Public Security Bureau. The rest of us were detained in the Huaizhong Secondary School for over three months by the Shanghai Municipality '*Wen gong wu wei*' – this phrase means, literally, 'Attack with words, but defend with weapons', and refers to a speech of Mao's wife Jiang Qing during one of the many phases of the Cultural Revolution in which the question of violence and 'anarchy' was debated. The idea was supposed to be that revolution-aries should not initiate violence, but should be prepared to defend themselves against reactionaries, by means of armed struggle if necessary. In fact, the political faction which adopted this phrase as its motto was never slow to employ violence for any purpose at all. Jiang Qing's fine words became yet another justification for barbarity.

There was plenty of violence in Huaizhong Secondary during these months. As 'disciples' of Hu Dachuan, we were also the subjects of meetings to denounce him, during which we were punched in the face and had our arms twisted up our backs, forcing us into the position known as 'doing the aeroplane', that is, a sort of position like the one children adopt when they are playing aeroplanes. Also, once a week we were 'brought to trial', and during these sessions we were punched and kicked, and beaten with sticks and belts. Once, after I had been thrashed, I was forced to perch on my knees on an upturned stool and told that I must not lift my gaze from the floorboards. They screamed at me to confess my crimes, but I could not utter a sound.

'Are you dead or alive?' they yelled, and suddenly I felt

a blow across the bridge of my nose. Something sharp, metallic, perhaps a box or a steel can, or a pencil case. I really don't know to this day what it was, but for the moment it brought my trial to an end, as blood gushed out over my face and I tumbled unconscious from the stool. At that time I was not quite sixteen.

In July 1969 Hu Dachuan was sentenced to three years' labour reform in Yunnan Province, and the rest of our old gang was sent back by the '*Wen gong wu wei*' to Fenyang Secondary, under the surveillance of the 'revolutionary masses', in order to be reformed. In November Fenyang Secondary became a model for heeding Chairman Mao's call to go 'up to the mountains and down to the villages', and the school was geared up to go and 'wage revolution' out in Huma County of Heilongjiang Province, near the Soviet border. I was to become one of many millions of high school students who left the cities to go out into the poverty-stricken countryside, to 'carry the revolution into the village', but I was one of a special category 'escorted' by Red Guards and kept under close and constant surveillance. During a preparatory mobilisation rally, the leader of our 'worker's Mao thought-propaganda team', Hong Shifu, told his 'little red generals':

'This time your assignment is to form the front line of the anti-Soviet revisionist army. But your assignment is not only to confront the Soviet revisionist invaders, but to also challenge dangerous elements within our own ranks, such as Fang Xiangshu and his ilk. You must keep a sharp lookout and dedicate your very life and your last drop of blood to defending our motherland, which takes its shape from the iron resolve of the proletarian dictatorship.'

Before departure we were permitted a few days to pack our things. My mother used this time to sew some clothes for me, and while she sewed she recited a Tang poem:

Loving mother, thread in hand,
Sewing clothes and silent, yearning,
Finely stitching, time and again,
Each stitch to wish a son's returning.

Her other son sat and watched. Yang Xiaoping had been in and out of hospital many times over the last two years or so, and, since he had documentation certifying that he was unfit for travel, he was in no immediate danger of being sent to some remote village. My sister wanted to come home from Chongming Island to see me off, but she was refused permission. We had not seen nor heard from Dad for two and a half years, since that terrible 'struggle meeting' in the local auditorium. My mother looked very grave, and said, 'Since you are going a thousand miles away, and we don't know when we will see you again, there is something I must tell you. Long ago, before your father was arrested, he and I discussed how we would handle the situation if he was pronounced a counter-revolutionary. We decided that it would be best if we got divorced, to save you kids politically. As for my problem, I think I am in less serious danger, since I was only a foster daughter of your grandparents, and my own natural parents were very poor and had to sell me, so I am a victim of the old society.'

Suddenly I felt as if I had grown up.

'Mum, if you are going to cry, do it now. I don't want any tears shed in front of them tomorrow. And I will be back.'

'That's my boy. My son's tears are not lightly shed.'

So it was in December 1969, when I was sixteen, that I set out for Heilongjiang, and Gold Mountain Commune, in order to receive 're-education'. The Shanghai Red Guards gave the local leaders a run-down on me and, as a result, my movements were strictly supervised, leaving me no opportunity for independent action or movement. I was assigned to a road-building brigade, for forced labour. Most of this brigade was composed of the 'black five' categories: landlords, rich peasants, counter-revolutionaries, bad elements and rightists, both men and women. Our task was to go into the virgin forests of Huzhong County to construct a road for hauling pine logs. Our living conditions were extremely harsh, and because there was no road we had to carry many of our tools, explosives, provisions, tents, etc., on our backs, thirty kilometres into the forest.

For the first few months the weather was below freezing, but at least, by the standards of that place, where winter temperatures often fell to fifty degrees below freezing point, making any movement impossible, the conditions were tolerable, and, since the Huma River was completely iced over, we were able to use it for dragging some of the equipment on sleds.

In May, after the thaw, everything had to be carried, and once in every five days one of us had to take a turn at lugging food and explosives for the others working on the road. This was the most hated task of all, far worse than the actual roadwork itself. The bearer had to rise about midnight and, half-walking, half-running, carry their loads to the workers. They had to take it from the point at which provisions had been dumped by a truck, at the end of the completed section of road, to their work station which, in our case, was some thirty kilometres across varied terrain of mountains, rivers and forest. For much of the journey the bearers were knee-deep in water. If they could manage their journey at some speed, they could get back to the depot by one or two in the afternoon, and have some time to themselves. Most of us, however, got back at about three or four in the afternoon.

On one occasion, not long after the ice had thawed, I had to carry a 30 kilogram bag of wheatflour. I had been walking for more than ten hours, until around dusk I arrived at the work station. The temperature dropped below zero after sunset as I crossed the last ford, some 200 metres from our tent. This was simply a tree, which had fallen conveniently across a narrow part of the river. I was absolutely exhausted. Many others had used the little 'bridge' before me, and water from their soaking shoes and trousers had formed a thin layer of ice over the surface. The tree was swaying 5 metres above the current, which surged around some large boulders at the deepest point of the narrow stream. Suddenly my feet shot from under me, and I tumbled, wheatflour and all, into the current. Fortunately, because I had been sweating earlier I had unbuttoned my cotton-padded jacket, and so I was able to get myself free of both the jacket and the bag of flour which was tied around it. I was swept downstream for 20 metres or so, frantically clutching at passing branches, until finally I was rescued from certain doom by my fellow-workers, who grabbed me and helped me climb up onto the bank. My arms were scratched and torn by the branches, I was unable to speak a sound, and my skin had turned purple with the cold. But my greatest problem was that I had wasted provisions – a great crime, according to Chairman Mao, who always said that waste was every bit as much a crime against the people as corruption or embezzlement. As a consequence, my punishment was to report the very next day for carrying explosives. Normally of course, I should not have had another turn for four days.

At the work station we were woken at a quarter past five, to the shrill blast of a whistle and the distorted cacophony of loudspeaker music. We jumped into our clothes, rushed down to the square, and lined up to sing 'The East Is Red' in front of a picture of Chairman Mao, which had been cut out of a magazine and pasted on to cardboard.

> The East is red, the sun is rising,
> Mao Zedong appears out of China,
> He brings great happiness among us,
> He is our saviour.

The Communist Party is like the sun,
Wherever it touches, it brings light
Wherever there is a Communist Party
There shall be a liberated people.

In fact, there usually was a very beautiful sun rising in the east. But no one ever noticed it, because of even more picturesque smoke rising from the kitchen fires where the cooks made preparations for our eight o'clock breakfast. All eyes were upon it as we raised our voices in reverence to Chairman Mao. At half past five every morning, we went off to work on the road for two and a half hours before returning for breakfast.

Only the hungriest person could anticipate food like ours with any pleasure. On 1 May (International Labour Day), 1 July (the birthday of the Chinese Communist Party), and 1 October (the anniversary of the founding of the People's Republic), each person received a special ration of 150 grams of sugar. Apart from an occasional supplement of fish when a group leader threw a bottle of explosives into the river, this was the only variation in a diet which was grossly inadequate for the demands of our labour. For a whole year there were no fresh vegetables or meat. But that was not the worst of it. Even our pitiful rations of wheatflour were contaminated, after being mixed up with explosive compound powder in the bags carried to the work site. *Mantou* [steamed bread] made from this concoction was so bitter as to be inedible. You just couldn't get it down your throat. We adopted the strategy of leaving it in a cotton bag outside the tent overnight, so that it froze. By taking a quick bite every now and then during the next day you could force it down.

We finished at half past eight at night, with half an hour for breakfast and lunch. Even our meal-breaks could not be spent idly eating. We had to listen to Propaganda Team recitations of the works of Chairman Mao and other central government documents and, on occasions, attend 'criticism meetings'. We were divided into military-style units of organisation, and I remember once a young girl of about sixteen, a member of the female platoon of our company, was forced to undergo 'self-criticism'. To my surprise, she had been charged with stealing, the crime of 'gain without labour'.

Some days before, she had been sick, and had been allowed to go back to her tent to rest for an hour and a half. She made the most of her time and took a half-teaspoon of sugar out of the jar of each platoon member to top up her own supply. Unfortunately for her, the second-in-command of the platoon was also resting (for which she needed no authorisation except her own), conveniently hidden by a mosquito net. She reported the girl's misconduct.

Some time after the criticism meeting I saw the girl sitting on a rock in the forest, a load of wheatflour at her feet. She looked exhausted and ill. I stopped to chat with her. She avoided my gaze, and began sobbing.

'Don't talk to me! I am a thief.'

'Oh come on, don't be silly! Tell me who is not a thief?'

'What do you mean?'

I produced a piece of dried venison which had been given to me by a member of my old school gang. He had himself 'liberated' it from provisions intended for cadres at brigade headquarters. She was very surprised as I handed it to her.

'Where did you ge—'

'Don't ask! Just eat it, and remember – you are no more a thief than any of the others who watched you confess, and certainly no more than those who made you feel ashamed. Just promise me you won't do it again, because you are obviously no good at it. For a start, a smart rabbit doesn't chew the grass around its own burrow.'

Despite my best efforts to sound like a seasoned old

campaigner, I was really unsettled by this girl, and I became conscious of my hair again. Although it had grown back reasonably well by now, it was in very poor condition. After we met once or twice more, I decided to crop my hair very short to make it look uniform, and overcome the patchy look. On one occasion I told her how I came to be in the camp, and encouraged by our growing friendship, I asked her to tell me her circumstances. To this point I had always imagined that I was the more sophisticated of the two of us and that she would follow my lead. But to my surprise and confusion she suddenly took charge of things.

'Look! Don't misunderstand me. You are the nicest boy I have ever met. You've been very kind to me. But you have had your tragedy and I have had mine. Let's not start another one together. We're like two lotuses that float together on the pond for a moment and then drift apart forever.'

I went on my way. For days after I thought of this girl whose name I did not even know, and remembered the Tang poet Bai Juyi, who had joined Pushkin and Du Fu in the flames at home that day. He had written a poem in honour of a lute player, a former courtesan, who had told him of her youth,

> *We are vagrants together at the ends of the earth,*
> *What more do we need to understand each other?*

The remains of a first romance lie buried deep in the virgin birch forest of Heilongjiang.

There were no safety regulations. Every now and then somebody was injured by an explosion. In our team, somebody was blinded, and another lost an arm. Nor were there any medical supplies or personnel. There was one time when half the work station had diarrhoea, and I was among the sufferers. My guts hurt so badly that I rolled around on the ground. I tried charring my *mantou* in the fire inside the

100

tent, so that the blackened bread would help to bind me up a little, but this was not very effective as a remedy. Every day I had a dozen or more attacks, and often I had no time to find a place, or remove my trousers. Finally, my trousers were caked in stiff, black filth, and the stench was terrible. But, after a while even the smell became a normal part of life, and there were so many who were afflicted that no one even noticed any more.

At the end of 1970, after our task was completed, the road-building team went back to the commune. I found that the majority of the Fenyang Secondary School contingent were preparing to go back to their families in Shanghai for Spring Festival. I made an application to the commune leader so that I too could go home, but my request was denied. The reason was that people of bad background were not permitted to mingle with their bad families, but had to continue receiving re-education to reform their thinking.

In August 1971 I received a letter from my family, to say that my father had been released from prison after four and a half years. The upshot of it all was that my father remained in the category of an 'antagonistic contradiction' among the people, but that, in order to demonstrate the leniency of the Party, he would be considered an 'internal contradiction' (a much less serious variety of opposition to the Party). This was supposed to be in accordance with Chairman Mao's dictum, 'Learn from past mistakes to avoid future ones, and cure the sickness to save the patient.' As a result my family were restored to the ranks of 'the people'. I rushed over to tell the commune leaders this great news. The leaders wrote off to Shanghai to verify the information, and found that it was indeed true. I began to experience a little freedom. I was allocated some different work, as a shepherd and a swineherd, and was permitted some unsupervised movement.

Then came the Richard Nixon visit to China. Beijing,

Shanghai and other big cities began to promote the study of English. English textbooks were published and became readily available in the larger cities. My brother began self-study in English, and sent me a set of textbooks so that I could do the same. In due course he also sent history and geography texts for me, and I could be seen almost any day studying my books as I tended sheep, goats or pigs.

I very quickly discovered that, although my family was basking in the warm glow of the Party's leniency, I still had to suffer a good deal of discrimination. My parents also felt that only by moving to another place could I be rescued from the 'sea of bitterness' that engulfed me. My father wrote to the leader of Fangqiao Commune in Yixing County, Jiangsu Province, asking for permission for me to join my grandfather in our ancestral home, Bow Hill Village. There were many twists and turns along the bureaucratic path to this solution, and many a cadre had to be 'consulted'. The greatest factor in my favour was that the exodus of city youths into the countryside had imposed an intolerable burden upon Heilongjiang Province, so that many rural units were just looking for any excuse to get rid of us. The central government issued a directive that students should be encouraged to join relatives in rural areas in order to relieve the crisis. As a result my father's request for me to go and stay with my grandfather in Yixing was eventually approved at the end of 1972.

At the beginning of 1973, when I was nineteen, I returned to Shanghai to see my father for the first time in six years. His features had not changed much, but his hair had turned completely white. On the other hand, he could hardly recognise me. My mother and brother were also at home, and although my sister was still on Chongming Island she was permitted regular visits home. I stayed in Shanghai for a couple of months. In the evenings I had concentrated

English instruction from my brother, who was also teaching himself not only English but French and Japanese. During the day he worked in a small neighbourhood factory, packing chewing gum, for which he was paid 70 fen a day, barely enough for his most basic needs. Then, in March 1973, I left for Yixing, taking with me the family's ancient gramophone on which I could listen to my Linguaphone records – and a good supply of medicine. I had learnt a hard lesson in Heilongjiang. In Yixing the medicine was extremely valuable, not only for my own health, but in establishing goodwill with the peasants, who often came to me when they had sickness. I was regarded as their own 'barefoot doctor' – a person capable of treating the most common village ailments.

I also took with me a number of ancient history and archaeology journals. Apart from the fact that I had become fascinated with these subjects, the journals had the advantage of being politically respectable and freely available. These things helped me to dream of the past, but I was in constant contact with the harsh reality of the present. Yixing is often called 'the land of fish and rice', but there was no fish and very little rice for the peasants, just pickled vegetables and thin rice gruel. At the same time, they had to endure a very heavy burden of labour to produce food for others. The land was never idle, and neither were they. Both the peasants and the soil were exhausted by the system of crop rotation, but Chairman Mao addressed himself first to the problem of the soil.

Our production team had tried everything to revive the spent dirt on which everything depended: we had coaxed it and teased it with everything from human manure to dog droppings, river silt and wood ash, but it still remained feeble and impotent. At last the Great Helmsman himself showed the way – 'Every pig is a little fertiliser factory. We must popularise the cultivation of pigs.' The trouble was that even fertiliser factories needed fuel. So we opened up new land on slopes unsuitable for other crops in order to grow sweet potatoes. But even sweet potatoes needed nourishment. So we started to collect all kinds of animal and vegetable waste from nearby Wuxi and float it back to Yixing in seven-tonne cement-shell boats.

The trip to Wuxi took two days, and was sometimes an absolute delight when there was a breeze and you could put on sail and skim across Lake Taihu. After arrival in the city, however, life became anything but idyllic. It seemed that all the Yixing peasants had the same idea, and there was suddenly a huge demand for all this rubbish and household waste. When the half-a-million-strong residents of Wuxi realised that household waste was a sought-after commodity, the neighbourhood committees quickly decided they should be charging us for it. But there was no way that the peasants could be persuaded to part with their hard-earned money for trash, so we had to find a way to collect the waste when members of the neighbourhood committees were not around.

We tied up in the canal for periods of up to twenty days, sleeping jammed together in the covered section in the bow. We were so cramped and bent that you often felt a toe probing for a berth in your nostril. At 4.30 in the morning we would leap out like pirates raiding a coastal town, but the object of our daring raids was the local latrines, and the finest loot we could expect to capture was an unharvested crop of night soil. After the booty had been stowed away, we would celebrate our triumph with a splash in the canal and a riotous feast of ten fens' worth of bean-curd milk and warm sesame cakes.

After breakfast we went from door to door in search of household scraps to put in our baskets, carried on shoulder-poles. At about this time the locals were starting up their little coal stoves, and they needed first to clean out the ash from yesterday's fire. They usually brushed the ash into a dustpan already half-full of food scraps, and left the pan sitting just inside the door for collection by the neighbourhood workers. If we offered to take it before the usual collectors arrived, they were often quite happy to be rid of it, although they seldom said so.

'Granny, do you have any scraps or rubbish? Can I help you empty your dustpan?'

'No, nothing left. It's all gone long ago.'

Often the man of the house would intervene at this stage. 'Hey, peasant, I've got some good stuff for you. You can clean up the muck in the fowl-house.'

There was always something else that had to be done before we could collect our 'pay' – 'Shift that pile of bricks while you are at it' – and we were always sent packing at the end of the job, with no please or thank you about it, by some surly neighbour, who would dart out of an adjoining house like a mad dog. 'You dirty little yokel, I know damned well you stole my nylon socks yesterday. Thieving shit! If I catch you around here again, I'll break both your bloody legs!'

I must admit we were not entirely innocent. We were sort of 'fences' for missing clothing, which was often sold to us very cheaply by the thieves. We couldn't really refuse them or they would be quite likely to sink us in the middle of the night by heaving boulders into the boat and holing the bottom. We just didn't have much to bargain with in dealing with the fine folk of Wuxi – if we tried to stick up for ourselves against this sort of treatment we were the ones who ended up in the police station, not our assailants.

Each crew wanted to fill up its boat as quickly as possible and get back to the village, so we tried to finish our other work and get down to the vegetable market by about ten o'clock, as business was winding up. We cleaned up their mess for them, while they sat and smoked and barked instructions at us. In the afternoons we walked for miles to some newly-built five-storey apartment blocks. Each floor had a kind of trapdoor at the end of the corridor through which household rubbish could be tipped into a large bin on the ground floor. There was a small door which gave entry to the bin, and we crawled in through here to shovel the garbage into our baskets. Frequently the garbage came tumbling down on to us while we were scurrying about like rats in a dump.

When the boat was finally full, everyone was delighted at the prospect of leaving. After some morning shopping to pick up some food for our relatives, we prepared to cast off early in the afternoon. Since we were against both current and wind, we had to rely on a combination of sculling and punting to make way until we got out of the city, and then we pulled the boat along the canal by means of ropes, yoked around our shoulders. One half of the waterway was crowded with boats and barges pulled by teams of men heaving and straining and chanting along a man-made track, at twenty-metre intervals, while the other half of the canal was alive with vessels flying along under sail. On our side all that could be heard were the numbing choruses of work songs, and all that could be seen were bent backs and straining ropes. In front of me I could see hard muscles beaten out like copper on my crew-mate's back, and little beads of sweat gathering, like the source of an ancient river, as we trudged barefoot along the thousand-year-old path of our ancestors.

At dusk we reached a little town on the banks of the lake. Everyone was exhilarated at leaving the petty tyrannies of Wuxi behind, and we dropped anchor in the long reeds and willows of a pretty little shallows. We took up a collection, and delegated two members to go into the town to buy some pig-head meat, trotters, peanuts and sweet potato liquor. When our friends came back laden with goodies, we gathered in a little circle in the stern, lit a fire and began to chew on our meat and drink our bowls of liquor. After a while, when a little of the edge had gone off our appetite, the talk began.

'Ah,' said someone, with a sigh of deep satisfaction, 'we peasants lead a miserable life, don't we?'

'Yeah, maybe our ancestors committed some terrible crime and now their descendants must pay for it.'

'That's our fate. We grow rice for city bellies, but when does a peasant get a full belly?'

'That's right. We even feed those bastards in Vietnam and Tanbodia.'

'You brainless hick! Do you mean Tanzania or Cambodia?' said the scholar of the outfit.

'Who cares? Anyway we feed both of them, even black bastards and foreign devils. One day when I'm rich—'

'Come off it, you clown, you've got more fleas than you'll ever have coins in your pocket', said Third Uncle, taking a playful swipe at the dreamer.

The scholar came to his rescue this time, 'Don't be so sure, cousin, look at the case of Zhu Yuanzhang. He was just a monk, not a penny to his name. But he became the first emperor of the Ming dynasty. He had one empress, two consorts and seventy-two concubines! Not bad for a bloke who started out as a monk, eh?'

'How many times do we have to hear this bullshit of yours about monks and concubines?' groaned Third Uncle. 'It must be like a whorehouse inside that head of yours.'

I was drinking from my bowl while this was going on, already half-drunk, not only with the liquor, but with the beauty all around me. There was a full moon just above the horizon, reflected in the ripples of the lake. There was a light cloud of mist above the water, and through it I could make out the kerosene lanterns of fishing boats, and hear the whistle of nets through the air, and the volley of little splashes as lead sinkers broke the still surface of the lake. Every now and then a cormorant split the water like a black arrow.

I was woken from my dreams by an insistent voice.

'Fang Xiangshu, we drink a toast to you! We salute you!'

'No, no', I protested, puzzled at this sudden formality. Usually they just called me 'Xiangshu', as did my grandfather and close relatives. In fact they *were* my relatives, since everybody in Bow Hill Village was related to everybody else.

'It is I who should propose a toast to you, Uncles.'

But the toastmaster was very serious now.

'They call me a scholar, but we all know it is a joke. I'm no scholar, but you are a different matter. Is there anything you don't know, Nephew?'

Third Uncle joined in the eulogy, 'He knows how to treat diseases with wolf's tail grass or winter melon peel—'

'Shut up, will you?' snapped the scholar, and continued in a lofty tone, 'I have given him many difficult characters to recognise and he has never failed, not even once, but I know very well that he could show me a boatload of characters that I do not know. For him it is as easy as eating bean curd! Come on, Nephew, a toast to you!'

After many toasts we were all getting drunk, and the scholar started up again.

'Nephew, we have all decided that you are not destined to remain among us. A small pond cannot contain a dragon, but when you become prosperous and powerful do not forget your poor old uncles, and if you can do nothing else you can at least inform the "Emperor" of our hardship! Then he will surely take pity on us and relieve our suffering.'

Whether overcome with alcohol or emotion I do not know, but I took some money out of my pocket and said, very elegantly, 'Honoured uncles, please accept my poor hospitality and join me in another drink. Let us send to the town for more liquor!'

A couple of uncles raced off to buy more grog, and, not just any old pig-head meat, but some ears and tongues. I also instructed the envoys to bring back a brush, ink and paper.

I was thinking of the famous essay on Yueyang Pavilion, by the Song dynasty writer Fan Zhongan, about the beauties of Dongting Lake, and the heavy responsibilities of being a true scholar. When they came back, breathlessly clutching more bounty from the town, I ceremoniously unwrapped the brush and paper and opened the little bottle of ink. With a dramatic flourish, I wrote the lines from 'Yueyang Pavilion':

> First to sense every care that is under Heaven,
> Last to know the joy that is free to all others.

I then took out my cherished seal-stone, which I had carved myself with the characters *Ren zhong dao yuan* [The load is heavy and the road is long]. I explained to my uncles what I intended by all this rigamarole, and then, drunk and tearful, plunged the seal-stone down upon the lines, incanting as I did, 'As this seal is my witness I swear I shall never forget the suffering of my beloved uncles!' After that there was a general uproar of approval and mutual affection, with pledges and oaths going off in every direction like firecrackers. We poured more liquor, ate more meat, and became rowdier and drunker and more emotional, until we all collapsed in a dead swoon on the boat or on the bank.

Apart from our expeditions into Wuxi, life in Bow Hill Village was a matter of routine, and one day passed much like another until the autumn of 1973. A young peasant woman called Yang Yujuan, also a distant relative, was bitten by a deadly pit-viper. When I found out I ran over to the fields and saw her lying motionless among the rows of sweet potato plants. She had been bitten on the finger.

109

I began to suck the blood from the bite, and afterwards applied a tourniquet to the wound. I remember praying that I did not have any cuts or scratches in the mucous lining of my mouth. I was terribly afraid that I might have swallowed some of the venom. I had with me a small box of orange powder called 'Jideshen snake potion', and, following the instructions on the box, I placed a small amount under her eyelids and on the bite. I also placed some of it under my own eyelids, just in case. We fashioned a makeshift litter out of a door removed from a peasant hut, and carried her across the fields to the commune hospital. The doctor said that my quick action had probably saved the girl's life, but it was an extremely risky thing to do.

The girl's father, whom we called 'Uncle Six-fingers' because he had an extra finger growing out of his thumb, was very grateful and asked the scholar to write an open letter to the commune leader, praising my deed. In order to improve my political prospects, they attributed my spirit of self-sacrifice to a thorough study of the works of Chairman Mao.

In the summer of 1974 the production brigade leadership finally permitted me to apply for entry to a university as a 'peasant student', and I went to the commune office to apply for enrolment as an archaeology student at Wuhan University. The secretary soon dispelled my dreams.

'No, no! You are eligible for entry only under the special categories for music, sport or foreign languages, in which there are severe shortages. In your case, we have permitted you to apply because we heard you knew some English. If you don't qualify for this, don't waste our time!'

'OK. English. Yes, of course. My English is not bad. I'm not especially set on archaeology.'

'Well, we'll know soon enough if your English is up to it, don't you worry about that.'

One morning, when I was spreading pig manure in the

rice fields, a production brigade cadre came cycling up to me and told me there would be an English test in the district central secondary school that afternoon.

I washed my hands and feet in the irrigation channel and went back home to put on my best clothes – the ones with the fewest patches – and a pair of PLA sandshoes. I ran to the bus stop, and then waited half an hour. When the bus finally came, it was almost full, and the conductor motioned to me to wait for the next one, but I wedged my hands into the door, forced it open and clambered aboard.

After about forty minutes we arrived at Zhoutie Bridge District Central Secondary School. The commune secretary was already waiting for me.

'Come on! Hurry up, you almost missed the start! The exam will get under way any second now.'

He pushed me through the crowd which had gathered outside the examination hall.

'Make way, make way, everybody. The Fangqiao Commune candidate has arrived.' As we pushed and shoved, he muttered to me, 'Don't worry, you'll be all right, you won't let us down. Just do your best.'

As we entered the hall, I noticed that they had set up a long table in the middle of the hall by placing school desks together. At one end sat three grand figures – obviously the examiners – and along the other three sides sat twelve very nervous candidates. I also sat down at the table.

One of the examiners stood up and introduced himself as Tang Yinxuan, the teacher of English in this high school. He introduced Liu Xiaohai, a lecturer in English from Nanjing Teachers College, who would be taking notes, and Chen Shifu, from the Yixing County Mao Thought Propaganda Team, who would be supervising the proceedings. Tang announced the commencement of the examination, and then began with the first candidate on his left.

'Please render into English "*Mao Zhuxi wan sui*".'

The first candidate bellowed, 'Long life to Chairman Mao!'

'OK', said the examiner. 'Now, what about "*Gong-chandang wan sui*"?'

'Long life to the Communist Party!'

The examiner repeated this process with the next six or seven candidates until he reached me. Even if I had not known the translation to begin with, I would have known it by heart by the time it was my turn to perform! But I felt that I could do better than this.

I stood up and said, 'A long, long life to our great leader Chairman Mao! A long life to the great, glorious and always correct Communist Party of China!'

The Yixing County examination supervisor sensed that there was something slightly different about this response, and murmured something to the English teacher. Tang whispered something back to him, and a broad smile broke out on his face. Next came the English alphabet. Each candidate had to recite the alphabet. We all managed this well enough. Then Tang asked us to count from one to ten in English. The candidate before me counted on his fingers, but somehow he managed to economise, and he got to ten by the middle finger of his second hand. He sat down in some confusion. Then we were asked to count from eleven to twenty. Only two were left standing at the end of this knock-out contest and the examiner asked my opponent if he could go on. He was forced to admit defeat, and there was a great groan of disappointment from the spectators peering in through the windows of the hall. The examiner turned to me, and I boldly asserted that I could go on. Applause and cheering broke out from the onlookers, and I felt like a high jumper at the Olympics heroically motioning to the officials to raise the bar to some new and unheard-of height.

The excitement had become contagious, and the supervisor yelled out, 'Just keep going until you cannot go any further! One, two, off you go!'

A hush fell over the crowd, and as I climbed steadily into the high twenties, they began clapping with each number and following along in Chinese. The news of this spectacle was gradually relayed beyond the examination hall.

'He's up to sixty-five!'

Still I went on.

'One hundred and five, one hundred and six—'

I was beginning to be alarmed. How long did I have to go on?

The supervisor was beside himself with excitement and looked as if he never wanted me to stop. I pushed myself on. I was almost out of the bitter sea of peasant life, I could see the shore – university – the city – 'one hundred and eighty-seven, one hundred and eighty-eight'.

The teacher was looking anxious. He said something to the supervisor, and finally he sprang to his feet and bawled, 'Hold it! I'll give you a number in Chinese and you tell me in English. Ready? *Si bai!*'

'Four hundred.'

'*Yi qian!*'

'One thousand.'

'*Yi wan!*'

'Ten thousand.'

Almost hysterical now, he screamed '*Yi baiwan!*'

I screamed back, 'One million!'

There was a gasp from outside.

The supervisor told Tang, 'Just concentrate on this Fang fellow, don't worry about the others.'

The other candidates were absolutely intimidated by my tour de force and never uttered a sound in protest. One of them said he had only come along for a bit of fun and he wasn't really trying. Tang gave me a textbook and asked me to read it out loud. In those days there were very few

113

textbooks, and I was very familiar with all of them from my self-study.

I took a quick look at the text he had chosen and then told him to take the book away. I began to recite:

Tom is a little American boy. His father is a coal-miner. Tom is at home with his mother. It is very cold but there is no fire in the house.

> Tom asks his mother, 'Why is it so cold, Mother?'
> Mother answers, 'Because there is no fire, Tom.'
> 'Why is there no fire?'
> 'Because we have no coal.'
> 'Why do we have no coal, Mother?'
> 'Because we have no money.'
> 'Why do we have no money, Mother?'
> 'Because Father is out of work.'
> 'Why is Father out of work, Mother?'
> 'Because our country produces too much coal.'

The spectators waited for a decent interval after I had finished, just in case there might be some more of these strange noises to come. Then, when they were certain the performance was over, they burst into a warm round of applause and excited chatter. Then came the last item – an English conversation. The English lecturer from Nanjing translated for the supervisor as we went.

Tang. 'What is your name?'
Fang. 'My name is Fang Xiangshu.'

Tang. 'When were you born?'
Fang. 'I was born on 11 November 1953.'

Tang. 'Where are you from?'
Fang. 'I am from Shanghai. My parents, a brother and a sister still live in Shanghai.'

114

Tang. 'When did you come to the countryside?'

Fang. 'I came in December 1969, in answer to our great leader Chairman Mao's call. I heard his words, "The countryside is a vast arena for the development of our youth."'

Tang. 'What have you learned since then?'

Fang. 'Since I came to the countryside I have learnt to tell wheat from weeds. I have also learnt a lot of farm work.'

Tang. 'What were you doing at eight o'clock last night?'

Fang. 'I was reading Chairman Mao's works.'

Tang. 'And what are you going to do tonight?'

Fang. 'I am going to help a poor old peasant to write a letter to his son, who is in the People's Liberation Army.'

Tang. 'This is my last question. Why do you learn English?'

Fang. 'Marx teaches us that a foreign language is a weapon in the struggle of life. We Chinese people are leading a happy life under the leadership of Chairman Mao and the Communist Party, but millions of people all over the world are suffering oppression at the hands of imperialists, revisionists and other reactionaries. It is our sacred duty to liberate all those people. Foreign languages are important in this great task.'

Tang. 'Excellent! Excellent!'

The supervisor took out an application form and handed it to me. He looked well pleased with his discovery of some local talent.

'Fill it in.'

My hand was trembling so much I could not write

properly, but the college lecturer told me to fill it in later and send it to Yixing County enrolment office. He chatted with me now like a fellow-ace.

'You've been listening to Linguaphone, haven't you?'

'Yes, how did you know?'

'I knew as soon as you opened your mouth – a beautiful accent. I can always tell. You can pick these things straight off, after a while, if you have a good ear.'

Tang Yinxuan came over to tell me, unofficially, that I would receive enrolment information in about three weeks, and that I should get myself organised to leave. I thanked everyone profusely, pushed my way through some admiring hangers-on, and went to the shops to buy some cigarettes and liquor for a little celebration at home.

About half an hour later I caught a bus home. Suddenly I realised that all the passengers were talking about a Shanghai lad who had taken part in the foreign language exams at Zhoutie Secondary School. It sounded as if they were discussing a being of mythological proportions.

'He must be a genius.'

'Oh yes, of course. I know him quite well. He is from Bow Hill Village.'

I turned round to sneak a look at the owner of this voice. I had never seen him before. But his next statement surprised me even more than the last.

'He knows ten languages.'

The whole bus tuned in on this.

'What? How is it possible?'

'Oh,' said the voice, with casual authority, 'every now and then one such person is born. They have one or two languages at their command even before they pop out of their mother's belly. Now this young man, for example. I saw him this afternoon with my very own eyes. He made fools of them all. When the examiner fired one sentence at him, he hit back with ten!'

I was really enjoying this, and I remained incognito to savour it all the more.

The news of my success beat me back to Bow Hill Village, and Grandpa was already beside himself with excitement when I got home. He was addressing a small crowd who had gathered outside our house.

'Haven't I always told you that Bow Hill Village is a place where tigers and dragons lie hidden under your very noses? Now you know what I am talking about! My grandson is mounting the ladder to the clouds, step by step.'

'Grand Uncle,' said one of his audience, 'how it is that those foreign devils only need twenty-six characters to say and write everything they want?'

There was a hush of expectation, while Grandpa cleared his throat rather thoroughly and prepared his answer. He was an old village teacher himself, and knew many thousands of characters, but he could never quite understand this twenty-six-letters business, although I had attempted to explain it to him on a number of occasions.

'Let me tell you. It is a sacred gift from their ancestors, like the eight trigrams of the I Ching, a work of unfathomable inspiration and genius. To understand things from another world, as my grandson does, is also a feat of genius. In history there are occasional prodigies – like the poet Li Bai of the Tang dynasty. The Emperor bestowed a gold pass upon him, enabling him to drink free in any wine shop in the land, in recognition of his talent with languages. That is the way of it!'

This did not entirely satisfy the questioner's curiosity, I thought, but it carried the day for Grandpa.

In three weeks, just as I had been told, I received a notice from Nanjing Teachers University to the effect that I had been accepted for enrolment in the foreign languages department.

Grandpa told me that we should arrange a banquet to give thanks to our ancestors for the good fortune they had brought upon our family. But Second Uncle didn't agree. He thought it would be a better investment to spend the money thanking the production brigade cadres.

Finally the day came for me to say goodbye to the whole village. Each family gave me cakes – *gao*, a homonym for the word 'high' – symbolising my ascent to the clouds. Years ago I had told my mother there would be no tears at our farewell, but this time I failed to restrain myself.

5 The Mouth Is the Source of Disaster

The last scene from my memories of Yixing drifted away and dispersed like the smoke from my cigarettes as I paced up and down outside the kitchen door. 'Look to the future', they said, and I kept seeing only the past – but then, the future was yet to be created. I looked at my watch; it was now nearly eight o'clock at night. I stubbed out my cigarette, and went in to tell my father that I was going out to see a friend.

'All right,' he said, 'but steer clear of those student demonstrations. Don't get involved.'

As I wheeled my brother's bike out through the gate I was thinking that nothing would ever change if no one ever got involved. I felt it could do no harm to go and have a look to form my own first-hand impressions of the demonstrations.

When I reached Yan'an Road, the crowd was so thick that I could not ride any further, so I chained the bike to a tree and started walking. In about forty minutes I reached the municipal government building in The Bund, opposite the waterfront. A crowd of about 2000 Fudan University students had gathered outside the building. They were singing 'The Internationale' in Chinese. Some had painted slogans on their bedsheets: 'Long live freedom and democracy', 'Protest against police beating students', 'Oppose the suppression of the student movement', and 'Jiang Zemin, you are in the wrong!'

On the steps of the building stood thirty or forty officers in the uniform of the People's Armed Police – but unarmed.

119

From a window somewhere high up a loudspeaker announced 'Students! Students! Please observe the traffic regulations. Preserve order, beware manipulation of your demonstration by troublemakers.'

The message was repeated so often it became obvious it was a recorded message, and the students began to mimic it, complete with whistling and crackling noises. A female student with a permanent wave began to lead a chant in very refined standard Mandarin: 'Jiang Zemin, please come out.' At first the students followed her lead, observing strict rhythm. She conducted them, rather in the style of an American college cheerleader. As she chanted 'Jiang Zemin', they chorused 'Please come out', and the whole thing swelled along rather gaily. Then she adapted the arrangement a little, and chimed 'Please come out', while they responded with 'Jiang Zemin'. This was a little too polite and artistic for some of the more robust Shanghai souls, and they began to bawl, 'Get out here, big shot!'

I noticed that a number of onlookers had gathered to watch the performance, without taking any active part themselves. I asked one of them how it had all started. He turned out to be very well-informed indeed. According to him, there had been a foreign performing arts troupe at the Shanghai Indoor Sports Stadium about a week ago. At the end of the performance, the foreigners had invited the audience to join in a dance with them, and about thirty Jiaotong University students had clambered over the ropes dividing the performers from the audience, and had begun dancing on the basketball court. Police, who did not understand what was happening, since they spoke no English, tried to stop them. The students explained that they were responding to the performers' request because they did not want the foreigners to think Chinese audiences were impolite. Some of the students were apparently less than complimentary about philistines who knew nothing about

Western culture or language, and police in turn had not taken too kindly to being told they were stupid blockheads who made China look backward. They radioed for reinforcements, waited for the foreigners to leave, and then arrested twenty or so of the students. Naturally the students protested, especially one, who seemed to know a thing or two about the Constitution and the rights of a citizen. They were all given a beating at the police station, and the severest beating was reserved for the constitutional expert. He was informed that he was guilty of 'obstructing a police officer in the performance of his duty' and 'resisting arrest'.

After their release the students went to see the president of their university, and asked for his support in lodging an official complaint with the Public Security Bureau. They demanded a public apology, but the president of the university refused to get involved. As a result, the students went on strike, supported by almost the entire student body, not only in their own university, but in every campus in Shanghai. The Mayor of Shanghai, Jiang Zemin, finally went to Jiatong University, to negotiate with student representatives. He claimed that he had not come as the mayor but as an old graduate of Jiatong. The students were not swayed by this, and told him he could not expect to 'join them at table in order to throw rice to the enemy'. If he really wanted to show his loyalty to his Alma Mater, they said, he should deal vigorously with those thugs in the police force. Jiang responded by saying that, as a former student leader himself, he understood that relations between students and police were not always ideal, but there was a right and wrong way of going about things, and so on. One of the students leapt on to the platform with him and told the audience that this 'Mayor' was an unelected official, that he did not represent students or citizens of Shanghai, and was just another 'running dog', like the police force.

I asked my informant if the students had struck Jiang,

because I noticed that he had a plaster on his forehead when I saw him on the television news earlier that evening.

'Oh yes, that's a laugh! After the negotiations, our dear mayor got himself in a real state and distracted the driver with his opinions about students. The driver braked suddenly to avoid a pedestrian, and Jiang bumped his head. The funny thing is that he's always so natty and fussy, he wouldn't dream of spoiling his appearance for the sake of a small cut. Now he's not only got a sticking plaster, he's given up his sophisticated Western suits in favour of his old Cultural Revolution style Sun Yat-sen jacket. I wonder what he's trying to tell us?'

As he spoke, I could actually see Jiang's features in my mind: the furtive little eyes behind glasses as thick as the base of a bottle, the thin smile in a great square face, and now his plaster campaign ribbon from the battle of Jiaotong.

I offered my source a foreign cigarette, thinking this might loosen his tongue even more.

'Thanks. Have you been overseas?'

'Yes, just came back from a few years away, and I haven't a clue what's going on here. Who is this Jiang Zemin anyway?'

He took a deep drag on his cigarette and said, very deliberately, 'Well, let's see. To start with, Jiang Zemin is the son-in-law of Carpenter Li—'

'Er, sorry, who did you say?'

'You don't even know Carpenter Li? You *have* been out of it, haven't you? All right, let's go back to the beginning. A river has its source, and a tree has its roots, eh? Early this century a certain Mr Li was a carpenter in Shanghai. Business wasn't very good, but he learnt some tricks of the trade, and got to be quite a shifty operator. In the 1920s he suddenly saw the light and joined the Party, and even took part in the Long March.* He wasn't all that prominent, but he survived the power struggles and eventually rose to be Minister of Finance in the new government. Not only did he survive through these early years, he kept on going through several dynasties – Mao, Hua, and now Deng. While others came and went like shadows on a spinning lantern, he just kept right on going. Now do you know who I'm talking about? That's right, none other than the President of the People's Republic of China himself, Li Xiannian.'

I was warming to this man's talents as a raconteur, and offered him another cigarette which he promptly lit with the butt of his old one. He went on: 'His old comrades and close friends nicknamed him "Carpenter Li". He seemed to manage financial and state affairs with great skill, but the same cannot be said of his romantic affairs.'

I was fascinated by all this, and although I couldn't figure out what it had to do with Jiang Zemin I didn't want to stop his flow. There was almost a festival atmosphere in the street, and a number of people had gathered around the storyteller by now. He began to address himself to them.

'This is the prologue. Now let me begin the first chapter. The first chapter in our story is entitled "In which the First Lady smashes her vinegar pot in a fit of jealous rage and the sour liquid is spilt all over the Dragon Throne, while Carpenter Li takes shelter under the presidential desk." '

---

* The Long March refers to the movement of the communist base from Jiangxi to Yan'an (October 1934–October 1935) while under constant attack from Nationalist troops. It is considered one of the great heroic exploits of the Red Army. Of approximately 100 000 soldiers and party cadres who left Jiangxi only about 8000 survived the trek. It was during this period that Mao Zedong began to take control of the party and the army.

123

There were hoots of laughter from an appreciative and rapidly growing audience.

While I would dearly love to have heard the rest of this tale, I was more anxious to know what was going on in the demonstration, so I moved on to another group. A student was standing on a box, and addressing his audience in very formal tones.

'My fellow-citizens, hear me! I ask you, what rights do people actually have in this people's republic of ours?'

I thought this must be the crux of the matter, something along the line of human rights.

'I repeat, what rights do we have?'

A well-placed stooge or two pitched in with the appropriate response.

'The right to eat!'

'Correct. Dead right, comrade! And what else?'

'The right to sleep!'

'Yes, exactly. Now, think hard, what else?'

There was hesitation this time, until someone shouted, 'The right to shit!'

'Splendid! Splendid! So, in this people's republic, you and I have the right to eat, sleep, and shit.' He paused for effect. 'Even pigs have these rights, my fellow citizens!'

With this he raised his palms behind his ears and flapped them about, grunting and oinking as he did so. The audience loved it and burst into laughter, then began grunting and flapping ears along with him. A banner was hoisted high in the midst of all this, a bedsheet with the words 'We want to be treated like human beings! Human beings! Human beings!'

The crowd stopped laughing, and a round of applause and approval broke out among them. I joined in enthusiastically.

I looked at my watch. Time was getting on, and I thought my father might be worried, so I went back to my bike.

I felt excited and happy with all these goings on, but I could not get Jiang Zemin's face out of my mind. I could not see the eyes behind those great thick glasses.

A few days later the talk everywhere was of the student demonstration. There did not seem to have been any serious repercussions. On the contrary, the official newspapers and news services did not even acknowledge that it had taken place. But one evening I read a notice in the *New People's Nightly* headed 'Shanghai Municipality Public Security Bureau Bulletin No. 3.' I wondered what had happened to Numbers 1 and 2. As far as I knew they had not been published in the paper yet. Anyway, No. 3 said:

Our constitution guarantees every citizen the rights of assembly and demonstration. In order to facilitate peaceful and orderly demonstrations while observing traffic rules, every demonstration or rally must be registered in advance with the Public Security Bureau. Organisers must attend in person to give seventy-two hours' notice of the route, numbers participating and other details of the proposed demonstration in order that the relevant authorities may re-direct traffic . . .

I felt a chill when I read this, but next day my sister-in-law, Chen Dandan, told me that the demonstrations had gone ahead without obstruction or incident, and without a single arrest. The police had behaved with exemplary restraint. Even when the students had gone a bit too far, there was no over-reaction. Chen Dandan also told me that there had been large demonstrations in Beijing, Wuhan and Hefei. I decided I would have another trip downtown before I left Shanghai, to see what was going on. These were interesting times. A new year was imminent, and maybe new ways.

One night after supper I rode back to the spot where I had chained my bike the time before. There had been demonstrations here every evening for about a week. This time I went to the People's Square, because I had been told this was where I would hear the best speeches. When I got there I found there was a police cordon to prevent anyone other than students from entering the square. They seemed to be adopting a moderate approach, allowing anyone who looked like a student to enter. Occasionally they would demand identification. One or two in the crowd demanded to know why, if the constitution guaranteed all citizens the right of assembly and demonstration, only students were allowed to participate.

'Don't give me "Constitution"!' said one officer. 'There are broad guarantees, and then there is the fine print. You aren't necessarily entitled to demonstrate as you please. It depends on the fine print. Anyway, just do as you are told and you won't be in trouble.'

'Well, the broad guarantee should take precedence over the small print! You also must do what you are told – by the Constitution.'

'Look, don't make my job any harder than it already is. If you are a student, come in. If not, just watch your mouth and don't try to be smart!'

I decided it would be unwise to try to get into the square, but contingent after contingent of students arrived from all directions, carrying banners and chanting slogans. I became more and more determined to get a good look at the rally. I walked down Xizang Road, and turned into Fuzhou Road. About twenty metres along there was a teahouse, and I thought I might be able to get a good view of the square from the second floor. I went upstairs. All the window tables were occupied so I decided to sit at another table and wait for a vacancy.

I ordered some Jasper Shell tea, a speciality of my home town, served in a special 'purple sand' earthenware teapot with a dragon's head on the lid, and some 'Idiot' brand watermelon seeds. These seeds are highly prized in Shanghai, where thousands of tonnes of them are consumed annually. The special seasoning was accidentally discovered by a man who was known locally as Shazi – a sort of village idiot. Whether idiot or savant, Shazi had the business instinct to market his product under the tradename – 'Shazi Guazi' [Idiot Melonseeds] – and grew steadily richer and richer. His little sideline began to assume company proportions, and to employ more and more people, until it was not clear whether he was a model of the new economic reforms or an evil capitalist exploiter. While the issue was hotly contested at the Central Party Academy, he just kept selling his seeds. The Academy debated the number of employees which distinguished socialist enterprise from capitalist enterprise. It was ultimately decreed that eight was still within the boundaries of socialism but nine was the beginning of monopoly capitalism. Finally, on the basis of this doctrine, Shazi was exonerated of the accusation, in the press, that he was a 'monopoly capitalist'. Some weeks later he was found guilty of tax evasion, and fined tens of thousands of yuan. I thought, as I munched on my seeds, that there was plenty of reason for small private shopkeepers and street-stall foodsellers and tradespeople to support reform. No doubt that was why so many of them had supplied the students with free icecream, bread rolls, cigarettes and cash donations.

The teahouse was full of smoke, to the point where visibility was limited. I lit up a cigarette of my own. I reflected on the Central Party Academy. Had they managed in their recent deliberations to come to a decision about the relationship between base and superstructure and political reform? Where would we be without the Academy? A popular Taiwanese female pop singer was going on about flowers – it seemed that each passing month the seeds of love brought forth flowers in her heart. I couldn't decide which was worse – the Academy, or Taiwanese pop songs – but I was quite sure that once the seeds of reform had been planted in the economy, political growth would follow.

A seat became vacant over by the window, and I moved quickly to grab it. As I settled in, I noticed that somebody had scribbled '*Mo tan guo shi*' [No talking affairs of state] on the wall near the window. This sign used to be pasted on the walls of teahouses in the old days. I had no one to talk with, but I could certainly watch political events unfold from here.

The view was terrific. About 500 students, arms linked, five abreast and singing patriotic songs, marched to the square. They carried banners, with the slogans 'Freedom of the press', 'Protect the Constitution, protect human rights', 'Give us back our democracy', and 'We represent the spirit of the future'. They were preceded by a police truck, with a loudspeaker blaring 'Your demonstration is not registered. It is illegal. Please go home.' This message alternated with 'Don't allow yourself to be deceived by troublemakers. Beware of bad elements disguised as students.' On the same truck were five or six plainclothes personnel, filming the students with video cameras. To my surprise, the students showed no sign of anxiety about this, and marched on joyfully. Behind the procession were more truckloads of police.

A number of processions passed, until it seemed that all the students had assembled in the square. It was now about ten o'clock at night. I noticed that more and more police were approaching the square, mainly on foot. They appeared to be unarmed. It was difficult to tell exactly what was happening, with so many people milling about, and so much commotion, but the loudest noise came from police loudspeakers requesting students to go home. As time wore on the number of students grew smaller and smaller, probably more because of the −3° centigrade temperature than police efforts to disperse them. The loudspeakers grew more and more agressive as the crowd grew smaller and smaller.

At about eleven I decided I'd better be getting home. As I turned into Xizang Road, there was a loud burst from the loudspeaker to the effect that the police were now going to clear the square. There was a volley of whistles, and all the police who had been on the perimeter of the square converged on the remaining crowd, flailing their belts and shouting warnings. I turned back into Fuzhou Road, and ran for my life.

After a few minutes, police vans came hurtling down the road, sirens blaring. Jammed inside the vans were rows of people with their hands on their heads. I darted into a lane.

After a few turns I was back on Yan'an Road. As I ran, I kept thinking of Carpenter Li, and those eyes of Jiang Zemin – surely the order for this crackdown would not have been initiated by either of these two. They were survivors, they would not take such a bold gamble at this stage. The directive must have come from a different sort of general. In any case, this demonstration business was over, and I knew I had to return to Nanjing.

In the afternoon of Friday, 2 January 1987, I got off the bus at Xikang Road, just outside the back gate of Nanjing Teachers University. The first thing I saw was a young man, wearing a padded PLA overcoat, turned inside out to reveal the white cotton padding, with the words 'We want democracy' painted on it. Outside the university there was a group of students from the nearby Hydraulic Engineering

College, all in very high spirits. I seemed to be reliving the very recent past. Now I knew exactly what it would be like to be able to tell the future – no one would listen.

It was very hard going just to get into the university, because the place was teeming with students, all the way from the back gate to the student dormitories up on the Western Hill. Political instructors were trying to persuade the students to stay on campus instead of going out into the streets to demonstrate.

'Fellow students, please go back, don't go out into the streets. The president of the university has arranged some end-of-term recreational activities for you, to demonstrate the university's goodwill. Free extra food rations will be distributed to each and every student – cakes and sweets will be provided from a special fund, and there will be a dance, and movies.'

Not surprisingly, the students reacted very badly to this rather limited offer, and demanded 'Democracy' instead. When they had wanted more food in the past, they were given more politics. Now that they wanted more politics they were given more food.

'Bread and circuses!' shouted some erudite soul.

'What a load of dog farts!' said another.

Suddenly an old man in a peasant cloth hat lunged out at one of the students.

'Xiao Gang, you little shit, I'll beat your brains out for talking to your teachers like that!'

In fact there were quite a few around who were obviously not students or staff. They were also having tremendous difficulty getting into the university grounds. Next to me a weathered-looking woman was shrieking, in her coarse northern Jiangsu accent, 'Is this how these good-for-nothing whelps repay their elders and betters? Shouting at their teachers? I knew there was something up when my little tart

130

had her hair curled like one of those stupid woolly foreign dogs. There she is! I'll tear the lips from her face! No wonder the authorities sent a telegram, now all of White Buffalo township knows about the silly bitch.'

Some of the political instructors were making a determined effort to clear a path into the university for these mortified parents and relatives, so they could apply a bit of good old-fashioned family pressure to the student activists, but there was general chaos, and nobody knew quite what to do or where to go.

I managed to force my way through the mob and back to my chicken-shit and lime store. On Saturday morning I went to the Foreign Languages Department office to show my face, and to see if I could pick up any news or rumours. The office was by no means its usual torpid self, but had been galvanised into action by some new policy directive. Now it resembled a military headquarters before some crucial battle. It seemed I was the only person with time on his hands. Party Secretary Kong spotted me and strode purposefully in my direction. There were no preliminaries.

'Did you take any part in the student demonstrations in Shanghai?'

'No, not at all.'

'Just as well! I'm warning you, Xiao Fang – don't make things any worse for yourself. You'll keep right away from these demonstrations if you know what's good for you!'

Suddenly a man's head poked out from the door of the dean's office. 'Xiao Fang. So it *is* you. When did you get back from Australia?'

Before I could reply, he said, 'I brought some food for Qiufang. She's so busy these days, what with being deputy dean of the department and all, that she doesn't take time for lunch. I've brought some myself to make sure she eats properly.'

131

Li Derong was the husband of Yin Qiufang, and both had been, like me, 'worker-peasant-soldier' students. We often grumbled together about our treatment in the past at the hands of bureaucrats and big shots. Now, after these two years away, I felt that I was listening to a different person. After a while it became obvious that his remarks were not for my benefit at all.

'And what about these students of today? They don't know when they're well off, do they, Xiao Fang? You must notice the changes more than anybody. You can see for yourself how things have improved. As far as I am concerned, they have nothing to complain about. Did you see the new overpass at Zhongyangmen? And the new hotel in Chang Jiang Road? By the way, that reminds me, have you tried our new bathhouse?'

Secretary Kong was rapidly losing patience with Li's account of the Seven Wonders of Nanjing.

'All right, I must be going. I've got things to do. Just remember what I told you, Xiao Fang.'

Li's ode to modernisation stopped abruptly when Secretary Kong left, and he went on to more useful information.

'Qiufang is far too busy these days. Even this afternoon, when everybody else can go home, she has to attend a meeting on the circulation of a Central Committee document.'

I made some excuse, and went off to get some lunch in the staff canteen. As I ate, I gave some thought to the most likely place for picking up some news about what was in this document. I could go to a toilet near the administration building and just occupy a booth until some chatty souls felt compelled, in the manner of all Chinese, to unburden their brains at the same time as their bowels. No, I didn't fancy that. If I had to perch in some place that inspired intimacy, a bathhouse would certainly be more to my liking.

132

At about five o'clock that afternoon, I put a singlet, underpants and towel into a plastic bag, put the bag into my washbasin, along with my soapholder and some nail-clippers, and replaced my shoes and socks with plastic sandals. The new bathhouse was built on the Western Hill, on the site of the old Canadian Embassy staff residence, which had been home to many foreign experts. As I slopped along in my sandals, carrying my washbasin, as I had done for many years in the past, I could not help thinking about those private showers in Western houses, where you could use as much hot water as you liked, whenever you liked. Still, as Li Derong rightly said, things had greatly improved here. Now at least there was no waiting outside in the cold in a long queue.

I paid my 20 fen for the privilege of the reserved staff changing room, which entitled me to a sort of deckchair and a box for storing my things. I stripped off and went out into the main pool with my basin. The water was only about waist-high, and bathers had to bend and flip water over their heads and backs, giving the whole place the air of a crowded duck-pond. Although there was more room than before, it was still necessary to defend your territory from others who were always ready to stretch their wings into your space. After a quick dip, I climbed out to do my soaping up, and then rinsed the soap off with a basinful of water from the pool.

After rinsing, I sat on a step about half a metre below the surface of the water and soaked myself in an enervating hot bath for about ten minutes. Some older men were steaming themselves on the bamboo grill covering the outlets from the boiler, hoping to get a bit of relief from arthritis. Younger ones, from the Music Department, were enjoying the rather flattering acoustics with spirited renditions of 'O Sole Mio' or songs from the *The Marriage of Figaro*.

133

It was always customary to have a partner in the bathhouse, for the purpose of scrubbing backs. From where I was sitting I could watch the procedure. Several teams had taken up their positions, with one of each pair leaning against the wall, as if being frisked, and the other setting about his back with a flannel wrapped tightly around his wrist, as if scrubbing a particularly stubborn floor. I looked around, but I couldn't see anyone I knew, so I had to go solo. I felt quite faint with the stifling heat and rather wished I was in Shanghai, where I could have paid one yuan to have an all-over scrub by a professional.

I soaped up again and went off to the next stage of the process, in the final rinsing-down room, where clean hot water ran continually from the pipes into a big tub, from which basins could be filled. After this I went back to the change room, and sat in my deckchair watching students from the Fine Arts Department sketching sleeping staff nudes. Some lecturers were warbling snatches from Peking Opera, and others were engaged in conversation. People tended to really relax in here. It was an ideal place for a bit of gossip and news about the last week's events, and somehow the normal reservations and inhibitions seemed to be shed, along with one's clothing. I took the pair of nail-clippers out of my bag, and started cutting my toenails, listening at the same time for any promising conversations. I went through all my toenails, and fingernails, but still I heard nothing of any real interest. Finally, I popped a cigarette into my mouth, and looked around for a light. The body next to me, which I had assumed to be asleep, sat up and fossicked around in its bag, eventually producing a lighter.

'Have you eaten?' I asked, relying on the normal Chinese opening gambit.

'No, not yet. I'm going down to the canteen after I'm through here.'

'The food seems to have improved in there, since this demonstration business', I said slyly.

'Oh, don't worry, that won't last for long. We'll soon be back to normal.'

'You don't have to tell me! Things are changing already, it seems. And now this central government document.'

'That's right.'

I threw him a cigarette as we talked, and said, 'Who cares anyway? All I'm interested in is a hot bath and a cigarette. They can keep their politics and their documents.'

'That's what I say too. Fang Lizhi! Who does he think he is? He's supposed to be an astrophysicist, not a political scientist. What would he know about it, anyway?'

Things went along in this vein for a couple of cigarettes. I didn't find out a great deal, but there was something about Deng Xiaoping naming Fang Lizhi and one or two others as the brains behind the demonstrations. Deng also said that although bloodshed should be avoided, we should not be afraid to spill blood if necessary. Our Polish comrades had shown us the right way of dealing with a crisis, and, as for foreign reaction, we should bear in mind that foreigners have short memories. 'They might squeal at first, but look how quickly they forgot about Wei Jingshen after we jailed him.'

'Well,' I told my companion, as I got up to dress, 'I just hope that this time, if there's a fire in the Forbidden City, it is not us small fry in the moat who get burned.'

'Here, here, my friend! You and me both! But who knows what's really going on? Perhaps Deng himself doesn't know. That's the nature of power struggles.'

Sunday, 4 January, was a perfectly quiet day. Everything had returned to normal. There was no sign of student activity, and the only unusual thing on campus was the number of peasants bidding their student-children farewell, with tearful entreaties not to get involved in any more trouble.

On Monday, 5 January, at 6.30 in the morning, I was woken by the loudspeaker near the student dining-hall. There was a blast of martial music:

> *The five-starred red flag flutters in the wind.*
> *How grand is the song of victory!*
> *We sing for our great socialist motherland,*
> *From this day forth she will grow strong and*
> *   prosperous.*

Then a vaguely familiar high-pitched voice began to recite an editorial from the *People's Daily*:

Again and again the lesson of history teaches us that only the Communist Party can lead China forward. It is this same Communist Party that led China out of the ten-year chaos of the Cultural Revolution by the frank admission of its errors. What other political party in the world would admit its mistakes in this way? This is the mark of a party which serves the people selflessly and wholeheartedly. Once more the Party has been quick to respond to the possibility of danger in the form of chaos and disorder, but some young people have the gall to burn the official organ of the Party! We ask, why are they so afraid of the truth, that they should wish to burn it? However, we stress that most of the students involved in the demonstrations are innocent, and naive, and have been manipulated by those they look up to as their mentors, those who have been abroad, those who have 'galloped through the flowers on horse-back' and imagine that they know it all, when they have only the most superficial impression from their brief sojourn in the West. We issue these people a stern warning – desist from spreading bourgeois liberalism or you will find that you have lifted a rock only to drop it on your own feet. The Party knows full well how much people suffered from political movements in the past, and we must reiterate here and now that the anti-bourgeois liberalism campaign is not going to be a political movement, and the open-door policy will continue, uninterrupted. In fact, our door will be opened wider, and it is for this very reason that we must carry the anti-bourgeois liberalism campaign through to the end. All those who are over thirty will clearly understand the need to prevent a re-emergence of the disorder that started with Red Guards – most of them university students – taking to the streets in the name of democracy. Preserve unity and stability, preserve genuine democracy with the rule of law!'

The editorial was followed by speeches from representatives of all walks of life – workers, peasants, academics and PLA soldiers – defending the Party and attacking Fang Lizhi 'and his ilk'.

There was another burst of song:

> *If there were no Communist Party, there would be no*
> *new China.*
> *If there were no Communist Party, there would be no*
> *new China.*
> *The Communist Party spares no effort on behalf of*
> *the people.*
> *The Communist Party wholeheartedly rescues China.*
> *It points the way to a bright future for the people,*
> *It has emancipated all of China . . .*

Then came the news bulletin:

Nanjing Municipal Public Security Bureau arrested Liu Jun, Wang Jiabin and Chang Keqin on the 27 of December, for damaging public and private property and jeopardising the safety of individuals during a student demonstration. All three confessed that, on the 25 of December, they pretended to be university students and spread malicious and false rumours to incite naive demonstrators. Despite repeated warnings from the Security Bureau, they not only stirred up student riots but actively participated themselves. There is an abundance of evidence that they are the ones who should be dealt with most vigorously under the relevant sections of the law.

I jumped out of bed. Things seemed to be getting out of hand now. I wondered what moves I should make in response to an increasingly threatening situation. At any moment, I might myself become a target for these attacks on troublemakers who had been abroad. I was still thinking furiously at ten o'clock, when there was a knock at the door. Someone had come to tell me that I must report immediately to the Provincial Higher Education Bureau.

About forty minutes later I was in the office of the director. I was told that there would be an enquiry into 'certain issues' arising from my time in Australia and that 'relevant personnel' wanted to talk to me.

I was led into another office and asked to take a seat.

I had to think this through. Of course, there had been quite a number of occasions in Australia when I had said things which were perfectly all right at the time, but which were now out of step with current orthodoxy. But surely there must be any number of people in the same situation? Even the general secretary himself had made comments which might be interpreted as bourgeois liberalism. Why should anything I said or did be considered so vital? But on the other hand, I told myself, I should not volunteer any information until I was quite certain what accusations, if any, had been made against me. I certainly did not want to put ideas in their heads.

As I was thinking, two middle-aged men came into the room. They looked very grave indeed, and without any

138

preliminaries, one started asking me questions while the other noted down my replies.

'So you are Fang Xiangshu, of Nanjing Teachers University? You were in Australia from the 21st of August 1984 to the 14th of December 1986?'

'Yes, that's correct.'

'You have been given the opportunity to confess since you returned, but you have refused.'

'I'm not sure what you mean by "confess"! Anyone can make a mistake, and I am always perfectly willing to submit a self-criticism, if others are prepared to point out my mistakes to me, but I don't know what I have done.'

'Yes, I know your style. You'd very much like to find out what we've got on you, wouldn't you? I can assure you, by the time we tell you what we know, it will be all over for you. You will live to regret not making a clean breast of it right now! You have already squandered one golden opportunity. This is your last chance, believe me. Don't waste it!'

'Look, I suppose I might have made a mistake, through not studying Chairman Mao – I mean Chairman Deng Xiaoping – thoroughly enough. Maybe I got a bit carried away sometimes—'

'Well, well, you really are a one, aren't you? You just will not shed a tear until you see your coffin, will you? All right, since you mention Deng Xiaoping, let me remind you of one or two things.'

He opened a very thick file, and began reading some sections aloud, including whole passages in English.

'On 26 March 1986 did you or did you not say the following? "In the past we studied Mao's *Selected Works*, now we study Deng's. And we all know what 'dung' means in English, don't we? And tomorrow it will be Hu's Works. Or is it 'whose works'? Who will be Hu in China the day

139

after tomorrow?" Do you remember saying anything like that, Fang Xiangshu?'

'Oh yes, but that was just joking! I admit it was stupid, but I was just trying to be smart, you know with puns, but it was definitely not intended to be against our leaders. After all, I didn't say anything against the Party, did I?'

'Yes, of course, a joke. I must say it sounds like it. But then a lot of your remarks are just jokes, aren't they? Let's see if we can find some more of your jokes in here.'

He turned a page. 'Did you ever say the following? "The slogan 'Long live the great, glorious and infallible Communist Party' is no longer a suitable slogan. We should change it to 'Long live the great and glorious Communist Party which made a mistake and frankly admits it, so now it is even more infallible'." '

'Yes, but that's just because I thought the slogan didn't really do justice – You know, it's not very logical, I didn't mean – the way I put it—.'

'Shut your mouth!' he suddenly screamed. 'You can spew out any rubbish you like about jokes. They are nothing but a pathetic thin disguise for your deep-rooted antipathy to the Party. I have it all here, and believe me, it is no joke!'

As he said this, he banged the file down on the desk and glared malevolently at me. I tried desperately to collect my thoughts. My interrogator's ability to use both English and Chinese had unnerved me terribly.

'You make it sound more serious than it really is,' I said at last. I was hoping against hope that the file was a phoney, calculated to rattle me, as used to be the case in the Cultural Revolution. I pointed at the file and said, 'Since you have such a thick file on me, you must know a great deal about me and my family. My parents were rehabilitated and moved into better accommodation, and I have myself become a university lecturer, and sent overseas, with the full trust of our government. Why should someone like me harbour any hatred of the Party? But anyone is capable of a mistake. If I have made a mistake of some sort, I'm quite—' I suddenly remembered the quotation from Chairman Mao that my father had used that day in August 1966 to defend himself, 'I'm quite willing to listen to criticism. That is one of my principles – "If we have shortcomings, we should not be afraid to have them pointed out and criticised, because we serve the people." '

As I spoke, my mind was searching through a tangle of dates and names and meetings, trying to find the right match – who could it be who had been present at both the conversations which had been quoted?

My interrogator was more formidable than any I had encountered in the storming, bullying days of the Cultural Revolution. He lit a cigarette, and chuckled, 'That mind of yours is really ticking over, isn't it? What else do we need to "factor in"?'

I had only heard this last phrase, which he pronounced quite emphatically in English, on one or two occasions – on American television programs.

'Of course we know everything about your family, friends, relatives, your movements, and so on. I wouldn't be surprised if we knew more about you than you do yourself!'

He flicked through the pages of the file, and while I was still trying to recover from his last remarks, said, 'But what we don't know, and what really interests us, is, as you say, why you should hate the Party. Don't waste your time trying to figure out what evidence we have and don't have. We've got all the evidence we need. All that counts now is your attitude. If you show some sign of genuine remorse, it will make our job less tedious, and things will be a great deal easier on you. But I warn you, for the last time, don't try

141

to hide anything. Every single thing is here in this file. Discussions, debates, speeches during political study sessions – even your little "jokes"!'

I decided, in spite of all this, that I would be better off, for the time being at least, to make some form of protest rather than to go into confession mode.

'I must make it clear that all my remarks during political study and so forth were not only permissible, but were actually encouraged by the Party at the time. It was Party *policy* to have a full and open discussion on political reform and various theories. I remember, in January 1986, during a student union meeting in North Melbourne, the First Secretary of the Embassy, Comrade Ni Chuanrong, delivered a message from the Party General-Secretary, Hu Yaobang himself. The message was "We must encourage intellectuals to take advantage of our new free and tolerant policy, to speak their minds openly, and not brand them or take the big stick to them." Not only that, but Ni Chuanrong stressed that he personally would hear no more reports on people. If my memory serves me correctly, the only stipulation was that we should keep basically in line with official Party policy when talking to Australians, or other non-Chinese, but that we could say what we liked among ourselves. If this "free and tolerant" policy was incorrect, how was I supposed to know? Naturally, if the policy has changed, I will do my best to bring myself up to date—'

'What rubbish! You talk as if the Party swings arbitrarily from one extreme to the other. The free and tolerant policy of '86 was meant to encourage the broad masses to work in wholehearted co-operation with the Party, to reform and perfect the political structure of our socialist system. It was initiated by Deng Xiaoping, and it was most certainly not incorrect! But it was never intended that the policy should permit people like you to indulge in a systematic, wholesale

142

and premeditated attack on the Communist Party, the Revolution and China itself, under the pretext of intellectual freedom!'

There was no turning back now. The charge was very serious.

'These are baseless accusations and rumours', I shouted. 'At the very least they are fantastically wild exaggerations! In view of the gravity of these accusations, I demand proof! In order to protect my good name, I am prepared to take this matter to the highest level!'

'Really? Well now, if ever I entertained the slightest doubt about the truth of these allegations, your performance today has completely removed it. You're covered in shit, but you're still hard underneath – like a rock in a latrine.'

As a last desperate effort, I decided to reach for witnesses. 'There are any number of people who can corroborate my story. Liu Aihua knows me very well—'

'Oh yes. Liu Aihua, your companion and colleague in Australia. I think you'll find Comrade Liu is a little too busy these days to be involved in your affairs. You do know, don't you? She's preparing to go back to Australia very soon.'

I was shaken and speechless. This prompted a burst of laughter from the interrogator.

'Just look at you! This is amazing! Such a tough character, I thought, and now I've knocked you flat with just a few little taps of my hammer.'

He took a few steps toward me, and offered me a cigarette. I refused because I knew that, despite my best efforts, my hands would be shaking.

'Come on now, let's not make this any harder than it has to be. You are only making things worse for yourself. Now tell me the truth. Did you ever say anything against Party policy?'

'No.'

'Not among your close Australian friends?'

'No!'

'Not even among Chinese students and friends?'

'*No!*'

'You do know our policy, don't you? "Leniency for those who confess, severity for those who are stubborn." '

'Yes, I know that.'

'Well then, do you remember anything at all that you'd like to tell me about?'

'No.'

'Don't give your final answer yet. Go away and think about it. Maybe something will come back to you. If it does, be sure to tell me straight away.'

I got up from my chair, and as I did he said, 'By the way, where's your wife now?'

'In Hong Kong I should think, visiting relatives, or maybe still in Australia, I'm not too sure.'

'Yes, she has relatives all over the place, doesn't she?'

He flipped through the file again, 'Hong Kong, Wisconsin, USA, Taipei, Keelung, and, oh, a place called Papua New Guinea. But when is she coming back?'

'In a month or so.'

'That's good. OK.'

I walked quickly to the door, and just as I was about to exit, he called after me, '—and when you come back, don't forget to tell me all about Shanghai.'

My stomach was churning as I left the Higher Education Bureau compound. I was frightened, angry, sick and desperate. At first I felt like confronting the issue and really sticking up for myself, no matter what the cost. On the other hand, I had to stay calm, and think – use the time I had been given. Half of me wanted to bring this thing to a head, and get it over, half of me warned against doing anything at all. I was trembling, and my face felt flushed. I decided that I would just walk.

144

It was a sunny winter's day, but by now there were no leaves left on the plane trees along the road to the Drum Tower. The trunks had all been painted with a kind of whitewash, as always happened rather mysteriously in winter. There was a lot of traffic, but every now and then a little convoy of curtained black Mercedes cut its way effortlessly through the jumble of three-wheeled trucks, Chinese mini-tractors, mule-carts, and cyclists wearing surgical masks to keep out the dust. By now I had calmed down a little, and I decided to stop at a roadside stall for a roast sweet potato. I ate as I walked, biting savagely at the peel and spitting it defiantly on the road – like everyone else. I needed some magic, like Hu Dachuan and his 'phantom footwork' all those years ago. It occurred to me that Hu Dachuan always knew exactly what move his opponent was going to make before he even knew himself. More than two thousand years ago our oldest military tactician, Sun Zi, said it all in his manual: 'Know the enemy, know yourself and you will emerge victorious from a hundred battles', and 'In warfare there is no such thing as "unfair tactics".' Concentrate on weaknesses, I thought, not on strengths. Hit where it is least expected. Could my weakness be a strength? What if I just hit back fiercely at the leaders, not out of emotion, but certainly in an emotional manner? I flung the remains of my sweet potato at the base of a tree, and turned back towards the university.

I burst into the office of the departmental Party secretary. Secretary Kong was reading someone's file, which she closed as soon as she saw me.

'How could you?' I demanded. 'How could you set a trap for me? All three of us were called back at the same time, but it was obviously only me that you were after. Did you think I wouldn't find out that Liu Aihua is going back, or that Gao Yong is still in Australia?'

'Hang on, what—'

'Even if the bureaucrats don't understand me, you certainly should. You've known me for ten years or more. Couldn't you have put in a word for me? You must have known that it's all about petty jealousy. Why didn't you give me a chance to explain. Surely—'

'Oh, I see, so they've told you. Why didn't you just tell them everything and explain the whole situation?'

'I could have. I had nothing to hide, but the trouble is they are not interested in facts, they are only interested in my "attitude". But you, of all people, know my attitude, you know that I can get a bit carried away with my smart remarks. Yet instead of explaining the situation, you wrote a letter and set a trap for me – now I am "an enemy of the people"!'

'Xiao Fang, that's not fair. When we were told there was a report against you in the Higher Education Bureau, we tried our best to defend you. I told them myself that there was intense competition between Suzhou University and us, and if there was a report on Nanjing staff by anyone from Suzhou it should be disregarded. As I told you last time, our department had no choice in the matter of asking you to come back. What else could we do? If we didn't comply with Higher Education Bureau directions they wouldn't allow us to send anyone abroad again. As it is now, it is out of our hands; you are no longer under our jurisdiction. Personally, I don't understand what all the fuss is about, but then again, you have yourself to blame to a large extent. How could you have been so stupid as to talk like that in front of Song Wenren? Everyone knows what a frustrated old goat Song is! If he wasn't so hard to get along with, he wouldn't be an old bachelor professor, would he?'

So that was it! Song Wenren, a professor of English literature and translation. I made some placatory remarks to Secretary Kong, told her that I understood her position,

146

and that I had been under a strain, and so on. Then I went back to my room to think this latest revelation through.

When I got there, I laid my broken stool on its side and moved it up against the bed, which could now serve as a desk. I took out some notepaper, and worked through the afternoon, jotting down everything I could possibly remember about my exchanges with Song Wenren, reconstructing whole conversations. I had never expected the trouble to come from his direction. As a professor, and a 'bourgeois intellectual', he had himself suffered a great deal from various reports and accusations, from the 1950s to the 70s, like so many of his kind. Now that I knew he had filed a report on me, I knew basically which conversation he had referred to, but I wanted to make sure I did not miss anything. As I made my notes, I kept wondering, as Kong had said, how I could have been so careless. But Song was a disarming sort of character, really.

In February 1986, two months after I moved out of my room at Frank Tate House in Melbourne, I heard that somebody called 'Baldy' Song had moved in. He was the latest participant in the exchange scheme. I didn't really approve of this nickname. Although I had done my share of name-calling in the past, I was still very sensitive about baldness, and my sympathy went out to him, so I asked one or two people how he was getting on. I was told he was a learned and amusing character, and that he was rather lonely and disoriented – in particular he was struggling to get used to the food. I offered to go and visit him, but since I was very busy I only did so a few times. He was good company on these occasions.

The first time I met him he put me at my ease immediately by asking me to call him 'Lao Song'. There were several other Chinese present. When I told him where I was from, he launched into a story about one of my colleagues: 'Nanjing

147

Teachers Uni, eh? Then you would know the Golden Locust? No, no, not the Golden Lotus, you young scamp – I said Golden Locust!'

These half-English, half-Chinese conversations were always great fun, particularly guessing at names across the two languages. I struggled to think what this 'locust' could be – did it refer to animal or vegetable, the insect or the tree? Surely no self-respecting Chinese would be named after an insect? Anyway, 'golden' must be 'Jin' something – of course, Jin Huai!

'You mean that very striking middle-aged spinster?'

'By George, I think he's got it! Yes, I always say, almost everything can be translated, including poetry, despite what linguistic defeatists say. You see, translation is both *re-creation* and *recreation*. This is a rather easy example, actually. The only real difficulty lies in the ambiguity of "locust" as a translation for "huai". In English, or I should say, in Latin, the botanical name of this tree is *Sophora*, and it is known by a variety of popular names, including "pagoda tree" when discussing the Japanese specimens, and "scholar tree" when discussing the Chinese ones. "Locust" on the other hand, refers to an insect and for some reason, the thorny variety of the scholar tree is referred to as—'

'Oh, come on Lao Song, never mind all that rubbish', groaned someone. 'Don't tell us about your trees and insects, give us another one about the Song scholar and the classical beauty!'

'Or better still,' said someone else, wickedly, 'tell us the one about the old professor and the lonely spinster!'

There were howls of laughter.

'All right, all right, but get some more tea for us all, Xiao Li. This may take some time.'

We waited in silence, while he composed himself. When the tea arrived, he took a deep and very noisy draught, and then began.

'I really don't know why people concern themselves about me getting married, and try to meddle in my affairs. I have plenty of candidates to choose from if I so desire, and there is certainly no shortage of go-betweens should I need the services of one. I personally never give it a moment's thought—'

'Perhaps you are just unwilling to compromise your high standards and settle for second best?' said our provocateur.

'Shut up, and let Lao Song tell his story', yelled Xiao Li above the merriment.

'In fact, those confounded amateur go-betweens sometimes go too far and arrange things without your knowledge. You can never be sure just who is a go-between and who isn't. Once, after a conference in Nanjing, just before the New Year festival, I had some difficulty getting a train ticket back to Suzhou, and an old schoolmate of mine, Professor Sun, offered to help. She managed to get me a ticket somehow or other, but she gave me a very funny look as she handed it over. I can still see the smirk on her face as she wished me bon voyage. When I sat down in the carriage, and took out the Yangs' translation of *A Dream of Red Mansions*, I noticed an overpowering smell of perfume opposite me. Naturally, I could not be so boorish as to look straight into her face, but I knew there must be a woman opposite, and I was aware of the movements of her hands as she flounced her hair about. Out of the corner of my eye, I also noticed that this hair was tightly permed. I buried my nose in my book. I felt this translation could stand some improvement. After a while I became conscious that another book was edging its way further and further into my field of vision. I couldn't help noting that it was in English, and had something to do with a dream of some sort. I became curious, and finally made out *A Midsummer Night's Dream*. A fellow-Shakespearean scholar! I looked up and saw a woman who had been at the conference. She was already looking directly at me, and said, "Excuse me, weren't you a speaker at the conference? I really enjoyed your treatment of literal versus literary translations from classical Chinese into English".'

Song paused for another prodigious slurp of his tea, and then resumed the tale.

'We engaged in quite an earnest conversation, and the time passed very quickly. Just outside Wuxi, she told me that she travelled from Nanjing to Shanghai every vacation, because she was single, and life was a bit dull without family in Nanjing. She said she would be staying with her parents in Shanghai, and then added, rather pointedly, I thought, that I was most welcome to visit if I happened to be in town. I began to get a little suspicious. Why had Professor Sun been so helpful about the ticket? Anyway, how did she manage to get one so easily? She was not noted for her pull with railway officials. She must have bought a ticket long ago – and perhaps she bought not one, my friends, but two!'

Song's audience responded dutifully to the denouement with catcalls and whistles and raised eyebrows. Lao Song was delighted.

'Or perhaps – yes, could it be – that my fellow passenger, Jin Huai, the Golden Locust herself, bought these two tickets – and passed one on to our mutual friend Professor Sun, with certain instructions!'

More cheers, then Xiao Li said, 'Come on, Lao Song, don't be coy, let's get to the action! What happened? Did you visit her in Shanghai, or did she visit you in Suzhou? Did the locust hop onto the scholar tree, or did the scholar tree fall on the locust?'

This brought the house down.

After this Song was plied with questions about why these women always failed to get their man. What could he possibly have against a handsome, intelligent woman like Jin Huai – a colleague who could share his enthusiasm for the delights of English literature, and the intricacies of translation?

'Well – let me tell you', replied Song, carefully. 'She might well be a good colleague and friend, but not a good wife, I think. A wife is a much more practical matter.'

At this point I jumped into the conversation, encouraged by the free and friendly atmosphere, 'Lao Song! What on earth are you suggesting?'

'Xiao Fang, you know a little about Francis Bacon, I'm told by my sources at Nanjing. Let me put it this way: "Wives are young men's mistresses, companions for middle age, and old men's nurses." I don't see how Jin Huai fits into the picture. I admit I'm a bit past mistresses, but I cannot settle for a mere "companion" and I'm a long way off needing a nurse! I am a man with a very healthy appetite, you know. But I will do without, rather than be left unsatisfied. On the other hand, give me enough of what I fancy, and I will really do it justice. I can polish off three great bowls of Suzhou wontons at one sitting!'

When the uproar subsided, I said goodbye to everybody, because I had to go and teach. Song thanked me for coming and asked me to try and come as often as I could. He suddenly looked rather serious, and said to me, 'You must realise, Xiao Fang, it's not good for someone like me to be stuck in here like a thrush in a cage. I need to get out a bit. I'm told you have a lot of friends here.'

After that I visited Frank Tate House every now and then, when I had time. Song never seemed to tire of telling stories, and I found him interesting, and sad. His youth, and his considerable talent, had been tragically wasted in the Great Leap Forward, then the Socialist Education Movement, the May Seventh Cadre School campaign and the Cultural Revolution, during which he was labelled a 'bourgeois intellectual' and sent to a labour camp..

As I became more and more familiar with Song Wenren,

151

I took the liberty of a few anti-Party jokes in his presence. I also allowed myself to differ with him quite vigorously on some issues. For example, I criticised Li Peng's strict regulations governing travel permits for spouses of students and exchange personnel. Since I was waiting for Bi Lijun to join me, I was most unhappy with any suggestion of a prohibition on overseas reunions. He, on the other hand, felt that no possible good could come of mixing business with pleasure, and that all distractions from work and study should be minimised. I was sure that he was making a virtue out of what, in his case, was a necessity, so I suppose I came on a bit strong, but he didn't seem to mind. He made some flippant comments about 'scholars and beauties', getting a little of his own back for the way we had teased him before.

It was a Friday, I seem to remember, and a public holiday in April, when I visited my colleagues again, to see if they wanted to do anything at the weekend. One wanted to go to St Kilda beach, the others thought the Arts Centre would be a good idea. Their house chef was not on duty, so they whipped up a nice lunch of stir-fried sliced fish, and spicy *Ma po* bean curd, while we argued the pros and cons of each itinerary.

'Look,' said Song, 'I don't care where we go, anywhere will do. Let Xiao Fang decide, he's been here the longest and knows his way around better than any of us – he even has his own car. You must know lots of fascinating places, eh, Xiao Fang?'

'Well, not really, but anyway, we can't go too far. The car's not up to it, it's only an old Volkswagen. Besides, it's not mine – I've borrowed it from a friend.'

'Really?' said Song. 'That's terrific! Driving is a very useful sideline skill. If another Cultural Revolution comes along, and we intellectuals cop it again, you can always go into taxis for a living.'

152

I laughed. 'That's right. You never know what's around the corner, do you?'

We finished our lunch, and then moved to the television room. At this point Song became a little more serious. 'What exactly *are* you going to do, Xiao Fang? Are you thinking of making a career in linguistics – or literature?'

'Well, now that you mention it, I've been thinking of asking you for your advice. Linguistics is useful, but a bit boring – I mean, you know "transformational grammar", "surface structure" and "deep meaning". I don't really think I could handle all that. On the other hand, I like literature very much, but it's a bit dangerous in China. If you want to play it safe, you always have to apply Marxist–Leninist literary theory. What do you think?'

Song deliberated for some time before he replied.

'Well, yes, this doctrinaire view of literature can be very destructive, I know, and various things must be taken into account, but the fundamental principles of Marxist–Leninist literary theory still apply universally, don't they?'

I hesitated, discouraged by Song's response. But he urged me to speak my mind. He said he enjoyed arguing with bright young academics, that it kept his mind sharp.

We began a debate which, although civil, gradually became a little heated. I was not surprised. After all, it was understandable that a man who had built his career upon Marxist–Leninist literary theory should stoutly defend it. Then we struck a real obstacle – the current situation in China. His mood darkened as I compared China unfavourably with the West.

I was pacing up and down, and, although Song was sitting, his hands and feet were engaged in an agitated dance as he tried to explain that I had been away from China too long to understand the real situation.

'I notice', he said, in some irritation, 'that you seem to put on your rose-tinted glasses when you are talking about anything to do with the West, but you have a pair of special dark glasses for China. I don't have as many friends here as you, of course, but I still have quite a few foreign friends, and I have found *them* much more sympathetic to China's circumstances than you are. They, unlike you, at least seem to appreciate our great achievements! And they quite frankly admit the shortcomings of Western society, whereas you seem to think even the moon is rounder here! I suppose you have simply been away too long.'

'Well, what about your foreigners then? They've been away all their lives! In fact the further they are removed from China the more enthusiastic they seem to become. On the scale of optimism about China we have foreigners at the top, then overseas Chinese, then our compatriots in Hong Kong and Macao, followed by us Chinese. At the very bottom of the list are high-ranking Party cadres, who demonstrate their faith in the motherland by embezzling money and using it to get their kids out of China. As for friends, yes I admit I have quite a few here, but what impresses me is not the way they talk about *our* government, but the way they talk about their own. I have a friend who swears every time he mentions politicians – "Bloody pollies, they're all bastards, all they're interested in is keeping their arse in a seat, at the taxpayer's expense." Whether this sort of attitude is constructive or not is one thing, but whether it is a right—'

'So, you really admire this sort of "right" do you? You'd like to curse and swear at our leaders like that yourself, would you?'

'No, not at all', I protested. 'I'm not interested in calling people names. That's not my point. And, anyway, while we have a leader like Deng Xiaoping there's no problem, but what I mean is – suppose we have a situation like under Mao, when he got senile and power-crazy? People should have the right to criticise their leaders.'

154

'All right, so we should think some more about rights and political reform. What do you suggest?'

'Oh, I'm no political scientist, and there are so many problems, but, to start with, it seems obvious to me that the Party should make its factions public, instead of pretending to be solid outside, and fighting bitterly on the inside. This might eventually lead to the development of a multi-party system when conditions are appropriate, and it might help to get rid of some of the cadres who squat on the pot without shitting.'

'So what are you saying?' Song asked contemptuously. 'Just copy Australia or America? What about "Chinese characteristics"? If we just slavishly imitate the West we'll end up with a worse situation, and lose our own strong points – we'll get AIDS and drugs, along with your precious Western-style politics!'

'I can't see the connection between what I'm talking about and AIDS, but maybe we would have to pay a price in some areas of traditional morality, just to be in the modern world—'

'That's your idea of "modern"?' he snorted. 'Well, I can tell you it certainly isn't mine. America and Australia have barely four hundred years of history between them, while we Chinese have more than four thousand years of recorded history! I despise their infant antics! What can they show us when we come here? Some stupid gold mines – discovered by Chinese anyway – or a so-called "historical" township built yesterday. Or "barbecues"! Tell me, how does that compare with—'

'Yes, yes, Lao Song. Don't tell me again about the Great Wall or the Forbidden City. I have had that all my life. If you want to look at it another way, how come we have taken four thousand years to get to third-world status, while they have managed a first-class standard of living in two hundred years?'

Song's face was now a mottled red.

'You seem to have something against the Great Wall, don't you? How can you call yourself a Chinese with that sort of attitude? The Great Wall is part of the birthright of every son and daughter of the motherland.'

I felt that I was beginning to lose control. I monitored my words, but they still grew into an angry speech.

'Lao Song, I have told you time and time again, and you know me by now – I will not be told what I must love and what I must hate. I will use my own judgement, and don't try to tell me I'm not a true Chinese, just because I do my own thinking. If you must know, since you mention these things, the Great Wall is a great obstacle – it not only shut us off from the outside in ancient times, but even now it allows people like you to be proud of their ignorance and isolation.'

Song's face changed to the colour of pig's liver.

'Yes, that's right,' he snarled, 'I know your kind. I've seen it all before. A "worker-peasant-soldier" student! One of the few who managed to profit from the Cultural Revolution – you wouldn't even be in a university, if it were not for a quirk of history. And now, thanks to another quirk, you are overseas. Not only that, you think you know it all! Infatuated with everything shiny and new and foreign! A bastard freak of the times, a mongrel breed that doesn't even know its own ancestors! And you have the gall to call me ignorant!'

I was shocked at his outburst, and, when I recovered, my mind was racing with insults to hurl back at him. This question of pedigree would have to be settled.

'Tell me, who are *your* ancestors? Chinese or foreign? The Yellow Emperor or Marx and Engels? You say I'm a freak, and a mongrel, but which of the "big-beards" seduced your grandmother, that you should claim them as ancestors? And you have the gall to tell me that it is I who worship things

156

foreign! And speaking of "quirks of history", I would say that China has been dominated more by foreign ideology in the last forty years than at any other time in the last four thousand. Look at our Constitution, and those "fundamental principles" you were going on about – Socialism, Marxism–Leninism, Communist Party, Dictatorship of the Proletariat – are any of these Confucian or Taoist? We've never even had a proletariat, but now we have a "dictatorship of the proletariat". That's what I call being "infatuated" with foreign paraphernalia. And not knowing it, is what I call real ignorance!'

For some seconds Song could not speak at all. Finally, he did say something, but in a weary way.

'You know very well that the four principles of the constitution form a boundary, a limit. If you insist on going beyond that point, then I don't want to be involved.'

I suppose I had worked myself up to a point where I could not stop, or perhaps I wanted to justify myself further. At any rate, I drove my point home.

'Our constitution guarantees us freedom of speech. If that is the case, we should be able to differ, shouldn't we? Surely that means we can criticise the government? I don't know of any regime that forbids its citizens to praise the government, so if the constitution means anything at all we should be free to criticise. Or are we only free to whisper a few intimate secrets in the wife's ear, in the privacy of our own bedrooms? As long as we don't go too far and suggest something unnatural, outside the four principles—'

'Enough', he said, looking up suddenly, and waving his hand. 'I can't take any more of this, I'm not well. My blood pressure is too high—'

I realised I had gone too far. I helped him back to his room, and asked if he needed a doctor. He said he didn't. I asked if he wanted me to stay with him for a while, but he said he would rather be left alone to get some rest. Before

I left I apologised for my temper and for my lack of respect to a senior colleague.

But Song had the last word after all, and nine months later I had to do some more arguing, not with him this time, but with the Higher Education Bureau.

6   The Summons

It was getting on for seven in the evening when I finished making my notes on conversations with Song Wenren, and with others who might have been implicated since. I went down to the student dining-hall and bought two steamed bread buns. It was too cold to go back to my room, but in the huge dining-hall, which could accommodate 3000 students at a time, there were some coal-burners made out of oil drums. I stood near one of them and, picking up a poker, stoked the fire up a bit, so that I could toast my buns. A cat ran squawking across the near-empty hall, and momentarily disturbed a couple who were cuddling surreptitiously in a dark corner. I knelt and warmed my hands near the small blue flames, and felt glad that at least this kind of secret romance was behind me, and I had had a short period of complete freedom. That was more than many others would ever have.

Then I began to wonder what Bi Lijun would be doing just at that precise moment, and the thought became painful. I couldn't even be sure that she was still in Melbourne. When they asked me this morning where she was, I was pretty sure she had not left for Hong Kong. Before I left Shanghai I had seen a letter she had written to my parents, saying that she was reasonably confident of enrolling at Chisholm Institute of Technology. If she was still in Melbourne, it must be about ten o'clock on a hot summer night, and she would be watching television with Jean and Ted – probably a movie. Perhaps they were having a drink, and chatting about me.

159

As I thought about the questions that morning, and the Bureau's interest in Bi Lijun's whereabouts, I suddenly realised what must have prompted their curiosity. If there were people outside China who were interested in my welfare, it might help my case. At the very least these connections might stand between me and the most severe penalties. So I decided that I must write immediately to Jean and Ted, asking for sponsorship to go back to Australia for study. This would set up regular communication and lead to enquiries and representations through the Australian Embassy. At the same time, if Bi Lijun were still in Melbourne these letters would convince her that I was hopeful of returning to Australia, and would keep her there for the time being, even if she failed to gain a place at Chisholm Institute. I finished my steamed bread in a hurry, and rushed back to the room to write my letter. Jean and Ted had often suggested that they could sponsor me, but I told them I had to return to China. I backdated the letter a few days to make it look like I had this idea before any suggestion of trouble.

Early on the morning of 6 January, I rushed down to the post office with my letter, bought some newspapers and then returned to my room to contemplate what the next moves might be. I had a lot of thinking to do. Although I had gone over the whole conversation with Song, this may not necessarily be the source of the greatest danger to me. Perhaps there were others, whom I had taken to be friendly, and to whom I had said far worse things. I also needed to study the newspapers very carefully to get a clear idea of what direction this 'anti-bourgeois liberalism' campaign was taking. There were reports of arrests in almost every major city, mostly workers and unemployed people and a handful of 'expelled' university students. Suddenly I saw a familiar name in a small headline – 'Li Shunxin, Deputy Director of Foreign Relations, Education Department, replies to the media.' My old friend from the Chinese Embassy in Australia. Perhaps he could help me – but then the last time I saw him was at the Melbourne airport the day I left. He was with some big shots that day, and somebody said they had been talking about me the night before. Of course, they must have already known there was a report about me.

I read the article anxiously. It was a question-and-answer routine.

Q. Recently, in a number of large cities throughout China, students have voiced their concerns, during demonstrations. Later the demonstrations were declared illegal, and this led to criticism both in China and abroad. Perhaps you could throw some light on this situation?

A. In late 1986, first in Anhui Province, and later other places, a group of patriotic students expressed their opinions about political reform. Some of their concerns were shared by the Government, Party cadres and broad masses, but as you know, the acceleration of socialist democracy cannot be realised without observing proper legal procedures. We never claimed that the student demonstrations were illegal in general, but that certain specific demonstrations were unregistered, and therefore illegal. This is the case not only in China, but in the United States, or for that matter, in Australia, where I have been stationed.

Q. There have been reports overseas that police bashed students during some of these demonstrations. Could you comment on this?

A. I have to say that some of the foreign media, including VOA, BBC, and some others I will not mention for the moment, played a dirty game, stirring up the students and spreading rumours. I reiterate here and now that there was absolutely no violence used to suppress the students, even when thugs and hooligans incited students to attack the police. Our police demonstrated exemplary restraint at all times. Not a single student was arrested, only thugs and hooligans. While some students were detained for their own safety, all were released when the danger had passed.

Q. *There were also reports recently of racial strife on campus between Chinese and African students. Would you care to make a comment on that?*

A. The policy of the Chinese Government is based on non-discrimination. We have always supported African nations in their just struggle for emancipation, independence and economic development. This policy is wholeheartedly supported by the whole Chinese nation, including students, so it is simply not true to say that there is racial strife on Chinese campuses. However, some people tried to claim the endorsement of the All-China Student Union to write letters full of prejudice and racial hatred, in an attempt to whip up the feelings of African students against China. This matter is under investigation. The whole affair shows quite clearly how easily naive young students can be manipulated by unscrupulous hostile elements from abroad, more often than not from across the Straits. Let me take this opportunity to emphasise that the open-door policy is not in question. Those who wish to come here from overseas are more than welcome, and I am quite sure that those who do come will find things here to be open, friendly and peaceful. As they say, 'seeing is believing', and anyone is welcome to come to China to see the truth for himself.

As I read this, I felt a little relieved. Obviously the government was still concerned about foreign opinion, and did not want to jeopardise joint ventures, investment, etc. If this was the case, my own foreign connections might well prevent them from acting too harshly, for the moment at least. As I was thinking this, there was a knock at the

162

door. A junior clerk told me that I was required to report immediately to the Foreign Languages Department office. I said I would be there in a moment, but the clerk insisted that I get on the back of his bike and he would take me straight away. As he pelted madly through the college grounds, he rang his bell almost continuously, as if it were a police or ambulance siren. Unfortunately for him, and his fantasy, no one paid the slightest attention to his frantic little tocsin, and he was forced to weave ignominiously from one side of the path to the other to avoid pedestrians, who simply turned their backs on him and strolled along with absolutely no thought for the great affairs of state that they were impeding. I would have got there much faster had I been allowed to walk down myself.

I dismounted from the courier's bike, under the roof of the sheltered corridor, just outside the Department office. He seemed reluctant to give up his part in this little adventure, and locked his bike to one of the red wooden pillars so that he could accompany me in to see the Secretary. I suppose he was hoping he would be asked to hang around just in case I turned dangerous. He announced my arrival, but Secretary Kong dashed his hopes of some sport with a dismissive wave of her hand.

'What's all the hurry about?' I asked.

'No hurry. Take a seat will you, Xiao Fang?'

She smiled apprehensively.

'Well, what do you want me for, Lao Kong?'

'Oh yes,' she said, thoughtfully, avoiding my eyes, and scrabbling through her diary, 'let me see. That's right, now where did I put that draft timetable?'

This performance made me feel that she was either extremely nervous, or she was deliberately trying to look amateurish in order to let me know that she was an unwilling participant in a rehearsed routine.

'We've just been looking at the timetable, and I suddenly

realised that we could do with your wife back here as soon as possible.'

The investigator from the Higher Education Bureau had acted very quickly indeed to block my next move. This kind of person was used to playing several games at once, and often did not even need to look at the board to know which move his opponent had made.

I was really alarmed now, but I had no choice other than to go on with it.

'Look, they say I was called back because I was needed urgently, and yet I haven't been assigned any duties yet, and now you tell me my wife is needed. What's going on here?'

'Xiao Fang, you are no fool. I don't have to tell you again why you were recalled, but your wife is a different matter entirely. Naturally, since you were due back we assumed the two of you would be coming together, and we have made arrangements on that basis.'

'But I remember Bi Lijun told me that she had been given a whole year's leave, and she was encouraged by the university to study overseas, with private sponsorship if possible. I've heard that this policy about private sponsorship is still valid—'

'Yes, yes, private sponsorship is permissible, with the proper authorisation and so forth, but you just said your wife had been given a year's leave. I must say I don't remember that. Can you show me some sort of documentation?'

'Well, of course I don't have it on me. Bi Lijun would have it with her, but I certainly remember seeing something signed by the university or department.'

'Oh yes, I see – there's been a change of leadership – probably she had some unofficial arrangement or understanding. Things were a bit confused during the changeover period – you know it's hard for people to keep their minds on the job when they are about to retire. Anyway, there's a new central government regulation which stipulates a maximum of six months' leave for spouses and Bi Lijun is already one month overdue.'

Both of us knew that this was a lie, but she had her part to play, and I had to go through the motions as naturally as possible, trying not too look either too anxious or too casual about it.

'You said that's a central government regulation, so it applies to everyone, but Gao Yong's wife and son joined him in Australia in 1985 and they're still there. She's more than a year overdue.'

'She's not from our university. If others want to breach the regulations that's their affair, not ours.'

'Well then, Su Jin is from our university, currently studying in Columbia University, and his wife is from our university – from this department. She joined him in America about the same time as Bi Lijun came to Australia, so she must be a month overdue too.'

'Yes, that's perfectly true. It's a new regulation, and it's taken us time to catch up with it, but we've already written to her, and you'll see her around here again in a few days.'

'Have you written to Bi Lijun?'

'No. Well, we weren't too sure exactly where she was.'

'OK. I can give you an address, both in Australia and in Hong Kong.'

'No. Look, you write to her, will you? It's better coming from you.'

I stood up, and said. 'All right, then I'd better be getting back and write this letter.'

'Hang on, there's something else I want you to do. Let's see now,' she said, fumbling through her diary again in a very obvious sort of way, 'yes, of course, now I remember—'

My heart was pounding now. I knew that the casual afterthought usually turned out to be the most dangerous threat of all.

'You know we are most anxious to establish links with foreign colleges and so forth, and it is the university's policy that all personnel returning from abroad should write down the names of all contacts and acquaintances made overseas. Don't forget to do that, will you?'

'Do you mean everyone? Or just people involved in education?'

'Well, who knows? All kinds of people can turn out to be useful. Better to put down everyone you can think of. By the way, have you been in touch with any of these people since you returned?'

Without a moment's hesitation I replied, 'Yes, I have.'

Her face clouded. 'What did they want? What did you say?'

'I wrote to some of my friends to ask for private sponsorship. I suppose they will be making enquiries—'

'You did what? You asked about private sponsorship? Who authorised you to write letters of that kind?'

'Well, no one told me not to. I had no teaching to do, nothing to do at all. Just wasting my time, sitting around—'

'So you have written to several people? When?'

'Some time ago, when I was in Shanghai.'

'Aiya! On my mother's – God, you are nothing but trouble, you damned young fool! I really have been too soft on you. You don't know the trouble you're in for – get out of my sight! Go back and write everything down as I have told you. God, why did I give you leave to go to Shanghai? Get out, I'll speak to you later when—'

She stopped speaking, and slammed her diary shut, looking very grim. I went out frightened, but feeling that things hadn't gone too badly. I don't know what I would have done if she hadn't shown any interest in my 'foreign contacts'.

I walked around the campus. Students were on their way back from the dining-hall, their bowls steaming with rice

166

and cabbage. There were girls in noisy chattering little flocks like sparrows, and boys on their way down to the sportsground, bouncing a basketball as they went. Voices poured out of the dormitories – everything seemed normal. What had happened to all this student unrest? Now they seemed oblivious to everything outside the campus, but in the meantime the workers who had supported them were suffering beatings and imprisonment. Were they really such superficial, spoiled little brats? Was it all just for a lark of some sort? Had they been bought off by dances and movies? Did they really want democracy – or discos? Was it all over after an indulgent pat on the head from authorities who forgave *them* their youthful high spirits, but were busily breaking workers' bones in stinking, blood-soaked dungeons?

It set me to thinking – the powers that be never ran out of excuses to protect people they needed, no matter how great their offence, and they never ran out of justifications for destroying those who stood in their way, no matter how slight the offence. It was all a matter of timing. When the need arose to make an example of a certain group, during the heat of a political campaign, all other considerations of guilt and innocence became irrelevant. If I could just survive this present crisis, I might manage to crawl into bed with that favoured group of intellectuals who 'erred once but have learnt from past mistakes' and who were so vital to the Party's self-esteem. As I walked up the hill to the Chinese Language Department building, I worked on my strategy for survival. From tomorrow on I must begin to bend with the wind of anti-bourgeois liberalism. They might think me a precious source of informed, experienced anti-Western propaganda, to be protected and cultivated. Even if they had already decided to make an example of me with some harsh punishment, it was obvious that they were waiting on developments with Bi Lijun before they made their play, and

167

that gave me some time at least. I would have to be careful –anything might happen at the top in the coming weeks, and the whole political climate could change overnight with the rise or fall of particular individuals. In the meantime, I might also be able to make my immediate enemies nervous about Bi Lijun's influential relatives in Taiwan.

I began to feel that there was still some hope of surviving this mess. I thought of my father, and all he had been through. My mind went back to that autumn day in 1965 when we were walking along together, and I asked him how to deal with the propaganda campaign going on in my school. He had said I should just read the newspapers, and copy them, like everybody else. I had never forgotten that lesson of course, but now I saw its value more than ever. Today was Tuesday, and tomorrow afternoon we would have political study, so I needed to get ready for *biaotai* – a declaration of my commitment.

On 7 January, at 9.30 in the morning, I went to the Department office to get first use of the newspapers and magazines which had just arrived for our reference room. I wanted to make sure I had a head full of the right slogans. When I got to the office there were already several people there, waiting for their mail. The junior clerk – my escort of the day before – was putting letters into the staff pigeon-holes, teasing some of the younger women as he did, with taunts about billets doux, etc. Suddenly his expression changed as he picked up a very thick envelope. He shoved it sourly into a pigeon-hole shared by me and a retired staff-member. I took it out and looked at it. It was for me, from the International Teaching Fellowship Association – a thirty-page address list of teaching fellows for the past four years. As I glanced over it a hand slid past me and popped another letter into the slot. I opened this one, and read:

19 December 1986

Dear Mr Fang,

I am writing to let you know that I will pay for all expenses associated with your attendance in court in Melbourne on the 23rd and 24th February 1987. This includes return airfare from Nanjing to Melbourne, accommodation and other associated expenses.

Yours faithfully,

Trevor Hay
Director
Melbourne College of Advanced Education
  China Project Centre

I was taken aback. I thought I had finished all the necessary business with Trevor's case. But then again, he did tell me just before I left that he would be writing to me, and to the president of the university, if it was necessary for me to appear in court in person. In fact he had written just five days after I left, and it had taken nearly three weeks to get to me. But of course, it was holiday season in Australia – and political season in China. That would account for the delay. I had no hope of getting out of my cage and back to Australia, now that I had been shut in again, but, from the point of view of my strategy, this letter was a godsend. Now the bureaucrats had not only Bi Lijun to worry about, but Trevor – and his institution. Not only would this situation focus attention on how I was treated, but it had the potential to threaten a foreign exchange agreement. And after all there was a matter of Australian law involved in this! I wanted to show the letter to the authorities immediately, but then I decided I'd better restrain myself and keep it quiet for a while. No, I couldn't just keep quiet about it, because Trevor had said he would write to the president of the university as well.

I needed to think this new situation over. I was not sure what all the implications were, and how to handle things. I found myself a chair in a corner of the reference room, took an encyclopaedia down from the shelf and studied the letter from behind its covers. After twenty minutes' thought, I decided that I had little choice but to tell the department. If I did not, I could always be accused of concealing something. I worked out what I should say, and went off once more to see the secretary.

I knocked at her door, but there was no answer. Suddenly she appeared in the corridor.

'Xiao Fang, I've been looking for you', she said calmly.

'Secretary Kong, there is something I must talk to you about.'

She smiled, knowingly. 'Remembered the names of a few foreign friends, have you?'

'Oh yes. I haven't quite finished, but I thought I'd better let you have something to go on with', I said, handing her the list of International Teaching Fellows I had just received from Victoria.

'There's another matter I meant to raise with you yesterday', she said, looking very pleased with herself. 'Do you have any idea what Bi Lijun's relatives do for a living? Did you have any contact with them? In particular I am referring to the ones in Taiwan.'

'No, I didn't, not at all.'

Kong looked relieved.

'But Bi Lijun did, of course', I added.

'What – who – what are they? I mean what position do they have?'

'I'm not sure about Second Uncle, but Fourth Uncle is a Taiwan National Congressman, and Fifth Uncle is a manager of a steel plant – well, in fact, that's just a front.

Really it's a munitions plant. Fifth Uncle's son – that is Bi Lijun's cousin—'

'Did you say "Congressman"? You know, we have a full name list of Taiwanese congressmen, and we can easily check it out—'

'Oh, yes. Look, why should I lie to you about that? Wu Shenwu was elected as Anhui's representative to the Nationalist Congress in the 1940s, and then he fled to Taiwan just before Liberation. Since they couldn't hold another election in Anhui, he has held his seat in absentia ever since. Naturally I don't want anything to do with that kind of old parasite, but my wife thinks that it's important to work for the unification of the motherland. I guess that's why she is delayed in Hong Kong. She probably arranged to meet her relatives there.'

'OK. What's his name again, this congressman?'

'The Higher Education Bureau will have all the details in their file, but his name is Wu Shenwu.'

'All right', she said, noting something down in her book. 'And I presume you have written a letter to your wife as I asked you?'

'Yes, I've written it, but I haven't sent it yet because I want to talk to Bi Lijun's parents, in case they want to pass anything on to their relatives.'

'Don't worry about that, just send it,' she said sharply, 'this afternoon!'

'Yes, of course', I said, pretending to fumble absent-mindedly in my pockets. I finally 'found' what I was looking for – Trevor's letter.

'Secretary Kong, this morning I received a letter from Mr Hay—'

'Mr Hay? What does he want?'

I explained the contents, since she had no English. She examined the piece of paper and started to move away, muttering about seeking advice.

'No, look, just hang on a minute! I want to explain. I'm not asking for leave, I'm not asking for anything. I just simply don't know how to handle this, and I need some directions. I have no preference or point of view about it, I will simply do as I am told.'

She left the office. I don't know where she went, but she came back in five minutes and stated emphatically, 'From now on, I have nothing further to do with this matter. As you know, I have no English, and anyway this is a matter for the Vice Dean in charge of foreign relations. She has taken it up, and is at present seeking advice from the relevant authorities. Would you please wait in the other room?'

I sat in the reception room. I was pretty sure that a telephone conversation was going on between the Vice Dean and the President of the University. Or perhaps the investigator from the Higher Education Bureau was also involved. After about twenty minutes the Vice Dean came out. It was Yin Qiufang, whose husband had complained to me last Saturday morning about her preoccupation with new responsibilities. Without any attempt at preliminaries, she said, 'Now, about this court business. First of all I must inform you that this department, in principle, has granted you two weeks' leave. As is normal procedure, this application should go to the President's office. So we need all the relevant documentation and details concerning this affair.'

'No, but I'm not applying for anything—'

'Yes, all right. But we need all this information, just the same.'

I couldn't believe that they were seriously considering leave, that they were prepared to 'let the tiger go back to the mountain'. I tried to explain the whole situation to Yin Qiufang, but when I got to the bit about the subpoena, she stopped me.

'Shub-what?'

I didn't know myself what, if anything, it was called in Chinese, so I had to repeat it in English.

'Subpoena – a kind of court summons.'

'That's quite serious, by the sound of it', she said. 'Go and get it now, will you, so I can talk to the office about it? I'll wait here for you.'

I borrowed a bike, and brought the subpoena from my room. When I returned Yin Qiufang was waiting outside in the sheltered corridor. I gave her the paper, and she read it carefully from top to bottom and back again.

'OK. Is that all the relevant documentation?'

'Yes, that's it. Oh, well, that is, except for one or two letters from a solicitor. I don't know where I put them. Perhaps they're still back in Australia.'

'What's in these letters?'

'Let's see. I think they were about the hearing date, and my evidence.'

'Where's your passport?' she asked me, abruptly, as if it had suddenly occurred to her.

'I still have it—'

She looked apprehensive.

'Your passport is still valid, isn't it?'

'Well yes, but there are no visa pages left in it. As you know, since you've been overseas yourself, this kind of passport is good for one trip only, plus a litle bit of space for urgent extensions or transit stops. In my case I stopped in Hong Kong on the way out, and had extensions in Australia. The only use for it is to confirm that I have been overseas and I'm entitled to duty-free purchases. I only kept it to buy a few things in Shanghai during the vacation. I can give it back, but could you let me have an official certificate of some kind to replace it?'

'No, don't worry. I didn't mean that. Naturally, everybody hangs on to his passport for a while. Keep it by all means.'

She started out towards President Gui's office, in the next building. I called after her that I would be happy to go with her to see him and explain the situation. She said it wouldn't be necessary, and I could wait until she returned if I liked.

I sat in the reception room and thought things over. If they were genuine, all I needed was a letter from the President, to give to the Security Bureau, in order to get a new passport. The whole thing should only take one or two weeks, as in Bi Lijun's case a year before. Two hours passed, during which I went through a mental list of all the people they were likely to contact. Finally, Yin Qiufang returned. This time she looked quite relaxed.

'President Gui's instruction is that we should discuss this matter with the Foreign Relations office. Since we have already made our decision in principle, the whole thing now rests with them. I expect a decision will be made in due course, when all relevant factors have been taken into account.'

'But, I heard from Bi Lijun that a thing like this only takes a couple of weeks. All I need is a letter from the University to the Security Bureau—'

'That's different. The Security Bureau only issues passports for privately sponsored visits.'

'But this *is* a private sponsorship. Mr Hay is paying for this himself. Naturally, no government organisation is going to pay for it.'

'Just the same, it arose out of your official exchange position, didn't it? It doesn't matter who pays for it, it remains essentially an official activity.'

'All right', I conceded, not wanting to argue any more than was absolutely necessary. 'Thank you. That clarifies the situation considerably.'

That afternoon, about 4.30, after a rather unconvincing performance in the political study group, I went to the Foreign Relations office, to see if they had made a decision yet. I kept telling myself not to entertain the slightest hope of going back to Australia. Realistically, it was out of the question, but at least I could pretend to go along with all these phoney procedures, in order to buy time. The office was located in a new building for overseas students, on Southern Hill. I couldn't be sure of my reception. My relationship with Lao Zhu had changed considerably since I helped him with the sister-college business, but on the other hand I knew it would not take him long to start being bumptious and silly again, just as he was two years ago when he assisted me with information about where to get family-size tubes of toothpaste.

The office had been greatly enlarged, and there were many new staff I did not recognise, so I went across to a sort of reception desk.

'Comrade, could I see Director Zhu, please?'

'He's busy at the moment', she said. 'What's the problem?'

I tried to explain the situation as briefly as I could.

'But that has nothing to do with us', she said, with great condescension. 'We only deal with officially-sponsored trips here, you know. If your trip is privately sponsored then it is no concern of ours. What's more, if you apply to us, the procedures will take at least three months – by the time we have assessed your application, it will be too late for you to go anyway. The right place for you is the Security Bureau. I just don't understand why people can't—'

'But I was instructed to come here by the President.'

'Oh, really? I see. Well, just wait here a moment, will you?'

A few seconds later she came out, waving a few sheets of paper in her hand. She told me Zhu was busy, and 'very upset about something'. He was apparently beginning to curse in Shanghai dialect, which was always a very bad sign. He wanted me to translate into Chinese all the documents that had been submitted to his office, including the

175

subpoena. I took the papers from her and mumbled a few well-chosen Shanghai oaths of my own as I left. When I got outside I noticed that in addition to the documents I expected, there was another letter – from Trevor Hay to President Gui Hong, also dated 19 December 1986.

Dear President Gui,

Thank you for your recent expression of sympathy and concern. I am very grateful to you and my friends at Nanjing Teachers University for your kind support at this very difficult time. I am taking leave now for eight months to rest and write a book based on materials I have been collecting for some years. If you would like to write to me, please use my home address, which I have written above.

Our college is looking forward to receiving Mr Hai Ru early next year. I have arranged accommodation for him from 21st February 1987. Please ask him to let me know when his departure date is confirmed. As you know Pat Meehan is also looking forward to staying in Nanjing next year.

As to the matter of Mr Fang, I want to let you know that I will pay for all expenses associated with Fang Xiangshu's attendance in court, including his return airfare, accommodation and other expenses during his visit to Melbourne. He is required to attend the court and give evidence on 23rd and 24th February 1987.

Thank you once again for your understanding.

My best wishes to you and your family.
Yours faithfully,

Trevor Hay
Director
Melbourne College of Advanced Education
  China Project Centre

In the left-hand corner of the letter there were some handwritten instructions in Chinese:

Please convene a meeting between Foreign Relations and Foreign Languages Dept to handle this.

Gui Hong
7/1/87

Obviously this was intended to show that the university was taking genuine steps to deal with Trevor's request, in case there was any suggestion of obstruction. And, if there was any difficulty, naturally it was just red tape that was to blame, nothing more than that.

Bright and early next morning, 8 January, I raced down to the Foreign Relations office with my translations. The receptionist had just arrived, carrying her thermos. She seemed a little more cheerful than yesterday.

'You're early! Can't wait to get to Australia, eh?'

'Yes, that's right', I chuckled, trying to give the impression of being thoroughly at ease. 'Er, comrade, could I see Director Zhu now please?'

'Well, it's a bit early. I'm not sure if he's in yet, but you can go and have a look if you like.'

I went down the corridor and saw a sign indicating the Director's office. The door was half-open. A voice came from within. I couldn't understand what was being said, perhaps it was a foreign visitor. It took me a little while to figure out it was Russian – and when I peered around the door I discovered that the voice belonged to Zhu himself. He was sitting astride the back of his chair, reading some phrases, which I gradually recognised as being from my old Russian language textbook:

Ivan.   On what days will you be working?

Nadia.   I am not working now. I am resting.

Ivan.   Good. You will be in the factory club on Tuesday?

Nadia.   No, it's too dull there. I want to dance all day and all night.

Ivan.   Don't you want to listen to the lecture on Marxism–Leninism?

Nadia.   Oh yes, indeed I do! I had forgotten about that.

I was quite surprised. Lao Zhu seemed to be handling this rather well – certainly better than any of his ill-fated sorties into English. His entire English vocabulary concerned food, and, no matter what difficulties it caused, he always insisted on using it during banquets with foreigners. I had been present on a number of occasions during his visit to Melbourne in 1985 when this had caused endless confusion and embarrassment. Once, when asked if he wanted fish or chicken, he stopped me in mid-translation, thought for a while and then said purposefully, 'Kitchen, please.' We all had to visit the kitchen and meet the chef because of that. Our hosts assumed this was an old Chinese custom, Lao Zhu assumed it was an old Australian custom, and we all toasted and applauded the bewildered chef before we had eaten a single bite. But the worst incident that I ever heard of happened in Nanjing, during the visit of some American early-childhood educators. There were a number of dishes spread out on the table, including all kinds of things that looked rather exotic and threatening to these ladies, I suppose. Whenever the interpreter tried to describe a dish to the group, relying on poetic Chinese titles, Lao Zhu would interrupt and attempt a crude literal description. Various bits of animals were beginning to cause alarm among the guests. Finally, Zhu picked up a dish of flour-coated peanuts, which he felt would be very familiar and reassuring I guess, and said loudly 'Penis!' He repeated this confidently several times, but he had no takers.

I knocked at Zhu's door.

'Yes, come in.'

'Good morning, Director Zhu. I must say your Russian is very fluent. Are you getting ready for a trip to Moscow?'

'Oh, no, no! I'm a bit rusty these days, it's been so long since I last used Russian, you know.'

He seemed in quite a cordial mood, even asked me to sit in one of the big armchairs, hidden beneath its white cotton prophylactic sheath.

'Comrade Fang Xiangshu,' his tone was serious, and formal, but not the slightest bit hostile, 'I have been very busy since you came back, and haven't had much time to talk to you – particularly about this matter of my friend Mr Hay, and his court case. Tell me, how did you get involved? Tell me everything, from the beginning, in detail.'

This was going to be difficult. I collected myself, and began. 'On the 26th of July 1986 I went to Mr Hay's home, early in the morning. We – my wife and I – were going to a place called Wilsons Promontory, a sort of national park by the sea. Trevor – Mr Hay – and Mrs Jenny Hay had arranged a weekend trip for us long ago. Originally it was to be a welcome for my fiancée, but then it became also a farewell for us both—'

'Just a minute, please. When did you say this was all arranged? How could it be a welcome *and* a farewell?'

'Well, my fiancée arrived in May that year. From mid-June to the end of that month we received two letters, one from the department, and one from your office. Both letters asked me to come back in September – that is, they asked me, Liu Aihua and Gao Yong to come back. So in early July I booked with Cathay Pacific for the 27th of August.

179

In fact, I was asked to go and see the First Secretary of the Embassy, Ni Chuanrong, about this time. I reported every detail of our travel arrangements – I'm sure he would remember quite clearly—'

I was being a bit long-winded in my explanation to Zhu, but I needed names and dates and so forth to corroborate a story that was certain to be subjected to a great deal of scrutiny and suspicion.

'Comrade, you still haven't answered my question about this welcome-and-farewell business. I want to know when it was all arranged.'

'I don't know exactly, but I guess the Hays arranged this some time before Bi Lijun's arrival in Australia.'

'Yes, I see. Thank you. Now what happened on the 26th?'

'At about half past eight we arrived at the Hays' house, and rang the doorbell. There was no answer, so I used a key which I knew would be left for us in the usual place, and we let ourselves in. I assumed they must have gone to do some last-minute shopping.'

Zhu took out a book and began making notes.

'You must be very familiar with the Hays?'

'Well, yes, but not only me – they're very hospitable to everyone from Nanjing. I stayed there for months, but not only me. Others have stayed there before, and one of your very own staff, Niu Ling, is staying with them at present. They have never asked for a cent from any of us. So I think there's nothing special about me, it's being from this university that is the special thing.'

'Yes, I know. Don't misunderstand me. I know very well that Mr Hay has made a great contribution to the relationship between our two institutions. Now, what were you saying? You let yourseves in. Now what did you say about last-minute shopping? Is this place very far from Melbourne?'

'About three or four hours' drive from Melbourne, I

think – like from here to Zhenjiang or Yangzhou. We were going to drive there on Saturday, because they only work five days a week—'

'Yes, I know all that!'

I had made a little slip. Zhu was very proud of his knowledge of foreign ways, and my condescension had nettled him.

'Then you must have intended to stay overnight? In a motel, I suppose?'

He used the English word 'motel' very deliberately, to demonstrate his sophistication. It seemed he had extended his vocabulary from food to tourism.

'No,' I said, 'we were to stay in a "lodge".'

This stymied him, but the last thing he wanted was to display any uncertainty.

'All right. Come to the point, please! What happened after you let yourselves into the house?'

'There was nobody home. We looked everywhere. Both cars were gone. The house was in a mess. Cupboard drawers were left open, and clothes were lying around, as if they had left in a hurry. About half an hour later they came back, and we watched them from the window as they pulled up in the drive. When Trevor got out of the car we were shocked at his appearance. He had bruises and dried blood on his face, and he seemed to be moving with great difficulty. As he came in through the door we asked him what had happened, and he told us that he had been stopped by two policemen on his way home from work the night before. They had taken him to the police station and beaten him up—'

'Hang on, why did they stop him? Why did they beat him up?'

'Some traffic offences. They said he was driving carelessly, and they wanted to take him back to the police station. He wanted to know why, and—'

181

'But the police wouldn't beat somebody up just for something like that. They must have wanted to teach him a lesson. Was there an accident?'

'No. Trevor wanted to know what the charge was. Look, this is very difficult. Are you asking me to provide an explanation, or do you just want me to tell you the facts as I know them? I don't quite know how to—'

'Both. Tell me first what you were told.'

'Trevor said they were very aggressive towards him, as if he had done something really serious. They said they were taking him to the police station. When he asked them what he had done, they pushed him into their car. He tried to get out of the car so they handcuffed him. They took him to the police station. He said he was going to make a complaint—'

Zhu stared at me, and then asked, 'What do *you* think happened?'

'Well, I don't know. Perhaps there was some sort of mistake. Perhaps they got Trevor's car mixed up with someone else's – perhaps he argued with them. They were young, and you know police don't like that sort of thing. Trevor is a bit sharp-tongued sometimes—'

'All right, let's move on. You were all together in Trevor's house that morning after the incident, but you were not directly involved in the affair, were you?'

'No, but I just didn't know what to do. I still don't really know if we did the right thing even staying in the house. I don't know if Western people regard guests or friends as intruders in that sort of situation, or if they need your support.'

Zhu was writing something down '—and so you made no attempt to leave the house at that time—'

'No. Look, hang on, you can't just walk out, can you? Even if you intend to leave, you can't just do it like that.'

'OK. Just go on, tell me what happened next.'

182

'Bi Lijun and I were sitting in the lounge, trying to figure out what happened to Mr Hay the night before. He himself was ringing people – friends and relatives – trying to get advice about lawyers and so on. His wife was making coffee for all of us. And then he rang his brother, who is a senior policeman in South Australia.'

'Ah, yes, I see. His brother is a sort of high-ranking cadre in the police force?'

'Yes, I suppose so. But during this conversation we could tell that Trevor was very emotional, and Bi Lijun whispered to me that she thought he might be close to tears. We kept very quiet, and then we heard him say something about photos and cameras. He called out to Jenny to see if she could find the camera and check if there was film in it. We said we had brought our camera with us—'

Zhu interrupted me again.

'So *you* offered to take some photos?'

'No, I didn't. It was actually my wife who made the suggestion, but I can't see what was wrong with that. We had brought our camera, to take some shots of Wilsons Promontory – I mean, why not help Mr Hay by – it seemed the obvious thing to do.'

'Yes, all right. So your wife made the suggestion.' He wrote this down in his book. 'What next?'

'When Mr Hay had finished on the phone, I took the photographs. Mrs Hay and Bi Lijun held a white tablecloth behind him to reflect a bit of light, and I took eleven shots of his cuts and bruises, from a variety of angles. The following Monday I took the film to be developed.'

'Did you stay on with the Hays for a while?' asked Lao Zhu.

'Yes, we did. On Wednesday I gave Trevor the photos, and two days later he told me that they were important evidence in his case.'

'I see, yes, of course. With these photos, and a brother

183

high up in the police force – those police would be in some trouble, wouldn't they? So what's the complication? It all seems pretty straightforward. I guess Mr Hay made a report on the incident and forwarded it to their superiors?'

'Well, it doesn't work exactly like that. Trevor did write a report – or "complaint", as they call it. He did that on the night of the incident, before leaving the police station. But the complication is that it is not the police who are in trouble – it is Trevor. They charged him with assaulting them! He needs these photos to defend himself against their charges, not just to discipline them.'

Zhu still could not grasp this entirely. But his attitude seemed to have changed. He appeared less interested in my role now, and genuinely curious about this strange and interesting business. He was mumbling to himself, 'Yes, in another state – that would make a difference. No matter how big a whip his brother has, he can't make it crack in another province – that's like trying to arrange something in Shanghai, from here—'

'Lao Zhu, it doesn't work that way. Mr Hay's brother is not the real issue. Even if he were the Prime Minister, he could not—'

'Oh, don't give me that! Some things are just the same everywhere, and don't try to tell me any different. Now, let's see, this doesn't look very promising—'

'No, but Mr Hay does have a good chance, you see, because these photographs are evidence—'

'You must be joking! If he can pull strings that's one thing, but don't tell me that he can defend himself with "evidence". If they want to find him guilty, they can do it easily, even if he has mountains of evidence – and photographs.'

'All right,' I said, 'if you say there's no point in me presenting these photos in evidence, then that's it. Of course, I won't go.'

'Comrade Fang, don't put words in my mouth! We are evaluating the situation. Try to be patient and we'll work it out. What I don't understand is – you just happened to be there to take these photos, and now you have given them to Mr Hay. OK, but what more does he want with you, and why didn't you just come back as soon as you had given him the pictures?'

So this was it, the point that was going to give me so much trouble.

'I couldn't just give him the photos and come back. A week or so after this, I was told that I would need to appear in court, otherwise my photos would be considered "hearsay" evidence. That is, unless I could verify, in court, that I was the person who took them, there might be some trouble about "admitting" them as evidence. I responded immediately that I was not in a position to decide this matter for myself, and that formal approaches would have to be made to the relevant authorities. My departure date was for the 27th of August, three weeks away, and I thought that a decision would have to be made in that time. I couldn't take it upon myself, one way or the other.'

'Well, as for this "admitting" business, we can discuss that later, but I only want the facts at the moment. What happened next?'

'A few days later, I received copies of three letters written by Mr Hay's solicitor, one to Mr Len Jenkins of the Victorian Education Department, one to Ni Chuanrong at the Chinese Embassy, and one to Chen Dongyu at the Jiangsu Higher Education Bureau. These letters requested an extension of my stay, in order for me to appear in court. Meanwhile, I was informed that I was to be "subpoenaed". I didn't understand this really, but as you know, we International Teaching Fellows were often reminded of our duties as "ambassadors" and I felt that I could not possibly shoulder the responsibility for a possible breach of Australian law.'

185

'Yes, I see. So you decided to stay?'

'No, no! I went to see Mr Jenkins in his office, to discuss it with him. He told me not to worry about it, and subpoena or no subpoena, I should just leave according to schedule, and he would take care of things.'

'So,' said Zhu, ominously, 'if you had instructions from Mr Jenkins, why didn't you just come back?'

'But look, as I told you, it was still three weeks before departure. Naturally, I had to tell Mr Hay about the instructions I received from Mr Jenkins. He was very upset. His solicitor telephoned Mr Jenkins, and she was told that I had left the country—'

'Ah, a "contradiction" emerging among the foreigners themselves over this?' said Zhu, looking very smug.

'Exactly. Among themselves. But the problem for me was knowing who I should listen to.'

'You should have paid attention to Mr Jenkins; you were under his jurisdiction.'

Zhu made more notes. The interview was becoming extremely dangerous, and Zhu's record would no doubt be used again and again in repetitions of this discussion. I had to try to make the strongest possible point, in order to have any hope of surviving future interrogations.

'I was only in Australia for two years, but I have to spend my whole life in China. If I must disobey someone then it had better be my Australian boss, rather than my Chinese boss. You were present when our President Gui Hong gave us all instructions that we should co-operate with Mr Hay in every way possible, because he is very special to us, and has been a great help to our university.'

'You know perfectly well President Gui didn't mean a situation like this!'

'I wasn't too sure then what he meant. If I got it wrong I would have more trouble than I could handle in one lifetime. So, naturally, I sought advice from Comrade Niu

186

Ling, of your office, who had just arrived in Australia, and was at that time staying with the Hays.'

Zhu sneered, 'But Niu Ling was not in any official position, he was only in Australia to study. Don't try to take shelter behind him.'

'I wasn't expecting him to shelter me, I can assure you. But he was a colleague, and I thought we could discuss this business among ourselves at least. Comrade Niu suggested – well, that is, we reached agreement – that the best thing was to get some instructions from the Embassy. I have to say that the discussion between us was completely personal and private. There was no suggestion—'

'Yes, all right, all right – you were talking about the Embassy. Go on.'

'Well, I telephoned Ni Chuanrong and explained the issue, and his instruction was that I should "Handle this sensitive issue properly, and with extreme caution." He also told me that he himself was not able to deal with it, and he would have to seek instructions from the relevant authorities. I then wrote to you for advice – as you know.'

'Yes, that's true, you did. Let's look at that letter again.'

Zhu went to his desk and rummaged around, finally producing a letter.

'Yes, this is dated the 8th of August, and you said you would be coming back on the 27th. But you didn't. You cancelled the booking. On whose instructions did you do that?'

'I had to make a decision. And the matter was sensitive. I had to use my own discretion. You told me yourself, before I left, that there are no minor matters when it comes to foreign relations. You said every little thing is crucial – and this was far from being a little thing. As the First Secretary said—'

'Yes, I'm not saying you were right or wrong. Just give me the facts. Did you make this decision yourself?'

'Yes, but—'

'Thank you', he said, and wrote something down in his book. 'Right! What happened next?'

'On the 8th of September I was informed that, within days, a subpoena would be served on me. Sure enough, on the 1st of October, it arrived—'

'Wait a minute.'

He picked up my translation of the document, and began reading.

'Who wrote this? Did you go and get it from someone in the Australian Security Bureau? How—'

'No, not at all! Someone I had never seen before in my life knocked at my door one night, asked me if I was Mr Fang, and gave me this piece of paper, and two dollars.'

'Well, what if you said you were not Mr Fang?'

Again it seemed that Zhu could not make up his mind if it was the 'facts' he was interested in, or the details. I attempted to explain, but I didn't really understand myself how this system worked. After a while Zhu lost interest and resumed his hunt for the facts. Or perhaps he just didn't believe a word of what I was saying.

'Surely by then you must have received a letter from your department, instructing you to write out some sort of statement of your evidence, and then to come back?'

'Yes, I did get that letter, at almost the same time as the subpoena, but—'

'I see. Well then, you had instructions from Mr Jenkins. You said you preferred Chinese instructions. You got your Chinese instructions – and you disobeyed them!'

'But the whole situation had changed! The department was not aware when they wrote – look, here, you see, on the document – the penalty for disobeying this order is a big fine, or imprisonment, or both. So it's not just a matter of obeying my superiors, it's a matter of obeying the law! How could I just deliberately break Australian law, and end up in jail in a foreign country?'

188

'They wouldn't dare touch a representative of the People's Republic!'

'Well, anyway, I didn't just ignore my instructions, I was making arrangements with Mr Hay's solicitor, but it took time. Of course, Mr Hay was also aware of my predicament, and he promised to write to the University making it clear that this whole situation was beyond my control. Finally, I did what I had to do, booked my ticket and came back as I was told. That's all there is to it. And here I am.'

'Yes, you came back', said Zhu slowly. 'That brings me to my final question. You left Australia on 14th December, and Mr Hay's letters to you and to the President of the University were both dated 19th December. Was that a coincidence, or did you know that he was going to write these letters?'

'Well, he did tell me that he had received a letter from President Gui, and that everything seemed to be okay for me to come back if necessary. He said that he wasn't too sure yet if I would be needed or not, but he would write to the University about it—'

'So you did discuss the arrangements for your return to Australia before you left? And four days after your departure Mr Hay decided that you were needed after all!'

'No, we didn't discuss anything like that in detail. It's just that he wanted to let me know there was a possibility, I suppose.'

'All right, so much for the facts. Now, about this evidence business – and "hearsay". As far as I am concerned, once you have written your statement and left it behind for the court, that's the end of the matter and that's all there is to it!'

'But, I don't know – I mean, I suppose you're right. But – well, maybe Trevor was over-reacting. I don't want to argue about that. You just tell him it's not necessary for me to go back to Australia, and I won't go.'

'No, no. We have promised that if you are needed, you will go back – and we are people who keep our word. But we have to know if you are genuinely needed or not. You said you thought Mr Hay was over-reacting, so it seems that you don't believe – '

'No, I don't mean that. Obviously Trevor was terribly upset and anxious, and would do everything possible to defend himself, and not take risks with evidence. That's why I said maybe he was over-reacting. But I just don't know, that's the whole point. It seems to me that he thinks I am needed, and you think I am not. As for me, I have no opinion at all. You just tell him what you think, and I will just do as I am told. If I go, that's OK, if I don't, that's OK too. As far as my department is concerned, they have already made arrangements for two weeks' leave. And if you think I planned this whole thing before I left Australia, why on earth was I so stupid as to come back?'

Zhu laughed contemptuously. 'China and Australia are both members of Interpol. If you had any thought of staying on in Australia, all we would have to do is pick up the phone to our friends, and we would have you back, quick smart! That is not a concern. But, frankly, I can tell you that your attitude to this whole matter will prove to be of great importance in the future. You are a bit out of touch with your homeland, I think.'

My mind was racing with responses I could not utter, but finally, I said, 'To me the principle of obedience to my superiors is far more important than a passing acquaintance with a foreigner I may never see again. Such contacts are like clouds and smoke.'

'Very well', said Zhu, sharply. 'Go away, and think the whole thing over. Write a report on the entire incident and your involvement in it. Bring it to me tomorrow – no, I'm busy tomorrow – bring it to me on Saturday morning.'

By the time I left the office I felt quite relieved and

satisfied that I hadn't handled things too badly. I was quite sure of my own safety while this court appearance business was being deliberated.

Late that afternoon I felt in need of some relaxation. I could always do the report next day, and there didn't seem to be any point in rushing it. I decided to go for a drink at the Shanxi Road Club, run by the provincial military. These days, with their budget cut, PLA units were encouraged to use their renowned self-reliance in the interests of making money. By selling once-revered second-hand military uniforms, opening the rifle ranges to private fee-paying shooters, and running bars that enjoyed complete freedom from the attentions of the Public Security Bureau, they generated quite a lot of income and, of course, greatly enhanced their reputation as a people's army. I left the university by the back gate, and caught a bus down to Shanxi Road.

Outside the entrance to the club there were glass display-cabinets, containing charts of military equipment and photographs of Deng Xiaoping meeting various members of the top brass. Inside these cabinets there were charts demonstrating the waltz and the tango. I stopped to examine the placement of the footsteps, but I found it quite bewildering. Above the charts there were slogans to the effect that 'Healthy recreational activities mean healthy youth.' I went into the club. There was a huge hall, half was completely empty and the other half was cluttered with tables and chairs, most of which were occupied. I sat down at a table and studied the drinks list. The waiter came – this was new to me, for a big place like this to have waiters. Normally you waited in a queue for a ticket for food or drink. I ordered four glasses of Nanjing beer. These days I had to consider price, not just taste, even if it meant drinking the local 'horse-piss'. But at least they served it in

191

glasses and not in bowls. I also bought some dried beef to chew, and some cigarettes.

After a glass or two I began to take a keen interest in my surroundings. I noticed that there were many healthy young people enjoying healthy recreational cigarettes – especially the teenage girls. You would not have seen that a few years ago. They were drinking from long, thin cocktail glasses, with plastic ornamental straws. According to my list, a cocktail cost about 6 yuan, more than everything on my table, including the beef and cigarettes; 6 yuan was then a little less than $A3, but still more than a day's pay for the average local person. I decided I could do without a companion with those sorts of habits. At about 7.30, when I had almost finished my drinks, and was thinking of leaving, everything went dark, and then coloured lights began to flash around the room. Loud disco music started up – something about 'the waters of Babylon'. All the tables were suddenly vacated and the other half of the hall was filled with a mass of swirling synchronised figures, occasionally parted by some great flapping intruder who was drunk, or unco-ordinated, or simply trying too hard to be free. In the filtered rainbow light of the murky dance-hall they looked for all the world like a school of tropical fish.

I watched, fascinated, for another half-hour or so, until the atmosphere became too stifling, and I had to go outside for some fresh air. Near the club there was an outdoor roller-skating rink, also playing very loud disco music. I suddenly felt very lonely. Months before, at the Myer Music Bowl in Melbourne, Bi Lijun and I had watched some ice-skaters. We were reminiscing about the time years ago when we had been together in a roller-skating group. Suddenly she said, in English, 'Unfortunately, I fell in love with you that afternoon.'

'What? You mean that was my lucky day?'

Somehow this combination of gentle sarcasm and

192

romance seemed possible in English, but I could not imagine talking to her like that in Chinese.

'Yes, I was a little bit naughty that day. Mum came to see me, and asked me to go home with her. I knew that you would be going to the skating, so I told her that I had to attend political study that afternoon. Of course, this was a very bad beginning – telling lies to my own mother. I had never done such a thing before!'

'Wicked! And once you start that kind of thing, who knows where it will lead? Just one black lie after another!'

'You corrupted an innocent young girl with your sophisticated Shanghai tricks!'

'I always thought so too, and I was rather proud of my skill, but now you tell me you were up to no good long before I got to practise my craft. Who was tricking who – I'm sorry – whom?'

'What "craft"? Just what are you talking about now, Mr Fang?'

'Literature, of course. Everyone knows that lending someone a book is an excellent way of getting acquainted, because a book has to be returned – and discussed. Why do you think I—'

'Of course! First *Winds of War* by Herman Wouk, then the sequel, *War and Remembrance*; altogether seven volumes in Chinese translation, one at a time. You scheming fox—'

'Seven volumes! Just to get one girl to meet me by the Yangtze. At this rate it would take *Encyclopaedia Brittanica* to—'

'If I knew then what I know now, not even a whole library would get me down to the river.'

Seven volumes to get her to the river. Yes, and in a way it had taken a library to get her across the ocean. Months and months of waiting, and worry, and documents. First I had to talk to the Victorian Education Department. Since they were the ones who had raised the issue of my extension, they were sympathetic to my request for a reunion, and there wasn't much of a problem in principle, except that Bi Lijun was my fiancée, not my wife. Then there was a suggestion that a marriage could be arranged in absentia, or proxy, or some such thing, so that she would be my wife when she arrived. I told everyone this would be fixed, but what did she do? She refused to have a 'phoney' wedding. Unfortunately she didn't tell me. In the meantime there was a complete misunderstanding at the Chinese end. They thought that the Australians had arranged a wedding in Australia as some kind of diplomatic publicity stunt, strengthening the ties between us and so on. When she finally came, the Education Department gave Mrs Fang a bouquet of flowers, various people threw parties to welcome the new bride, and took us away on weekend trips with them – and I had to arrange an Australian wedding in secret so that they would not be embarrassed or offended when they found out they had been encouraging us to live in sin. A church wedding was out of the question, because that would create political difficulties, so we had to think in terms of a civil marriage. In any case we had to wait a minimum of forty-one days to allow time for the declaration of any impediment to the marriage.

I was giving some thought to all this when I received the letter from Nanjing, informing me that I had to return to China in November. After taking everything into account, allowing for finishing off my work at Victoria College, and leaving some weeks for a honeymoon in Australia, I decided upon a date – 10 August 1986. I worked out a very small guest list, including essential participants and a few friends. Ted was to give Bi Lijun away, his daughter Linda would be one witness and Trevor would be the other. Since Niu Ling was staying with the Hays at the time, he would need to be asked, and he could act as a sort of Chinese representative. I was still busy teaching, so Bi Lijun made the necessary arrangements for the wedding – when she was not occupied with various celebrations to welcome her as my wife. One of my students, Ann, offered us the use of a house at Dromana Beach for our honeymoon, and some of my Australian-Chinese friends organised a combination celebration and farewell.

On 10 August everyone assembled at Ted and Jean's place. I had not seen Bi Lijun during the morning. Apparently it is considered bad luck to see the bride before the ceremony. Curiously, our Chinese representative rang me the day before, and said that, since he had an oportunity to go to some beautiful historic spot called Williamstown, he felt sure that I wouldn't mind if he didn't come to the wedding – after all we knew each other pretty well, and it was no big deal. But our next-door neighbours, Hilda and Karl, who had only known us a few months, were delighted to come, and in fact Hilda had tears in her eyes when I greeted her at the front door.

The wedding march started up on the tape-recorder, and Bi Lijun was escorted into the lounge-room by Ted, in his new suit. She was wearing a burgundy velvet cheongsam, and she had flowers in her hair. Our celebrant made a short speech, and then, at our request, recited 'The Prophet' by Kahlil Gibran.

Then Ted joined our hands, and we made our vows:

'Bi Lijun, I take you to be my wife, from this time onward, to join with you and to share all that is to come, to give and to receive, to speak and to listen, to inspire and to respond, and in all the circumstances of our life together to be loyal to you, with my whole life, and with my whole being.'

'Fang Xiangshu, I take you to be my husband. I promise to be with you, in all that is to come, to love and to respect, to care and to console, to share the sorrows and the joys that lie ahead. I promise to be faithful to you, and to be honest with you; I will share my thoughts, and my life with you, and I pledge myself, and all I am, in love.'

As I recalled these solemn words, and our little flippant conversation that night watching the skaters, I wondered what it would take to bring us together again. Not a library, but perhaps just one small brown book with a photograph and a stamp – and a few pages for a visa.

As I had promised, I returned to Lao Zhu's office on Saturday morning, 10 January, to give him my report on my involvement in Trevor's case. Last time I had seen him bright and early in the morning, but this time I did not want to create the impression that I was at all anxious. In fact, I wanted to appear not only relaxed, but co-operative. I arrived at his office about eleven o'clock, and gave him my report. I stressed that if there was any difficulty about my going to Australia, if it interfered in any way with my 'teaching duties', I could discuss the matter with Mr Hay myself, and personally alert him to the difficulties of the situation. He informed me that his office had approved my leave and the Foreign Languages Department had made arrangements to cover my teaching. I was rather curious about which staff member had been burdened with non-existent duties, but I said nothing.

Lao Zhu went on to say that the matter of my court appearance now rested entirely with the relevant provincial authorities, and asked me to go with him to the reception desk.

'Xiao Ding, where are those documents I gave you yesterday?'

'I've already sent them to the printers, and asked them for three sets—'

'No, wait a minute – please ring and tell them that Comrade Fang will be over there soon to pick up – let me see, one to Provincial Foreign Relations, one to Foreign Ties Association, Central Admin., State Security, and the Higher Education Bureau. Altogether five, for the moment at least. By the way,' he said, turning to me, 'have you been in touch with Mr Hay yet?'

'No, I haven't, because I didn't know what exactly to say.'

'Well, now you do. I think he must be very anxious. You'd better contact him as soon as possible, and let him know what's going on. Oh yes, don't forget – your Department wants to have a word with you, go and see them when you are through here.'

He handed me back the envelope containing my report, which he had not even opened.

'Look, you'd better photocopy your report while you're at it. That might help to clarify things, so ask the printers for five copies of that as well.'

Twenty minutes later I returned to the office with five copies of each document. The receptionist was busy and looked at me rather sourly when I handed them over. She suggested that I might like to collate them for her and place them in their correct envelopes. I was anxious to find out what was going on in the department and I really didn't want to waste any time, but I had to appear co-operative so I quickly sorted the papers, stapled them and placed them in the appropriate envelopes. Then I went to the Foreign Languages Department.

Secretary Kong told me that my teaching duties had been covered in case of absence, and the problem of my accommodation would be resolved shortly. I left her feeling that this Hay might have some clout, after all. On my way down the corridor someone called out to me, 'Xiao Fang, just a minute! Wait, I want to talk to you.' It was Hai Ru, almost concealed beneath a pile of books and magazines he was juggling under his chin. I noticed *The Beauty of Australia* and the 1982 *Year Book of Australia* among the collection. As he reached me he dropped the whole lot, making such a racket that several heads peered out from their office doors, including that of Secretary Kong.

'Teacher Hai,' I said, observing the correct form of respectful address to my own former teacher, 'what can I do for you?' I bent down and helped him regain control of his unruly cargo.

'Oh, I – I have just been informed that—' he panted, removing his spectacles and polishing them with his handkerchief, 'that – Mr Trevor, that is Mr Hay, your friend, has already arranged accommodation for me from next month, but I just don't understand why they are taking so long with my passport.'

'So do you want me – I mean, I can't do anything about that – look no one understands this problem better than me, but I can't—'

'No, no, I don't mean that! I know you can't help with the passport, but have you heard what they have asked me to teach in Australia?'

'No, what?'

'English literature, if you please!'

'Well, that's all right, isn't it? You are very competent—'

'Oh, come off it, Xiao Fang! Teaching English literature in Australia is like teaching your grandmother to suck eggs. How am I supposed to handle a situation like this? Just imagine some Australian ignoramus coming here to teach Tang poetry!'

'Well, as a matter of fact some Australians *are* know-ledgeable about Tang and Song poetry, and some English translations are easier to read than the original classical Chinese.'

'Oh, Xiao Fang, don't talk such drivel! You know

198

perfectly well that I'll be a laughing stock! You're the only one who can help me out of this jam. I heard that Mr Hay is a very close friend of yours, and that he is director of some "centre" or other. Could you get him to change the curriculum—'

'But Teacher Hai, he can't change the curriculum! He is not the director of the college, and anyway even the director can't—'

'Look! Is he a director or isn't he? And what's the point of being a director if you can't direct things? Just do your bit for me please, if it doesn't work, I won't hold you responsible.'

'All right, I'll write to him for you.'

'Oh, thanks ever so much, Xiao Fang. I really appreciate it. And if you don't mind, please write me a letter of introduction, so that I can go to him for help if they decide that I must teach not only my grandmother how to suck eggs, but my grandfather as well!'

He laughed, said goodbye, and scribbled out his address for me, so that I could go and visit him before he left. I assured him that I would do whatever I could for him. After all he had always been very kind to me, and in fact he was the one who had recommended me for a teaching position in the university.

As I walked back to my room I thought about this business of Trevor and his influence. Even if others were inclined to overestimate the importance of the China Project Centre, that in itself was a kind of power. I was very glad I had suggested to Trevor that he did not call himself a 'co-ordinator'. 'Director' had much more impact on the Chinese side. Even Gui Hong had a habit of giving the thumbs-up sign at banquets and saying, in English, 'Mr Hay, now Director!' I don't imagine Trevor would have made the same mileage out of 'co-ordinator'.

Back in the room, I lay down on my makeshift bed and

amused myself with a few thoughts along these lines, until suddenly I remembered Niu Ling's friendly warning, back in Australia: 'Xiao Fang, we Chinese should never make the mistake of thinking that influential foreign devils can shield us from our own masters. If they want to they can always crush us like so many blades of grass, and they don't care who is watching.' Yes, of course, I could not afford to place too much reliance on protection from foreigners. The investigator from the Higher Education Bureau might tread warily for a while, but when the moment was right he would act, and no one on the outside could do a damn thing about it. And even if they were concerned about Trevor for the moment, they might decide at any time that he was dispensable.

The more I thought about this, the more nervous I became. I tried to tell myself that I was imagining things, but what could anyone really do about it if I just disappeared? How would they know anyway? I could have a sudden illness. After a while I convinced myself that I was over-reacting. The bad old days were still with me, and Dr Wang's stories about kidney transplants and secret executions were playing on my mind. Perhaps I had even underestimated the effect of culture shock. I calmed myself down with these thoughts, but nevertheless I did not sleep that night, and in the morning I had a terrible headache. I remembered that when I went to visit Mu Yi in hospital he had offered me his bed in the dormitory. So, on Sunday, 11 January, I moved out of the storeroom.

I introduced myself to the two others in the dormitory as a friend of Mu Yi. In fact, I had often seen them around the campus before I went to Australia. They were quite curious about why someone of my age and experience should not have had a room, or even a flat, allocated to him. I assured them that the matter was being looked into, but they were rather outspoken in their criticism of the university

200

administration. I was surprised, in view of the recent demonstrations, that they were so bold. I became alarmed when they went on to a general denunciation of the government, and described Hu Yaobang as a 'puppet emperor' who had been manipulated by Deng Xiaoping, the 'Old Buddha'.

I certainly didn't need any further trouble of my own, so I climbed up into my bunk and busied myself fiddling with a mosquito net. There were no mosquitoes left in January, but as our leaders kept saying, we had to screen out the 'flies and mosquitoes of liberalism and pornography'. In fact, my net only seemed effective against the former of these two pests. It failed completely to block out a conversation about nude models in the Fine Arts Department.

Li Ning, a photography teacher, sighed and said, 'We finally got somewhere, just towards the end of last year. In fact you could say we had established a beachhead on this question of art and nudity.'

If only they could see some of the beachheads in Australia, I thought. His friend, Wen, a physical education teacher, joined the lament, with more than a tinge of sarcasm, 'Ah yes, that's right. Now you must start all over again to win back the ground you have lost since the crackdown.'

'But look, you have to admit it doesn't make sense. We can have nude models for painting, because Zhou Enlai said it's OK. But why not for photography, what's the difference? I mean, if anything, you have more time to get impure thoughts when you're painting than when you're taking a photograph.'

'I always thought professional photographers were allowed to take nude photos, but not to display them in exhibitions. I've seen plenty of your bare-arsed masterpieces in my time.'

'Well, yes, but the angle is the thing. In the past we could

201

only take shots from the back. Then we could take them from the front, but side on. We had just made it to frontals, with a lick of tasteful covering draped here and there. I think we were on the brink of artistic freedom. Now look what's happened! What a load of fucking dog-shit!'

'OK, OK, take it easy! Anyway, who's going to supervise your "angle"? The Engineering Department? Don't tell me you can't just please yourself and take your own good time about it! What I want to know is how you get to choose the girls—'

'Oh, for God's sake – what – can't you think of anything else? Who says they're always girls?'

There was a snort of derision at this. From my position up on my bunk, where I had dropped the net and tuned in to the conversation, it seemed that this point didn't carry much weight. Li Ning continued, undeterred by his friend's sarcastic observations about the level of interest in male nudity among the Fine Arts staff.

'Some of the cadres from the admin. office sit in, and monitor the sessions! They say they are aware of bad elements who ocasionally peep in through the windows, so they go around drawing the curtains. When you need a bit of extra light, they stand at the windows and hurry any passers-by on their way. You can imagine how conducive all that is to an artistic atmosphere!'

'So how long do you expect it will take to regain your "beachhead", Mr Li Ning? A year or two, before an artist's life is worth living again?'

'You know as well as I do, smart arse – it could be a month, a year. It could be tomorrow, with a change of leadership. "A storm may arise from the clearest of skies." '

'So we should just watch the sky, eh? No point in us mortals worrying ourselves!'

Listening in on this little chat made me feel a great deal more comfortable. Obviously things had not gone so far that

202

people had stopped talking, at least among themselves. This indicated to me that we had not gone back to the 1960s. And there seemed to be a general dissatisfaction, so I need not feel isolated – after all, my opinions were no more counter-revolutionary than many others I had heard openly expressed. I entirely agreed with my colleagues. Nobody knew what the future might bring like a bolt from the blue. Today's villain might well be tomorrow's hero, just on the whim of the 'emperor' – or the 'dowager'. In fact, the whims of emperors and dowagers didn't worry me much – they were too far removed to cause me much bother – but I certainly had to be careful of the eunuchs and concubines. I had to know who was in charge of my business: Lao Zhu, Gui Hong, or the bureau investigator, or Li Shunxin, or my big sister's Auntie Fang Fei? Five copies. Maybe several of these had been given material. The higher up it went the longer it would take to come back down again. If my file went to a really big shot it would sit on his or her desk for some time, perhaps forever – or at least until things had cooled down. The real danger was the investigator from the Higher Education Bureau. He could swing his axe at any moment.

I began to think that the best way of handling things was to announce that I wanted to go back to Shanghai during the vacation, to look after my sick mother. That way they might decide that I could be persuaded to stay in Shanghai until after the trial – and it would be my personal decision, not that of the university, if I was unable to help Trevor. They might be willing to go easy on me about the other business if I provided them with this demonstration of my 'attitude'.

A few days later, on the evening of 16 January, I went next door to watch the television news, as I had been doing every night. I felt fairly relaxed, since there had been no dramatic developments, but the sight of the newsreader in a Sun Yat-sen jacket, instead of his customary Western-style suit, filled me with foreboding. The other disquieting sign was that the reader did not look at the camera at all – he kept his head down, and simply read the news item from his text.

Comrade Hu Yaobang has submitted his resignation to the enlarged conference of the Party Politburo on the grounds of ill-health. His resignation was accepted by the conference, and Comrade Zhao Ziyang has been appointed acting Secretary-General. During the conference Comrade Hu Yaobang made a self-criticism concerning his mistakes in violation of the principle of the collective leadership of the Party, and other major issues. Comrades attending the conference also made serious, frank and genuine criticisms of Comrade Hu Yaobang . . .'

I left the room in some haste and confusion. I went back to my own room, and lit a cigarette. What were the implications of this? One thing seemed crystal-clear – the 'liberals' in the Party were on the run. The power struggle had passed its critical stage, and most likely a purge would follow.

After some time my two roommates returned. They were talking softly, and looked quite grave.

'The bastards! You know that "enlarged conference" was completely unconstitutional. Unless there is a vote to determine a two-thirds majority of Politburo members in favour of a conference, the Secretary-General has the right to dismiss the meeting.'

'Of course it's "unconstitutional"! The big decisions are made every year when they have their little party at the beach at Beidaihe. Theoretically the Politburo makes decisions, not the old goats at the top, but who gets to be in the Politburo? The ones who are recommended by the old goats! Obviously somebody decided that Hu Yaobang was out of line, so he goes, Constitution or no Constitution.'

'Violation of principles of collective leadership, blah, blah! I can tell you who really violates collective leadership. The "Old Buddha" told a foreign journalist that he wanted to step down but his comrades wouldn't let him. Hu Yaobang was naive enough to take him at his word, and I heard that in *Shenzhen Qingnian* magazine there was an editorial entitled "persuading Comrade Deng to retire". Since this magazine has a close connection with Hu Yaobang, it was only a matter of time before he got the push.'

My roommates talked on a bit, but I didn't join in. I just sat on my bed, smoking and thinking. My options were running out. I couldn't afford to rely on foreigners. I couldn't rely on a favourable change in the government – so I had to rely on myself.

On Saturday, 17 January, in the afternoon of the last day of the semester, I went down to the Department on the pretext of checking my mail. As soon as I arrived my old friend, the despatch-riding clerk, rushed over to tell me, with an air of grievance, that Secretary Kong had been looking all over for me. I wondered what she wanted this time – after all she had been at some pains to tell me that the matter was out of her hands. I went to her office to find out.

'Where the devil have you gone to these days?' she demanded. 'I sent the clerk over to your room several times, and he couldn't find so much as your shadow. Have you moved out? Why didn't you tell anyone?'

'Oh, I'm sorry. I didn't realise I had to notify you—'

'No, no. I'm not saying that you have to, but after all, it is common sense that every staff member should leave his address in the Department, in case of emergency.'

I told her my room and dormitory number and, as she was writing this down, she told me that she had been trying to contact me to tell me that my accommodation problem had been solved. She took out a list with several addresses on it, and asked me to choose. I looked quickly through it, and selected a place I knew, where the houses had been built from Ming city wall bricks during the Great Leap Forward. I knew that an old schoolmate lived there. I asked for the key, but she told me I could not have the key just yet, because the flat had to be repaired and painted, and anyway, it had been allocated not just to me, but also to my wife, on the understanding that I had written to her and she would be returning very soon. She grew very annoyed at this point and began to raise her voice even higher, in an accusing tone.

'I have personally checked with all the relevant heads, and they assure me that no one has any knowledge whatsoever of your precious Bi Lijun getting twelve months' leave!'

I didn't argue the point with Kong, since I had no proof of my claim anyway.

'There's another thing', she said, calming down considerably. 'As you know, there is a regulation that anyone who studies overseas for two years or more gets an automatic promotion of one grade. Your regulation promotion has been granted in principle.'

'That's wonderful, but I have to be honest with you. I'm not sure I qualify, because I didn't study full-time for two years—'

'Yes, yes, I know all that! Nevertheless, we have decided that you are entitled. The only problem is your second foreign language. You need to pass a test. As it happens there is going to be a French test towards the end of February.'

'Er, is there a Russian test too, Secretary Kong?'

'No, only French. That should suit you down to the ground.'

'Well, but – you see, I don't speak French, only Russian.'

'What? But I just checked with Xiao Bai, and he tells me you used to attend his classes—'

'Xiao Bai? "The genius"? Yes, I did go to some of his

classes, to observe his teaching method, but I couldn't understand a word he said.'

'Nonsense. Look, it's not difficult for an English-speaking person to understand French—'

'I wouldn't say that. Mr Hay had learnt quite a lot of French, but he hid whenever he saw Xiao Bai coming.'

'—all you have to do is to memorise twelve articles. They will choose one of the twelve for translation from French to Chinese. You can use dictionaries, and you can take the whole afternoon to do it, if you want to. What could be simpler than that? French is just a dialect. You speak Mandarin and Shanghainese and you understand Nanjing dialect, don't you? English and French – it's just the same thing. My only concern is that you should not miss out on this opportunity.'

'I see. In that case, thank you very much. Yes, I suppose I still have a bit of time up my sleeve. I'll get on to it straight away, but I'm afraid there is something else I must tell you.'

Kong looked grim, but I knew she would be very pleased with what I had to say next.

'I will, of course, do my very best to prepare for the exam, but I may not have enough time. You see my mother is sick, and I was thinking of going back to Shanghai during the vacation '

'Your mother? Of course, I understand. Care and respect for our elders is the great foundation-stone of Chinese civilisation. We can always arrange another test for you at a later date. By the way, what about this court hearing business?'

'I really don't know. I'm afraid I can't just leave if my mother is sick. I'll go and see her, and make up my mind about the situation then, but I think it's pretty unlikely I would be able to go if she needs me here.'

'Mmm. Well, in that case, I think you'd better go and talk to Lao Zhu in the Foreign Relations office.'

'Yes, that's exactly what I had in mind. I'll go over there in a moment. There's just a few things I want to do here first.'

When I saw Lao Zhu a little later he did not seem at all surprised at my news about my mother. He did, however, go on at some length about the importance of our relationship with the Melbourne College of Advanced Education, and his concern for Trevor. After quite a long-winded and confusing speech, he wound up by saying that I had a moral responsibility to look after my mother, but I had my duties to the university too – and then the business of staying here or going to Shanghai was a bit complicated now because we had made all this documentation available to the authorities, and we couldn't very well pre-empt their decision.

I left his office none the wiser.

As it happened, that day was Bi Lijun's twenty-third birthday, and her parents had invited me over. I had seen them for the first time a few days after I returned, but only for a very short time, to pay my respects. I had given them a very expensive ginseng root from the north-east and a bag of 'silver ears', a kind of fungus which cools the blood. Our first meeting had not been anywhere near as difficult as I thought, and I was quite relaxed about seeing them again, especially now that I could report some progress in the area of accommodation – just imagine what foreigners would make of an 'early Ming brick residence', I thought – and even the prospect of promotion, if I could master French in thirty days! After eating in the campus dining-hall for some time I was really looking forward to some home-cooking, and I was not disappointed, although Bi Lijun's mother kept apologising for using vermicelli noodles instead of sliced jellyfish. Her father kept plying me with a good Chinese brandy, and after a few drinks he told me that he did not drink nowadays because of his health, but since it was his daughter's birthday, and since she had given him this brandy as a present, we should use it to toast her. I was really enjoying the spring rolls, but he insisted that they were not as good as Bi Lijun's. For my own part, I thought his wife was a better cook than mine, and I sympathised with her when she grumbled that he was never satisfied with anything unless it was cooked by his precious little pearl.

As we talked, he showed me a letter he had received from Bi Lijun. She was still in Melbourne, trying very hard to enrol in a finance and banking course. My father-in-law told me that overseas opportunities were very precious and, although he missed her terribly, he was hoping that I would encourage her to follow up the matters she had mentioned in her letter.

I was very excited about this, because, although I had written as instructed, telling her that she should return as soon as possible, I had deliberately adopted a very officious and unnatural tone, gambling that she would take the hint:

I have been requested by the departmental leaders to inform you that you should return to China after the expiry of six months' family reunion leave. This is a new regulation which applies to all staff members. As you know very well, the leaders did not give you permission to explore the possibility of studying overseas and they have already allocated your teaching duties for the new semester, for which you are desperately needed.'

I was relieved that she had apparently understood my message, and that her father also wanted her to stay in Australia.

After that, I kept turning things over in my mind. Bi Lijun's time in Australia was not only a precious opportunity for her professional future, but a matter of our personal safety. She seemed to get the hint from my last letter, so I felt encouraged to try something a little more cryptic – and

209

vital – next time. If I could just prepare her to expect some kind of code, I might be able to send her quite complex messages. This might mean that I had to get at least the first one hand-delivered. I stayed overnight with my parents-in-law, since it was too late to catch the ferry back to my side of the river. Before I went to bed I went through Bi Lijun's jewellery box, looking for a gift I had given her on her twentieth birthday. It was a seal stone, which I had carved myself, after the style of Han dynasty tomb tiles. It was a rabbit, the sign of her birth-year. I had written a poem in her honour, stamped it with the seal, and wrapped the paper around the stone, which I presented to her during one of our secret trysts down by the ferry dock. After that, whenever she wrote to me, she used only the seal instead of her signature. I think this had more to do with romance than discretion, but it had given me a useful idea.

I found the stone without difficulty, and also a bundle of letters, tied with red silk, all from me. There were also some term-deposit certificates from the People's Bank of China, indicating that several hundred yuan were soon due for interest. I opened the other drawers of the box, and found her identity card, a letter from the University approving our marriage – and Bi Lijun's letter of application to the Foreign Language Department:

Dear Dean,

I, Bi Lijun, hereby apply for permission to study in Australia. As you know, I am going to Australia soon, in order to marry Fang Xiangshu. While in Australia, I would like to improve my qualifications, in order to make a greater contribution to our Department. I therefore request one year's leave (twelve months commencing from the date of my departure) in order to make the best use of my

*visit and take up an appropriate course of study. I
understand that I would be entirely responsible for
my own travel, living and tuition expenses, and
my aunt in the United States, Zhou Huifen, will
act as my official sponsor. I would also like to
take this opportunity to express my sincere gratitude for the prompt and thoughtful manner in
which our request to marry has been handled.*

With respect,
Bi Lijun

1985, December 22

On the bottom left-hand side, written in fountain pen,
were the words 'Comrade Bi Lijun's application is approved', and the signature of the Dean, Hao Zhenyi, with
the official seal of the department underneath. There was
also a date: '11/1/86'.

Of course, I had never believed Secretary Kong when she
told me that the Department had not given Bi Lijun
permission for twelve months' leave, but seeing the proof
of their deceit in front of me in black and white made me
very angry. So I found some paper, and wrote a very simple
note:

My dearest Jun,

*I'm writing from your place. Your father wants
me to remind you that a lost hour never comes
again, and not to worry about your mother or
him. Remember, when you see the rabbit, you see
me. No rabbit, no me.*

I stamped the letter with the rabbit stone instead of my
usual signature, and put the note in an envelope, with her

name and Australian telephone number on it. I would be seeing Hai Ru on Monday, to give him his letter of introduction to Trevor, so I could ask him in return to take this to Bi Lijun. I could put a cheap necklace in the envelope and tell him that it was a birthday gift, which should be delivered personally.

On Monday morning, at about eleven o'clock, I went back yet again to the Foreign Relations office. Since university vacation had already begun, there was only one clerk and no receptionist. He was reading a newspaper when I came in. I introduced myself, and he told me that Director Zhu had left the following message: 'Your freedom of movement is guaranteed in China, and you are, of course, perfectly at liberty to go to Shanghai to see your mother. Decision on other matters to be made in due course.'

I was uneasy about this peremptory response, so I went down to the Foreign Languages Department, to hang around in the hope of bumping into Secretary Kong, who might throw a little more light on the situation. There was a group of people huddled together in the office. I couldn't see what they were doing, but they seemed quite animated. I went through into the reference room.

There was only one librarian on duty, as it happened a good friend of Bi Lijun. I asked her if she had seen Kong. She said she had, that she had been in a moment ago, to see if anyone had borrowed any French language textbooks, and if so, who. I decided I should borrow some while I was there. While she was getting the books for me I asked her what was going on, and why there was a little gathering in the office.

'You mean to say you haven't heard the news? It's Hai Ru. He's had a very nasty traffic accident.'

'What?'

'Yes, his wife rang just a little while ago. She and Hai

212

Ru went out to do some New Year shopping, on their bikes – you know he was going overseas, and they were going to have a special party, I suppose they weren't concentrating on what they were doing – well, anyway, suddenly this truck, a sort of army truck I think they said, came hurtling round the corner and sideswiped him.'

'How badly is he hurt?'

'Don't know. He's in hospital. The truck driver didn't even stop!'

I ran all the way back to the dormitory, destroyed the letter, and packed my things for Shanghai. Perhaps Hai Ru's accident *was* only coincidental, but it unnerved me terribly.

7   The King of Hell

Nanjing Station was choked with people, travelling for the Spring Festival holidays. Chinese New Year was only ten days away. Peasants were trotting along under their bamboo poles, toting great baskets of dripping fish, trussed ducks, and winter bamboo shoots. There were students everywhere, wearing their college badges, standing round in small excited groups. By contrast with the peasants their luggage seemed pathetic – just a small nylon or string net bag. I had a large foreign-made suitcase, with big wheels, which attracted quite a few admirers whenever I stopped. The booking office was jammed full, and lots of people were sleeping on bamboo mats, with luggage piled up around them. I tried edging my way towards the ticket-office window, but somebody told me it was no use, the tickets had all been sold. I looked up at the timetable, and everywhere there were red disks indicating that the trains were full, except for one or two freight trains which would leave about midnight, stopping all stations to Shanghai.

I didn't care what kind of train it was, or how long it took, as long as it got me out of Nanjing. I kept burrowing my way towards the office, and finally bought a ticket on Freight No. 1207. About 11.30 pm the passengers for 1207, who had been waiting out in the freezing cold square in front of the station, were led through a side gate onto the platform. When I finally boarded the train, I found it wasn't too bad. There was room enough on the floor to stretch out on a rice-straw mat. I put my suitcase against the wall and lay down, using my small bag as a pillow. From where I

214

lay I could see a bucket behind some mats hung in the corner of the car. I went to relieve myself, feeling better to be leaving Nanjing – although it certainly wouldn't take much for someone to find me in Shanghai. As I stood over the bucket, I wondered if this carriage was an illusion. Perhaps, like the Monkey King, I would find that, despite a mighty leap, I was still in the palm of the Buddha's hand – and worse, that I had been pissing on his fingers, thinking they were the pillars at the end of the world.

The train was slower than I had imagined. Each time it seemed to be reaching a decent speed, it stopped. I dozed, but never slept. The carriage was filled with peasants on their way to Shanghai to sell their goods. After a while, it was no longer possible to lie down, but in any case it was far too cold to sleep. At one stop there was someone on the platform selling steamed buns, and I got out to buy a few. There was a radio playing somewhere, and one news item in particular caught my attention. It seemed that two 'hoodlums' were arrested at Shanghai International Airport, while trying to use forged passports. The police noticed these two suspicious characters trying to board a flight to Vancouver. When apprehended, one of them shouted, 'If you delay my flight, it will cause an international uproar.' Our police told them very courteously that they would take all responsibility for any inconvenience. During detention the 'hoodlums' confessed that they had bought their passports for some thousands of yuan. The two police were awarded a 500 yuan bonus, and promoted one grade. Back on the train, I kept thinking about this forged passport business. I still had a genuine valid passport, of course, but it required extra pages – whether genuine or false – to be of any use to anyone.

I took the passport out of my bag, and examined it. It seemed to me that forging or falsifying any part of it would be extremely difficult. Suddenly I realised that the page entitled 'Observations' was at the beginning of the pass-port – not at the end. And the page at the end, which I had always assumed was for observations was, in fact, for visas. And this page was blank! I had never noticed this before, in all the times I had looked at my passport, possibly because at a glance the Chinese characters for 'Observations' and 'Visas' looked similar. My heart was pounding, and I tried to calm myself. An empty visa page, in a valid passport, is at most only half the battle. I needed a visa on this page. To obtain a visa from any foreign embassy I needed a legitimate reason for travel – and I had such a reason. The subpoena!

But where was it now? I had given it to Lao Zhu. Yes, and that day he said he had given it to the receptionist, and she – the printing house! They had only given me five copies of the documents, and I had handed them all back to the receptionist. The originals must still be in the printers! I felt like jumping out of the train and running back to Nanjing. Why hadn't I managed to keep a copy for myself somehow? Perhaps I could find some excuse to talk to someone in the printers about giving the originals back to me. Anyway, it was a holiday, and they knew I was going to Shang-hai – perhaps I could break in and get the documents. No, of course not. Too risky, and anyway I didn't know where they were. The best thing would be to try to convince them that I was doing a job for the Foreign Relations office – interpreting or translating or something. I hadn't paid much attention that day because I wanted to see Secretary Kong, but I was sure they regarded me as someone who was working for Lao Zhu. As I thought about this, I recalled the way the girl came out of the printers, handed me the copies, uncollated, and gave me back an envelope which I assumed contained my report. Come to think of it, it had seemed a bit thicker than the original.

My hands were shaking as I searched through the bag I

had been using for a pillow on the train. Yes, there was the envelope. I was really fumbling, I couldn't get the sheets out, and, when I did, it was so dark that I could hardly see. But I knew this was not just the report on my involvement in the court case. There were three other sheets. The letter from Trevor to Gui Hong. The letter from Trevor to me. And the subpoena!

I walked past the American Consulate in Shanghai. There was a queue of about twenty people waiting to go in. They varied in age from teenagers to old retired people. Some were sitting on little bamboo stools, others were chatting about how to handle interviews with American immigration officials. I made several trips around the triangular park between the French, American and Australian consulates at the junction of Huaihai, Urumchi and Fuxing Roads, trying to make up my mind. I was careful not to get too close to the entrance to the Australian Consulate, in case the guard noticed me. When I stopped, I did so at the American Consulate, so that I could mingle in the group of people waiting in line. I struck up a conversation with some of them.

'Excuse me, but how long does it take to get an interview, and how long does the actual interview take?'

'Well, that all depends – if it's a J-1 application, it doesn't take very long at all, but if it's F-1, that's a different matter altogether.'

'What's the difference?'

'You've got a lot to learn my friend, haven't you? J-1 is for government-sponsored students and therefore the holder cannot change his status in the US, while F-1 is private-sponsored and the holder can convert to an H-1 visa on completion of his study.'

'So H-1 is the one you need to stay in America?'

'No, not exactly. That's a Green Card. But it's sort of

217

close. Anyway, it's not easy to get an F-1. It's up to the American interviewing officer to decide if you have the intention to immigrate – and they have "absolute discretion". They don't even have to give you their reasons. You can argue that your wife and child are staying behind in China, or that you have a plum job to come back to – say what you like, it all depends on whether the interviewing officer takes a fancy to you or not. There's one we call the 'King of Hell', because he won't admit anyone to Paradise. He seems to enjoy shutting the gate on you. He doesn't even read your application. Thank God he's on holiday back in the US at present, that's probably why there's so many people here this week.'

I walked into the park, and sat on a bench for a while, admiring the elegant 1930s European-style houses bordering the park. The phrase 'absolute discretion', which my informant had pronounced very deliberately in English, kept ringing in my ears. I must have absolute determination, I thought. But I didn't think anyone would suspect me of intending to immigrate. After all, I had just returned from overseas. Why would I have done that if I was intending to stay? It was already the 22nd of January, and I was supposed to appear in court on the 23rd of February, so there was no time to waste. Arranging for an overseas trip on a month's notice was cutting it extremely fine, in Chinese terms. I collected my wits and set out for the Australian Consulate. After all, if anything went wrong I could always argue that I was only trying to find out some precise information about the necessary procedures. I could say that I just wanted some detail so that I could make my excuses to Trevor if I was unable to get to Australia in time for the case.

I looked confidently into the eyes of the guard on the gate. He was very young, perhaps eighteen or nineteen, tall, slim and suntanned.

'Comrade soldier, I have an urgent matter to discuss with the Consulate staff.'

'Ah, no, no, no', he bumbled, in a strong rural Shandong accent, apparently very unsure of himself. 'You – it's only – I mean, inside – that's only for foreigners' business.'

I showed him the letters from Australia. Clearly they had something to do with foreigners.

'I'm sorry, but I just don't understand that stuff – there's no point in me looking at it. But anyway, I can't let you in.'

I took out my passport and I.D. card.

'Look, Comrade, I'm a lecturer in English at a university. I've just come back from abroad, and there's a very urgent matter I must deal with. I have to go back. Look here, in the corner, you can see my President's orders, in Chinese.'

He didn't seem to take much notice of the note in the corner, but he did seem interested in my passport. He could see from the stamp that I had just returned from overseas.

'Look,' he said, 'I'm not trying to be difficult, but I have to be careful. Only a few days ago, somebody came here asking for political asylum.'

'What? How disgusting! It's a disgrace. The man was obviously insane.'

'That's right! In fact they took him away and locked him up in one of those places, you know – a sort of hospital for loonies. That's how mad he was.'

I was taken aback by this, in spite of my own remarks.

'You see, Comrade, I'm not actually making an application for a visit to Australia. It's just that my boss wants me to find out the procedures for it, that's all – I need to know how long it takes, and so on. Perhaps you could just make a few enquiries for me, but if it's too difficult, forget it. I'll just go on my way. It doesn't matter a damn to me. I've had enough of bloody foreigners to last me a lifetime.'

'OK, OK, just wait here a minute.'

He stepped into the guard hut, and picked up a telephone. A few seconds later, he stuck his head out through the doorway. 'What was that you said a moment ago? There was something about a court order, or something—'

'Yes, court order. An Australian regional court, in the Australian city of Melbourne.'

A moment later he emerged again and said, very cordially, 'All right, it's all clear. You can go in now.'

He pointed to a black cast-iron double gate. It was bolted in the middle, but there was a smaller door to the side, and I was able to push it open. I stepped through, and despite my anxiety to get inside, I made a great show of closing the door carefully behind me. I prayed that the Australian Consulate would not have a 'King of Hell' on duty today.

It was strangely clean inside the gates, and the garden was well cared for. I walked along a neat little path, and entered through the front door of the Consulate. It was quiet, and still, and warm, and I actually thought I could smell Australia. There were some half-familiar pictures and photographs on the walls, and I walked slowly along a corridor, wondering which office I should enter. Someone called out abruptly, in Shanghainese, just as I approached a staircase, 'Hey you! What are you doing here? Where do you think you're going?'

It gave me quite a start, and I turned to see, not the face of the 'King of Hell', but the face of some cruel old stepmother, straight out of a Chinese legend. I felt as if I had been caught pilfering leftovers from the kitchen.

'Sorry. I didn't see you there. I wasn't trying to sneak past—'

'All right, all right. What seems to be the problem?' She spoke from behind a window, like a bank-teller. I approached her and slid my documents under the glass, and gave a very brief explanation of my circumstances.

She swung half-away from me on a swivel chair, and

looked partly at something she was doing on her typewriter, and partly at the documents. She scanned the papers very quickly and said, 'The court case referred to here is on the 23rd of February, and it's now already the 22nd of January. You must have received this letter early this month. Why have you left it so late to do anything? I thought you said the matter was urgent?'

I stammered through an explanation about not being able to do anything until the vacation period, which only started a few days before.

'But if it was so urgent and important why couldn't you have been given some leave to come and sort things out?'

'Please. Don't misunderstand me. I'm not really anxious to go. I've just come back from Australia. I don't really want to go again so soon, but I need to be able to give this Mr Hay some good reason. My bosses would also prefer that we handle things diplomatically, and not upset Mr Hay or his institution. So, if you, as an official representative of the Australian Consulate, think there's just not enough time, then I'm happy with that. That's the end of the matter as far as I'm concerned.'

'Now just hang on a second, Comrade. I'm not saying that. I'm only saying that this consulate does not handle unusual or special cases. That sort of thing is up to the Embassy in Beijing. We don't have discretion in such situations.'

'Oh, I see. Well, thank you very much, you've been very helpful.'

I took back my papers, and left the Consulate.

Go to Beijing! That would really be burning my bridges. How could I explain it, if I were caught? And now I knew that not only foreign devils but even more dangerous Chinese comrades haunted this diplomatic underworld of consulates and embassies. But if I did not take this risk I might regret it all my life – and I would not necessarily be any better off even if I did not take it. My sister-in-law had told me that, even with a valid passport, a Chinese citizen might soon require an exit visa from the Public Security Bureau before he or she could leave the country. The longer I hesitated, the more difficult things were likely to become.

I thought and thought for the whole of that night and next day. There would never be a better time. It was approaching Chinese New Year. Even if suspicions were aroused in the Australian Embassy, there was a good chance that key officials in Nanjing would be uncontactable, because of the holidays, and I might be able to slip through in the confusion.

On 24 January I took the No. 14 special express train to Beijing. As was the usual custom, a number of seats had been left unallocated, for sale after midnight on the day of departure. I had joined the queue before midnight, and bought my ticket about 2 am, but when I finally boarded the train at 4.30 that afternoon I could not even find a seat. Fortunately, the train was not too crowded – it was supposed to be a model of civilised transport – and I was able to sit down on my bag in the aisle of the compartment.

About midnight I was disturbed from a very light sleep by some rustling noises in the seat next to me. I tried to force my eyes shut again, because I knew I would need my rest, but curiosity got the better of me, and I gradually focused on a most intriguing sight. A man was standing awkwardly in the dim light, apparently wrestling with something inside the upper part of his padded cotton pants. On closer inspection, I noticed that he had unfastened his belt and was hanging on grimly to his voluminous baggy pants with one hand, while with the other he was lowering a very bulky something into position near his groin. He noticed that I was watching, and grinned sheepishly at me.

'God, this is a nuisance. I'm trying to get my hot water bottle in place. Heh, heh – my old winter legs have come back as usual. Arthritis, you know. I took some hot water from the boiler some time ago, but it's still a bit hot, so I just can't get comfortable.'

'Well, you'd better be careful', I said. 'You'll scald yourself.'

'No, it's not too bad, I'll be OK.'

After a while he settled down again, not to sleep, but to munch on a bag of special Shanghai five-spiced beans. By now I didn't have much hope of sleep either. He leaned over and offered me some beans.

'Do you know how much these bloody things cost? 4 yuan. You wouldn't believe it, would you? You need to carry a wad thick enough to wipe your arse if you want to buy anything at all these days.'

'Shush – be careful – look, I'm happy to join you in some five-spiced beans, and have a chat, but if you're going to talk like that I'll have to leave.'

'Right. Right, of course. Thanks for pulling me up. Quite right. Very good of you.'

He sighed deeply, and said no more.

About 9 am on Sunday, 25 January, I arrived in Beijing. I looked up a big transport map in the square outside the station to find the Embassy. I knew it was somewhere in Dongzhimenwai Avenue and, according to the map, a No. 24 bus would get me pretty close. I found a stop which seemed to include route 24, and asked some fellow-travellers if they thought this was the right number for Dongzhimen-wai Ave. A controversy broke out among several bystanders on this issue, and I was totally confused.

Suddenly a bus appeared. I couldn't see what number it was, but the crowd surged forward, running alongside before the bus came to a standstill. I had no idea where I would end up, but the person next to me urged me on, and I found myself clutching at the half-open doors and trying with all my might to cling to the bus, 'like a baby on a breast' as we say. One leg was still dangling in the breeze as the bus lurched off again, and I passed a 20-fen note to someone inside, with a request for 'one to Dongzhimenwai'. My call was relayed through the bus and then started making its way back, with my ticket and change. Each time the bus stopped there was a frenzied struggle from inside as some poor wretch fought to get off, like a wild animal caught in a trap.

I realised that I did not have such a bad position. I could see the stops clearly, and so I had some idea how much farther to go, and of course I wouldn't have to strain every fibre of my being to get off when the time came. The only catch was that I had to hang on to my position, in spite of repeated all-out assaults from people who wanted to get off before me. I couldn't afford to let go of my hold on the rail, and I certainly couldn't surrender my position to clear the doorway and then try to get back on. Every stop was crowded with rivals who would trample me underfoot in an attempt to get not only themselves but their massive suitcases and baskets and boxes on to the bus. The conductor always tried to persuade such people that there was an empty bus coming right along behind, but she was never believed.

I got off somewhere near Dongzhimenwai Avenue, and went in search of the Embassy. I wanted to locate it first, and then find a hotel room somewhere nearby. After five minutes' walk I saw the Australian flag in a compound guarded by a Chinese soldier. I crossed the road and went back the way I had come, until I saw the sign 'Dongzhi-menwai Hotel' outside a brand new apartment building. I went in and followed some arrows down several flights of stairs into a basement. Finally I saw a middle-aged woman at a counter, having a smoke.

I asked if there was a vacancy, and she told me there was – at 6 yuan per night. So far so good. Then she asked me for a 'letter of introduction' from my work unit, to establish that I had proper authorisation for travelling. Of course I didn't have one, but I fussed around, taking out everything I possessed and mumbling 'It must be here somewhere' and so on. When I placed my passport on the counter she said, 'Oh, you've got a passport, I see.' She was clearly impressed. In China not everyone is entitled to a passport.

'Yes, I've come to see the Embassy people about some urgent business overseas. That's why I left in such a hurry. I just don't know what I've done with the letter. Maybe—'

'Don't worry about it. That's OK. If you have a passport that's good enough for me.'

She noted some details from my passport, and then called out 'Hua Niu! Come here a minute, will you?'

A young female attendant appeared, and addressed the woman at the counter as the manager.

'Hua Niu, this comrade is in Beijing on important business. See that he gets a room to himself, so that he can look at his papers and things in privacy.' She turned to me, 'You just never know who you might get tossed in with otherwise, with all these blow-ins about the place.'

I was taken to a room with three beds. Not grand, but neat and tidy. As I was sorting through my things the attendant came back with two thermos bottles. I rinsed my soup cup with a little water from the thermos, and then poured some water on to some one-minute noodles I had brought with me. While I was waiting I read a notice on the wall:

BEIJING MUNICIPALITY PUBLIC SECURITY BUREAU REGULATION
GOVERNING CONDUCT IN HOTELS

Beijing is the capital of our great socialist motherland. In the wake of the four modernisations and the open-door policy, Beijing has become the centre of political and economic activities, both domestically and internationally. Hotels have an important part to play in the maintenance of socialist standards. To this end the Bureau proclaims the following regulations –

1. In your demeanour with foreigners be neither arrogant nor obsequious. Never discuss state secrets with them. Never conduct yourself in a manner likely to bring discredit upon your country or upon yourself.
2. Identification and letters of introduction must be produced upon request of hotel management and staff. If you have secret documents, or firearms, please inform hotel management so that appropriate security measures may be taken.
3. Do not leave valuables in the hotel room when you go out. If there are items which you must leave behind, please inform staff so that such items may be secured.
4. Explosives, poisons, animals, or any substance likely to endanger public safety or hygiene are strictly prohibited in hotels. Offenders will be severely punished.
5. Prostitution, gambling, superstitious or magic rituals, negotiation for the sale of women or children, or any other activity prejudicial to socialist morality, are strictly forbidden. Offenders will be severely punished.
6. Please contact the Bureau or hotel management concerning any suspicious activities or persons.

After reading this, I decided not to move around too much, in case I aroused suspicion. I ate my noodles, and lay down for a rest. I had not slept at all on the train the night before, so I crashed until early evening. When I woke I decided I would go out somewhere and get myself a decent meal. I noticed on my way out that there was someone new on duty at the reception counter. When I came back I opened the door to find that my room had been taken over by a group of four men and a woman, chattering away in a cloud of smoke. The man who was sitting on my bed was counting bundles of money and distributing it to the others, who were busily checking what they had already received. The only one who didn't seem to be involved in money was the woman, who was puffing away on a cigarette. As I entered the room, the men began shovelling notes into their pockets.

'Excuse me. I'm sorry to disturb you, but that's my bed.'

'Oh, sorry. Yes, of course, excuse me', said the man on my bed, as he stood and tidied the sheets a bit. 'We didn't know there was anyone else in the room.'

'That's OK, thanks.'

I felt a little awkward. I poured myself some water. The woman came over to me and offered me a cigarette, which I accepted. Now that the ice was broken, we could chat.

'Where are you from? What on earth are you doing travelling alone during Spring Festival?'

I didn't feel threatened by this group. They seemed pretty relaxed and casual, and their questions were perfectly normal for Chinese under these circumstances. Nevertheless, I didn't want to talk too much.

'Oh, it's just a bit of family trouble. I don't want to talk about it. What about you? What are you guys doing here? You don't sound like locals.'

'No. We're from nearby – Baoding, you know? We're just here on business. There are some accounts we had to settle up for the New Year.'

'Oh, I see. Well, don't let me disturb you. I was just on my way down to watch television. I'll see you later.'

The TV was on, but there were no other lights in the room. A man and a woman were sitting in the gloom, obviously related and not expecting company, because they were both in their woollen knitted pants, normally worn as one of the 'inner layers' of winter clothing. They sat one on each side of a table, nibbling at something from a bowl. The man greeted me, and invited me to sit down.

'My name's Ma. What's yours?'

'Fang.'

As I sat down I took a better look at him. He looked

227

about sixty. His head was completely clean-shaven, and he was not actually sitting on his chair, but squatting on it. He looked exactly like a character out of a novel of 'old Peking', like *Rickshaw Boy*. The woman was quite young, and was knitting. She didn't seem nearly as interested in the program as her companion. It was Peking Opera, and every now and then the man would clap his hands and bawl out, 'Well done, oh, beautifully sung!'

Finally the young woman said, 'Oh Dad, please! There's someone else in the room now. You're making too much noise.'

'Sorry, sorry', said the man turning to me. 'I'm getting a bit carried away. I just love the opera, it's a thousand times better than all that newfangled rubbish they put on the television. Of course my daughter wouldn't agree with me about that!'

I sat with them for an hour and a half thinking about the business of tomorrow morning.

At 8.30 on the morning of 26 January I left the hotel. On my way out I met Ma again. But to my surprise, this time he was attired in a Western-style suit and tie, and carrying a walking-stick. He raised his stick in the air, and called out cordially, 'Morning, Mr Fang.' This time, instead of looking like something out of the past, he seemed the epitome of a modern Taiwanese business executive.

About twenty minutes later I was outside the Embassy compound. I showed the guard my passport, and told him that although I had just returned from Australia I still had some important unresolved business, and I needed to discuss it with someone inside. This guard was very different from the one in the Shanghai Consulate. He listened without interrupting and did not seem at all concerned about the matter. He had a quick look at my passport, and then told me to see the receptionist in the foyer, where seven or eight people were vying for her attention.

The receptionist was Chinese, in her twenties, and she wore a striking powder-blue dress, and makeup – one of the fringe benefits of having a job that required her to create a good impression with foreigners. She appeared to be quite busy and efficient, sorting mail, handling newspapers and answering the telephone. From time to time she held animated conversations with other staff members who came into the Embassy. It seemed there was going to be some sort of social function to celebrate Chinese New Year, or perhaps Australia Day. She told the waiting people that if they had their documents in order they should just leave them on the counter and allow a minimum of two working days before returning to collect them from the box marked 'Completed visa applications'. This satisfied a few, but the majority were reluctant to part with their precious passports in such a casual way, so they hung around waiting for a chance to check the formalities with the receptionist.

While I was waiting my turn, I saw an old green Volkswagen pull up outside and park alongside a gleaming black Mercedes. Both had Embassy plates, but to my way of thinking, a black Mercedes was commonplace in Beijing, and warranted no particular attention, but an old green Volkswagen was quite another matter. There was something else which emphasised the foreignness of the place. The walls of the foyer were bedecked with pictures commemorating the history of relations between the two nations, including a recent photograph of a grinning Bob Hawke, shaking hands energetically with Hu Yaobang. Photos of Hu Yaobang would have rapidly disappeared from Chinese walls over the last week or so, since he had been ousted from his position as Party General-Secretary.

The crowd dwindled fairly rapidly as I stood there apprehensively. I watched every movement and listened to every remark around me. Finally it was my turn. I showed her my papers, and briefly explained the situation. She asked

me to wait while she went off to seek advice from her
superiors. As soon as she left I became extremely nervous.
What would she do? Would she ring someone in Jiangsu
and check up on me? I had heard that some of the officials
responsible for checking visas were actually Chinese, and this
could be my undoing. I waited, I don't know how long,
until suddenly a hand appeared at my side, clutching a brown
envelope, with 'Security Bureau' stamped on it, in red. I
froze. From behind me a man with a Shanghai accent called
out, 'Where is everyone? Isn't there anyone on duty at the
desk?' I said nothing, and didn't turn around.

The receptionist reappeared and asked me to wait a while.

'I'm in a hurry; I have urgent business', said the voice.
He took some papers out of his envelope, grumbling 'It's
already too late. I'll never understand why it should take
so long to fix up a damn passport. Bureaucracy, I suppose!'

'Too late for what?' asked the receptionist.

'For enrolment in an English course.'

Enormously relieved, I turned to look at the man. He was
in his mid-forties, I would say. The receptionist asked him
in some surprise, '*You* are enrolling for an English course?'

'No, of course not, I'm talking about my daughter.' He
pointed to a timid, frail-looking creature of about fifteen,
hiding in a corner of the room. I thought she looked too
young and helpless to get herself back to Shanghai, let alone
to Australia.

'She has never been away from home by herself before,
so naturally I've come with her, to give her a hand with
things.'

'Oh,' I see, said the receptionist. 'Well, let's look at her
passport.'

She checked the document, and said, 'Just go straight ahead,
and turn right; then take the stairs to the first floor. You'll
see the overseas students office. In fact, you may have noticed
the officer in charge. She passed by just a moment ago.'

'I didn't see any officer.'

'A black woman, just a minute ago.'

'Oh, yes. That was her? She is in charge?'

'Yes,' said the receptionist, beginning to get a little impatient, 'she can tell you what you have to do.'

'All right, all right', he said, and beckoned urgently to his daughter. 'Come on, let's go.'

Half an hour later, when everyone else had been attended to and I was left alone at the counter, the receptionist rang someone to see what was happening with my papers. Then she went inside, and reappeared almost immediately with some application forms for a visitor's visa. She asked me to fill them in and come back in a couple of days. I was taken aback because I had not actually asked for application forms. I had chosen my words very carefully, so that I could always deny that I had gone there specifically for the purpose of getting a visa. I wanted to be able to say that I was just enquiring into what kind of procedures might be involved. She invited me to take a seat in an armchair and fill in the forms.

'You'll find a pen on the table over there. When you've finished, please return the forms directly to me. Don't just leave them on the counter, because this matter is rather special and I don't want to get your papers mixed up with the others. Come back and collect it from that box in a couple of days.'

'You mean Wednesday?' I asked, scarcely able to believe that things could be so simple.

'Yes, Wednesday, the 28th of January.'

I went over to the armchair she had pointed out, and filled in an application for two weeks in Australia.

I left the Embassy in a state of almost uncontrollable excitement. But I had to think my next move through very carefully, or the whole thing could come unstuck. I went

231

back to the hotel. I had to make a phone call to Melbourne, and I did not want to have to fill in the usual forms at the post office. The manager was on the desk again. I offered her a prized Red Peony filter. She was all smiles.

'Now, what can I do for you, Comrade Fang?'

'Well, look, do you think I could make an overseas telephone call from here? I just can't stand the thought of going down to the post office and hanging around for hours while they arrange things. You know what they're like.'

'No problem. Just give me the name of the person and the telephone number.'

'The person doesn't matter. Anyone who answers will do.'

I gave her Bi Lijun's number and she tried it, but no one answered. Maybe Jean and Ted had taken Bi Lijun out somewhere for the Australia Day holiday. I gave her Trevor's number. But I had to handle this very carefully.

The manager got through without much difficulty. I took up the phone.

'Hello. Is that you, Trevor? This is Xiao Fang.'

'Oh, Xiao Fang. How are you? Everything all right?'

'Mmm, not too bad, I guess. What are you doing? Is there anyone else there?'

'I'm watching the cricket. There's only Jenny and me. Niu Ling has moved. He's gone to Hawthorn.'

'Good. Trevor, please listen carefully. I can't talk for long. I've just tried ringing Bi Lijun, but there's no one home. Can you ring her for me later, and give her a message?'

'Sure.'

'OK. Just tell her this – arrange an air ticket for around the 10th of February. Return ticket—'

'So it's OK then? But I'll make the arrangements for your ticket—'

'No, Trevor, just listen. I don't know whether I can come or not. I'm in Beijing at the moment, but don't tell anyone. You know what I mean. In case people get jealous.'

232

There was silence at the other end. I went on, 'I haven't finished my message. Tell her – return ticket, leaving Shanghai for Melbourne in about a fortnight, via Hong Kong, and the same route return for both of us, but leave the date open—'

'But Xiao Fang, she's made some arrangements for study with Chisholm Institute—'

'No. Just tell her to forget it, and make these arrangements as soon as possible. I have to go now. Goodbye, Trevor.'

I hung up. The manager was beaming at me, in admiration of my skill with this foreign mumbo-jumbo.

'God, that was marvellous! I couldn't understand a single word – oh, except "goodbye", I've heard that on television – and you just – just talked – like a machine gun. Fantastic.'

I offered her another Red Peony. That was the least I could do for her, I thought. She would soon enough hate me, when she was interrogated about this escapee, but at least she could say she didn't understand a word of what I said on the phone. Chinese bureaucracy is usually very slow and inefficient, but somehow it is always galvanised into dynamic action by this sort of thing. They would be round here like a shot.

Next morning I felt very agitated and restless. I had a day to kill before I could go back to the Embassy, so I decided to go to the Summer Palace. I took a bus to the zoo, and then another out to the Haidian District. My mind was in a turmoil – a strange mixture of minute detail and grand vision, of hard practicalities and poetic insights. At the Summer Palace I walked along the Long Corridor by Kunming Lake, and up to the Hall of Parting Clouds on Longevity Hill. It was Tuesday morning, and there were not many people about although it was a pleasant enough day, not particularly cold for winter. Dry, dead lotus reeds poked out of a few melting shards of ice on the banks, and in the distance one or two tiny boats floated like curled leaves on the still, grey water. Litter slapped back and forth in the shallows and there was an oppressive feel of ruin about the place, in spite of the fresh restoration work on the corridor and the Marble Boat. I stopped and looked out across the lake to the Seventeen Arch Bridge in the distance. Ruin and restoration. Not only palaces, but people are caught up in this cycle. But people come and go, like so much litter, while palaces at least stay put for a while to watch it all.

I thought of Wang Guowei. One of the most illustrious scholars in Chinese history, brilliant even among contemporaries like Cai Yuanpei, Chen Duxiu and Hu Shi. The generation of scholars which crystallised the best of Eastern and Western philosophy and linked it in their writings, like a jade belt. I had become familiar with Wang Guowei's name during my archaeology phase, back in Yixing. He was not only the most respected authority on ancient Chinese shell and bone inscriptions but he also introduced Kant, Schopenhauer and Nietzsche to Chinese scholarship. In 1927, despairing and disillusioned, he drowned himself in this very lake. He was a man who had pursued truth with a relentless obsession. He had once said that the search for truth was like an endless quest for love, and quoted some lines from Song poems:

> Rue not a slack belt and hanging robes,
> She is well worth your wan and sallow looks.

and

> A thousand times I seek in vain
> To find her in the crowd,
> I turn away, and she appears
> Suddenly out of the dim lantern light.

But why had he killed himself? For my part, I felt certain that, having resisted the temptation to suicide back in Shanghai when I was a teenager, I would never contemplate it again. Even an occasional glimpse of the apparition made life worthwhile.

On the morning of 28 January I returned to the Embassy for my passport. There were people at the counter, and the girl seemed busy, everything normal – but for me everything in the world depended on whether there was a small book with my name on it sitting in that box at the end of the counter. I looked in the box for a passport with two pieces of paper inserted between the covers – Trevor's letter, and the subpoena. I could not see it, and I struggled to compose myself. Something must have gone wrong, but I had to remain as calm as possible. There were twenty or thirty passports, most of them brand new, and just a few old ones like mine. I had resigned myself to defeat as I flipped through the old ones, and suddenly I found that I was looking at a photograph of a person with short-cropped spiky hair. I turned to the last page. There was the visa stamp.

Now I had to struggle to contain my elation. My first impulse was to get out of the Embassy as quickly as possible. But then I remembered the letter and the subpoena. Where were they? I didn't really want to go back to the receptionist, but I could not afford to leave these documents behind. I probably didn't need them myself, but what if someone in the Embassy found them and decided to contact my university to return them? I approached the counter, and the receptionist asked me if everything was all right. I told her that I might need the documents and asked her if she could photocopy them for their file, and give me back the originals. She left the counter and returned very shortly with another young Chinese woman, who was reading the documents. I asked her also if she would like to photocopy them. She simply said that was unnecessary, and handed me my two sheets of paper. Trying to look ever so casual and unconcerned, I thanked the girls and ambled out of the building. I made a nonchalant comment or two to the guard on the gate and strolled out into the street. My pace quickened as I got a little way down the road, and soon I found myself running.

Back in my room, I took out my passport and drank in every detail. It had been issued on 27 January, good for a single journey before 27 February, and permitting a maximum stay of one month. I wanted to shout for joy, but I stifled myself and began frantically throwing things into my bag. I dashed out into the corridor, and then suddenly remembered that I should try to be calm again. I sidled up to the reception counter and paid my bill, trying my best to look thoroughly bored with life. Once outside the hotel, I broke into a trot on my way to the bus stop. A bus came along almost immediately, and twenty minutes later I was at Beijing Central Station.

Everything seemed to be in my favour. I didn't even have to wait in a long queue. When I reached the window I asked for a ticket on the earliest and fastest train to Shanghai, preferably for a sleeping compartment. The ticket-seller looked at me in some surprise. 'Why on earth do you want a sleeping compartment? There's hardly a soul about at this time of year. You can have the whole damn train if you want! Just take your pick of sleeping places. Who cares?'

I bought a ticket for No. 13 Express to Shanghai, leaving in about two hours. Then I went to wait in the vast station hall. Loudspeakers were playing revolutionary songs from the 1950s and 60s. I thought they sounded just beautiful. I munched contentedly on some steamed buns, and read a crime story magazine called *The People's Police*.

The train came, and, just as the man had said, it was almost empty. I had quite a splendid New Year's Eve feast.

While I was proposing a toast to myself with Qingdao beer, I suddenly thought of Lao Zhu. No doubt, like every other Chinese, he was settling down to his New Year banquet, but he had a surprise in store for him when he lifted the lid on his cooking-pot. This bird had flown. I cackled away to myself, delighted at my own little joke. After dinner I dropped off to sleep, but I woke after midnight. It was freezing, and I took to jogging from one end of the train to the other in an effort to keep warm.

I was home by eight o'clock in the morning, the first day of the Year of the Rabbit. Shortly after that my uncles and aunts and young cousins began arriving at the house, and about eleven o'clock another feast had started. A crowd of squealing kids gathered around me in the lane as I lit fireworks with my cigarettes.

On 31 January I rang Bi Lijun again. I took my sister-in-law with me to the post office. I wanted her to make the call, have a short chat, and then just hand over to me, so that I could talk without registering details of my name and so on. It took about an hour to get through. Finally I had my chance to talk to Bi Lijun. I felt certain she must have discussed things with Trevor, and that she would have some idea of what was going on.

'Hello, Bi Lijun. It's Xiao Fang.'

'Hello, Xiao Fang.'

'Is everything arranged?'

'Xiao Fang, what kind of medicine are you peddling this time? Trevor told me—'

'Yes, I'm back in Shanghai', I said, persisting with English, in spite of her Chinese reply. 'Everything is all right. The business in Beijing was fine—'

'What sort of game are you playing? Stop being so mysterious! You mean to say you have a visa? But I had a letter from my parents to say the leaders didn't approve—'

'Shut up, will you? The telephone is expensive enough

237

without wasting time prattling on like that. Just listen to what I'm telling you, and don't interrupt.'

'All right, all right, there's no need to be like that!'

'Look, all I want to know is whether you have arranged things or not. If you have, I'll get you know what in a few days—'

'Yes, I have arranged it. I booked you a return ticket on Cathay Pacific. It leaves at 7.15 in the evening on the 12th of February—'

'I don't need to know all that stuff, it will all be on the ticket.'

'What's the matter with you, Xiao Fang? Why are you carrying on like this?'

I knew I couldn't go on telling her not to¹ say things without arousing the suspicions of those who might be listening in, so I told Bi Lijun very sternly that she could chatter as much as she liked, but she should just remember that it was costing us good money.

'So what?' she said. 'I don't suppose it will send us broke. Now please listen, and write down the flight details. Do you have a pen?'

'OK, go ahead.'

'Flight CX 101 from Shanghai, 12th of February, 7.15 pm, leaving Hong Kong for Melbourne at five past ten the same night.'

'OK. I've got all that.'

'Right. Now there's another thing I wanted to ask you. You told Trevor that I should just forget about enrolling at Chisholm. Unless I enrol my visa will expire before your court appearance, and I won't be able to come back with you.'

'All right then, enrol.'

'But I still need a letter of permission from Nanjing. You'll have to go back to Nanjing, and get it before the 12th—'

'Oh for – you – you are too stupid for words! You know they want you back in Nanjing for teaching. Of course they won't let you enrol—'

'Is there any need to talk to me like that?' she said, sounding a little tearful. 'If I can't enrol and I can't stay here, what am I supposed to do? You just tell me, and I'll do it.'

'Get yourself a ticket to Hong Kong and wait for me there. You can stay with your aunt for a while, and when I come we'll go to see your uncles.'

'But Xiao Fang, you know perfectly well there is only Fourth Aunt in Hong Kong, all my uncles are in Taiw—'

'For God's sake shut up, will you, you stupid woman!' Goodbye!'

I hung up. I turned to my sister-in-law very nervously. Her English was just sufficient to get the drift – and the tone – of what I had said. 'Surely Bi Lijun must have read something about the situation here with all this anti-bourgeois liberalism business and the purges?'

'Perhaps she'll figure it out afterwards. You've never talked to her like that before, and she must realise after a while, when she gets over it, that there's some purpose behind your manner.'

The immediate problem for me was that the conversation may have been noted and I might well walk into a trap at Shanghai airport. Fortunately it was still the holiday season, and security officials might be short-staffed or not quite in the mood to take their duties too seriously. Nevertheless, I could not stand the thought that, just when everything seemed within my grasp, I might be caught. I decided that next morning I would go to the booking office in Yan'an Road and see if I could get a ticket for myself, leaving a bit earlier on another airline – CAAC or Qantas.

I arrived at the booking office about nine o'clock that morning. I was told that there were seats on a Qantas flight to Melbourne on 9 February, but departing from Beijing. That was even better. Not only a different flight and time, but a different airport. But to buy a ticket I needed 2922 yuan in foreign exchange certificates. I had about $A4000 in my pocket – saved from the allowance I had received from the Victorian Government, and which I was supposed to turn over to Jiangsu Province. I rushed down to the Bank of China in Huaihai Road.

The bank was choked with people. The front rank was draped over every counter, frantically waving money at impassive tellers, who did not remain at the counter but wandered about, occasionally being prevailed upon to offer some service. I pushed and shoved my way through the rear ranks and yelled out to one young man, who finally poked a numbered metal plate in my direction. I took the plate out of a big bulldog clip, marked with the same number and replaced it with an envelope containing my money. Ten minutes later my number was called out.

'Number 501! Number 501!'

'Yes, here I am. 501.'

'Letter of approval please.' I handed my passport to him, over the heads of the other supplicants.

'This is not what I asked you for. You've given me your passport—'

'All right, I know, I'm just getting it for you.'

I plunged my hand inside my jacket in search of the non-existent letter.

'What I really need to know is, where did you get this Australian currency? Oh I see, that's why you've given me your passport. You've just come back from Australia. All right, no problems. You've got a letter there somewhere?'

'Oh, yes. I have everything. Even a customs declaration, to prove that I brought this money with me when I returned from Australia.'

'All right, that'll do. Just wait a minute.'

Another ten minutes later the same voice called out.

'501! 501!'

'Yes. Over here.'

'How much did you give me?'

'1500 Australian dollars.'

'Here you are.' He handed me a wad of foreign exchange certificates. I pushed my way back out through the crowd and counted it. There was about 700 yuan! I struggled desperately back to the counter.

'Excuse me, excuse me!' I screeched.

'What's the problem?'

'I gave you 1500 Australian dollars! The exchange rate is 2.25. You only gave me about 700 yuan!'

'So what's wrong? The exchange rate is 2.25 as you say. And I gave you 666 yuan and 67 fen in foreign exchange certificates for 1500 Australian dollars.'

'But no, it's the other way round! It should be more than double – you *multiply*, not divide!'

By now the other customers had forgotten about their own transactions and were paying a great deal of attention to this exchange.

'Oh, really? I see. OK, give me back the money. Take another number, and wait a minute.'

Five minutes later he came back with a much healthier-looking wad. I flipped through it very quickly, and fought my way back out into the street.

I jumped on my bike, and rode back to the CAAC booking office. My one remaining worry was this letter-of-approval business. Everyone kept asking for it. The best way to deal with it might simply be to say that someone had hung on to it, somewhere along the way. But there was no guarantee that this excuse would work. If I struck a particularly officious type, it would get me nowhere. When I got to the booking office I went straight to the international section. There were very few people about. I had a quick look at the staff, trying to size up personalities and decide who was likely to give me a hard time. Finally I decided on a young man who looked rather easygoing.

'Excuse me, Comrade. I was here a couple of hours ago, to get a ticket from Beijing to Melbourne on Qantas. I was told there were seats available, but I had to go to the bank for some foreign exchange certificates.'

'Where are you going?'

'Melbourne.'

'Where's that?'

'Melbourne, Australia.'

'Visa?'

'Yes, here it is.'

'Which flight do you want?'

'Qantas. Beijing to Melbourne on the 9th.'

He tapped away on his computer keyboard for some time. Everything seemed to be going very smoothly. Suddenly a loud northern voice broke the silence as a woman in her sixties asked, 'Excuse me, Comrade, where can I get a ticket to the United States, and how much is it?'

'What is the purpose of your trip?'

'Oh, just to have a look around, you know? Don't worry, I've got the money all right.'

'But that's not the point! It's not just a matter of money. You have to have the right sort of money – foreign exchange certificates. See here? Like this.' He pointed to my Chinese foreign exchange certificates on the counter.

'What? Oh, so that's what they call Hong Kong dollars, is it? Well, where do I get them?'

I was anxious to get my own business concluded, and the longer she held things up the more likelihood there was of something going wrong. Besides, it was becoming obvious that she did not take too kindly to this young man's offhand manner, and there was going to be a fuss. So I tried to reassure her.

'Auntie, don't worry. He's very busy at the moment. Look, just wait a minute until I get through here, and I'll explain it all to you. I've had a bit of experience with this sort of thing.'

'Hah! What's it to me? It's no big deal is it, this travelling business? I can go any time if I want to. What's he getting so hoity-toity about? What kind of attitude is that? Serve the people they say! Serve the people, my arse! And all on account of a few lousy Hong Kong dollars!'

'Blast!' said the attendant. 'Now look what you've made me do. You're just making a nuisance of yourself. Do you think I have nothing better to do with my time than coach you in the travel business? Money isn't everything, you know. Just because you've made a few bucks doesn't mean you know everything all of sudden. Look, you see here? A passport. I don't suppose you've ever even seen one of these before, have you?'

He dangled my precious passport before her, like a red rag to a bull.

'Don't give me "passport" you stuck-up little fart! I'll show you what to do with your bloody passport. I'll tear it to shreds, then I'll throw it in the—'

'No, no, good old Auntie, no!' I yelled, grabbing the passport. 'That's mine. I haven't done anything, have I? I want to help you.'

'Shithead!' she yelled at the young man.

By now the duty supervisor had appeared.

'All right, all right! Shhh!' he said, motioning to the desk attendant to calm down. 'Just take a break will you, Xiao Wang? I'll look after this. Now what can I do for you, Auntie?'

'Nothing! I don't want to go to the United States anyway! Even if you offered to carry me there in a sedan chair, I wouldn't want to go!'

The old woman stomped out of the booking office,

leaving me still only half-processed, and extremely worried that I would now get some really thorough type to contend with.

'I'm sorry, Comrade. Where were we?'

'Well, the young chap was just trying to confirm my flight for me.'

'OK. Right. That's it on the screen now, is it? Fang, Beijing to Melbourne, QF 172, 9th February. You haven't paid yet, have you?'

'No, I was just about to.'

'Right. 2922 yuan in foreign exchange certificates. Thank you.' He handed me my ticket, and told me I could use it to book my flight to Beijing at the domestic section of the office. But I decided to go by train. That way I would minimise the number of times my name appeared on some computer list – train tickets do not have passengers' names on them. I went a little farther down Yan'an Road to the railway booking office and reserved myself a ticket for No. 14 on 8 February – with a berth this time.

About one o'clock in the afternoon of 9 February I arrived at Beijing airport. The train had been reasonably comfortable, and I hadn't had much trouble getting a taxi to the airport. I only had one suitcase and a small travelling bag, neither of which were full. I had originally thought I might include with my luggage some recent newspapers containing various articles about the anti-bourgeois liberalism campaign. But although such things might have been of use to me once I was out of China, they might themselves lead to my detention, so I decided against it. The plane was due to leave at 4.45 pm, and I still had some hours before I could even check in. I stood on the balcony above the departure gates and watched the people milling about below. I wanted to be able to see what was going on without myself being observed. On the other side, I could look out across the runway, and there, sitting on the tarmac was a great white plane, the tail all red except for an elegant white kangaroo.

I wandered from one side of the floor to the other for a couple of hours. When I noticed that the crowd had suddenly dispersed below, I decided to go down myself and check in. I filled in the customs declaration – a camera, some Australian currency, a 24-carat gold necklace and ring. I handed the declaration to a very sloppy-looking young official. He yawned repeatedly as he went through the motions. He told me take the camera and jewellery out of my bag, and empty my pockets, but then made quite a point of not even watching as I did so. He simply told me to put everything back, and listlessly waved me on. I joined a queue to check in my luggage. There were two queues, one to Melbourne and one to Sydney, but the Melbourne queue was much shorter. My ticket was checked, my passport was checked, my luggage was taken, and then I was asked, 'Smoking or non-smoking?' Another step forward. I joined another queue. Security check. Chinese police.

The woman in front was in difficulty about something to do with a departure card. Did I have a departure card? In fact, I realised I did not, that I had left behind some sort of white card with green print that others were holding. I felt sick at the thought that this would be my undoing, after coming so far. After some time the policeman told her that she could fill out another one. When my turn came I told the officer that I had been given such a card in December last year when I arrived back from Australia, but I didn't know where it was now, 'I should have kept it of course, but—' He told me to fill in another one, and hurry up.

My hands were shaking. I went on to a policewoman sitting at a counter checking passports. I handed her mine, and my ticket, boarding pass and departure card. She put everything else aside and took up the passport.

I tried not to think or feel anything. She looked at my

photo, then at me, then back at the photo, then at me again, and then held the passport up to the light to check the seals. Her expression was grim. Then she placed the passport down on the counter, picked up a stamp and banged it down heavily three times – on the passport, departure card and boarding pass. The departure card went into a box. Someday soon they would be looking through that box, to find this trace of me, but by then I would be gone.

I collected the other documents, and walked as casually as I could manage over to the duty-free shops. Technically, I had crossed the frontier. I was out of China.

I wanted to cry. The day before I had seen my parents, perhaps for the last time. I visited my mother in hospital. Dad looked very old, his hair completely silver. There wasn't much to talk about. Mum said I must be sure to write often after I returned to Nanjing. I couldn't tell them that I might never see them again, but I knew they would still support my decision, even at this terrible cost.

An assistant broke in on my thoughts to ask me if I wanted to buy anything. I took all the Chinese foreign exchange certificates out of my pockets and put them on the counter. A cloisonné vase, a mahogany chopstick holder. I looked at my watch. There was still three-quarters of an hour to go. I was beginning to feel safe. But I could not afford to be seen by any Chinese Embassy or Consulate officials, or for that matter by any Australian friends who might innocently pass on that they had seen me. I went and sat in the departure lounge for Karachi, from which I had a good view of the Sydney/Melbourne lounge, through the windows. When almost everyone had passed through into the boarding tunnel I went over and gave the Qantas attendant my boarding pass, and made my way onto the aircraft.

Everyone was fumbling with luggage. I sat down as quickly as I could in my place, 37B. 37A, a window-seat, was occupied by a young Chinese woman, in her twenties.

37C, on the aisle, was empty. I kept looking at my watch. Eight minutes to go. The young woman told me excitedly that she was going to Australia to marry. I began to relax, and think of the drink I might order in a while. Then there was a loudspeaker announcement.

'Ladies and gentlemen, please be seated. There will be a security check. Please have your documentation ready for inspection.'

Two Chinese police started moving down the aisles, obviously only stopping to ask questions of Chinese passengers. My head was in turmoil. I was thinking of what I would say. I could yell out, 'I demand asylum, this is no longer Chinese territory. I demand the intervention of the Captain. I have explosives—'

'What's wrong? You look terrible. Can I get you something?' said a voice from the window seat.

'Oh, no, sorry – I was just thinking of my mother, you know, so close to leaving, it's a very emotional thing—'

'Yes, of course I understand. My own mother has not been well these last few years, and I don't know when I'll see her again.'

'Yes, that's right. Er, do you speak English?'

'Well, I'm learning. In fact I'm enrolled in English classes in Australia. I can speak a little, and write a little, but I just don't understand when people speak to me. They talk too fast—'

The police were now checking the row in front. I babbled on about methods of studying a foreign language. The young woman asked if I would mind getting her little red bag down for her. I stood up to get it, as well as my own, but one of the police motioned to me to remain seated.

'I was just going to get our things—'

'Are you together?'

I looked straight into my companion's eyes and said, 'Mmm.'

She didn't react.

'OK. Don't bother.'

When they passed I mumbled, 'Thank you.'

'Forget it', she said.

At 4.45 pm the aircraft began to taxi, and in the engine's vibration I fancied I could hear the droning chorus of boatmen heaving along the Grand Canal.

Epilogue

I remember some lines from a poem of Yue Fei:

> *All last night the autumn crickets kept up their beat*
> *I woke, alarmed . . .*
> *I too want to hurl my heart into a song,*
> *But few understand my music,*
> *And even if I played my lute till the strings snapped,*
> *Who would listen?*

During the last few years I have often woken in the early hours of the morning, and paced up and down, outside our bungalow in the back garden at Jean and Ted's place, wondering who would listen, if I sang my song. These years have been full of fear, tragedy and despair. There have been happy times too, and triumphs, but in the shadows of each crisis I have always returned to the thought, 'When will it all end? Injustice is ancient and modern; it is Eastern and Western.'

Yue Fei was persecuted a thousand years ago, and put to death on the word of a man who wanted him destroyed. His accuser, when asked what evidence he had to support his allegations, replied in three words that have become infamous in Chinese history: '*Mo xu you*' [There is no need]. And yet, how many times has it happened since, over and over again, that the accuser himself has been the evidence? Has some kind of family curse followed me to Australia, to settle on my life and those who are close to me? There was a time when the words, 'no need for evidence', drummed in my ears all night and deafened my hopes.

Yue Fei was posthumously rehabilitated, twenty-two years after his death. His temple and tomb have stood on the shore of the West Lake, Hangzhou, since the twelfth century. There is an archway, inscribed with the words, 'Blood of jade, heart of cinnabar', and beyond a courtyard there is a hall containing the statues of General Yue Fei and two loyal comrades, who, some say, were executed with him. West of the courtyard is his tomb. In front of the tomb are four cast-iron statues of the traitors who accused, arrested, tortured and executed him. They are kneeling, their hands bound behind their backs. Traditionally, visitors to the tomb used to spit on these statues, and throw stones at them. Around the tomb is a marble balustrade, and some cypresses, twisting in an ancient anguish. On two pillars are inscribed the words: 'Since ancient times the upright and the debased have contended like fire and ice. But innocence and guilt must await the verdict of posterity.'

As long as innocent young people who peacefully express their ideals and aspirations are killed, or tortured, or imprisoned, there will be more statues. We have seen the demise of the Goddess of Liberty for the time being, but perhaps one day there will be more figures of iron kneeling before the people and being spat upon. In the meantime they continue to accuse the innocent. And they have no need of evidence. But now I am in Australia, and Australia is a modern democracy. Or perhaps I have been trying to defect to a place that is more in the mind than on the map.

Since 10 February 1987 the strange event which brought me here has grown into a complex saga, and I have answered my summons. My wife and I became permanent residents in Australia in January 1990, after three years of struggle. But there is much more to it than that. The following pages will tell how it all turned out – but the tale can end here, or begin here, as the reader pleases.

The aircraft landed in Sydney, but I kept telling myself not to get too excited. I was not yet officially 'in' Australia, and would not be until after airport formalities in Melbourne. I stayed close to the young woman during these few hours. There were people who might recognise me, and might approach me if I were on my own. Finally, we boarded again, and landed in Melbourne about an hour later. I went through customs without incident, but I was startled to see a battery of news media representatives and their cameras out in the arrivals area. Flashbulbs were popping, video cameras stalked our exit, and there were several people with huge bouquets of flowers, calling out at the tops of their voices. It quickly became apparent that it was my companion, and not I, who was the object of their attention, and that the 'media' were gathering home-movie material for an excited bridegroom, not for some sensational news of a defection.

For the first few days I felt a combination of exhilaration and panic. I went straight from the airport to Jean and Ted's place. By now Bi Lijun understood the situation completely, and we immediately began planning our next move. We calculated that, from the point of view of Chinese authorities, a defection to Taiwan would be the worst possible outcome of the whole affair. For that reason, they might well be very cautious in their approaches to the Australian Government, to avoid forcing our hand. On the other hand, the best possible outcome for the Chinese side would be for us to remain in Australia and to go into hiding – that way we would be silent, and in time we might be tracked down and repatriated to China as 'illegals'. We resolved to go to Taiwan. We were not safe as 'illegals' anywhere, but least of all in a country which China regarded as 'friendly'.

In my moments of self-indulgence, while Bi Lijun was rushing about arranging transit visas to Hong Kong, booking tickets to Taipei and contacting her uncles in the Republic of China, I conjured up visions of the investigator in Nanjing, the President of the University, and Lao Zhu, pacing their respective corridors of power, puffing on their cigarettes and blaming each other for this 'incident'. Then the scene would shift to the Chinese Embassy in Canberra and even to bureaucratic lairs I had never seen, in Beijing. I realised with some satisfaction that I could predict their moves more accurately than they could predict mine. And I knew that the situation regarding Trevor's case would confuse and disorient them. The charges had been changed and made more serious, and Trevor now had to appear in court on 25 June, rather than on 23 February. The whole business was going to take much longer and be much more complicated – and expensive.

With this in mind, I was not surprised when Trevor received a telephone call from the Chinese Consul-General on 20 February, asking if it was 'still necessary' for me to make an appearance in court. Trevor refused to discuss the matter with the Consul-General, but I was quite sure they were now very worried that my stay in Australia might be at least temporarily legal, and that there might be further extensions. In fact, I did not need any further delay beyond June in order to make my arrangements. I had discussed the whole thing with Trevor and Jenny, and they said that this was a matter of life and death for me and Bi Lijun, and that our arrangements must take precedence over an appearance in court.

Three days later, my dreams of being a much-sought-after propaganda tool for the Taiwanese Nationalists were dispelled by a telephone call from one of Bi Lijun's uncles. Taiwan didn't want me. And the uncle himself was trying desperately to emigrate to the United States. 'Try to stay where you are. Australia is a democratic country. Perhaps you can get help from some humanitarian agency, you know, like the Red Cross or the Salvation Army.'

We were beginning to panic, but after discussion with the Hays and with Jean and Ted we decided to approach Amnesty International. Amnesty told us we 'had a case'. I was alarmed by this at first, and thought I was going to be prosecuted, like Trevor. Then I realised this meant we had a chance of persuading immigration officials to let us stay. We were advised to go and see the Legal Aid Commission immediately for advice.

We made an appointment, and two days later turned up at the Commission to see an immigration lawyer. He seemed very official, and a bit forbidding at first. But we had an hour's free consultation, and then the time stretched into two, and he didn't seem to mind. He told us that we could lodge an application for permanent residence on humanitarian grounds, and that once we had lodged our application we would be 'in the system' and no one could touch us. I will never forget my feelings at that moment. I could feel the tears welling in my eyes. He also told us that an immigration case could go on for a very long time with appeals and so on – sometimes for many years. Perhaps he knew, as we did not, that there would come a time when the pressures of waiting would seem unendurable, but at that moment all that 'several years' meant to us was sanctuary.

I had some savings in Australia from my exchange teaching years, and Bi Lijun was very thrifty, so we managed to survive, with the help of friends. In order to keep the lowest possible profile, we did not apply for a work permit. But we never changed our address in Mt Waverley. The Chinese authorities, including the Embassy itself, all knew the address and telephone number, but it was obvious that they thought we had gone into hiding somewhere. I heard on the grapevine that they were trying to find us through contacts in Melbourne. It was all rather like the classical tale from the Three Kingdoms, in which a famous strategist had confused invaders by throwing open the gates of his city.

His enemies could not believe that the city was theirs for the taking, and went away empty-handed.

In May we had an interview with the Immigration Department, regarding our application. The interview left me deeply troubled, but I could not really say why. I was fearful of interference from Victorian education authorities. I started reading *The Law Handbook* of the Fitzroy Legal Service. There was a section about authorities exceeding their powers, and I began to wonder what we could do to protect ourselves, if someone was manipulating things behind the scenes. I was also trying to figure out what was going on in Trevor's case, which seemed to have taken a strange turn, since the charges had been changed. My brother, Yang Xiaoping, often rang me from America. As a law student himself, he was able to help me to understand legal issues.

Everything was quiet for some time after the interview – for us at least. Trevor's case was postponed again. The police were not ready in June, and the committal finally took place toward the end of September. As I understood it, this was just a hearing to determine if there was enough evidence to justify a trial. I was not required at this stage, and I did not attend, but, from what I heard, the only evidence against Trevor was what the police themselves said. He had made a complaint of assault against them, and they had charged him with assaulting police. There were no independent witnesses. The hearing seemed to go very well for Trevor, as far as evidence is concerned, and his barrister cross-examined the police over statements they had made to their Internal Investigations Department, which was investigating the complaint. There had been a battle between the barrister and the magistrate over obtaining these documents, but finally they were produced, and the police were questioned about apparent inconsistencies between these and other statements they had made. But then, after three days, the magistrate said that the evidence against the defendant was 'quite clear'. He said that any inconsistencies in the police account indicated that they had not collaborated. Trevor was committed for trial in the County Court on a charge of 'recklessly causing serious injury' for allegedly kneeing a policeman in the knee and dislocating it.

My brother rang me again in October. This time we talked about Freedom of Information legislation, and the possibility of getting documents related to our application. Perhaps we could get proof that the Chinese side had put pressure on the Australian side to send us back. He advised me that I would need to throw a very long line if I wanted to catch such a big fish. I began to raise the issue with my solicitor, and in March 1988, just a little more than a year after I had returned to Australia, he made a request to the Immigration Department for all documents obtained by the Commonwealth Government in relation to our application. There was no response to the F.O.I. request, so my solicitor repeated it in April, and again in May.

On 30 May the Immigration Department sent me a letter rejecting our application for permanent residence. The Department's decision was based on an assessment by Foreign Affairs that, while my account of events in China was 'generally credible', I had exaggerated the dangers to myself and my wife. The Foreign Affairs assessment also emphasised that the demonstrations in China during late 1986 and early 1987 had led to the arrest of a relatively small number of people, and that, in any case, I had not been directly involved. According to Foreign Affairs, the disciplinary action likely to be taken against me would be the restriction of opportunities for further overseas study. The letter stated that Bi Lijun and I were now 'prohibited non-citizens'. I had been a 'non-citizen' for most of my life in my home country, and now my political pedigree had followed me to Australia and had been recorded on a new file in a language that had always been the language of hope.

I geared myself up for another struggle. We lodged an appeal with the Immigration Review Panel, requested a statement of reasons for rejection and repeated the Freedom of Information request. I went to see Amnesty International again, and they referred me to the Refugee Casework and Advisory Committee of the Jesuits. The Refugee Casework people helped me to obtain an expert assessment of the political situation in China, to counter the views of the Department of Foreign Affairs and Trade. I also visited some federal members of parliament. At least I was free to swim, even if the tide was against me.

On 8 August 1988, which according to Chinese belief is supposed to be the luckiest day of the century, we received word that Bi Lijun's father had died twenty days earlier. He had been ill for some time, but this came as a terrible shock. Bi Lijun sobbed and choked, while I could only stand helplessly at her side. That she had lost her father was one thing, but that she could not express her grief or mourn as a daughter should – that was unbearable. Late that night we stood out in the back garden by Ted's incinerator, and burned incense and paper money. It was raining quite heavily, but the smoke curled upwards into the darkness as Bi Lijun cried out to her father to forgive her.

This was the worst time. We had almost given up hope, but we got through each day by promising each other that we would win, that things would take a dramatic turn for the better soon. I told her that the Chinese authorities would also lose interest with each passing day, that they would become suspicious that Australian officials had no intention of sending us back, and were just playing games. I was not just comforting Bi Lijun, I really thought that, given time, I could get some proof that Chinese officials were out to make an example of us, and I could challenge the Foreign Affairs' assessment that my fears were exaggerated.

By early January 1989 I still had not received the documents I had requested. My solicitors protested to the Immigration Department, and gave notice of their intention to go to the Administrative Appeals Tribunal to get them. On 10 February, on the second anniversary of my flight from China, the Department released the documents. I devoured them, and found that they greatly exceeded my expectations. Not only did they provide me with the evidence I required, but they revealed the process of assessment and decision-making. Freedom of information! This was truly the language of hope.

The documents revealed that just a few days after I had lodged the application for permanent residence, Liu Aihua, my 'big sister', met privately with Len Jenkins, a Victorian Ministry of Education official. Liu told him of rumours that I had applied for asylum in Australia on the basis that I had no accommodation and no job in China. She also told him that I was thought to be in Sydney. She told him of the Jiangsu Government's concern at my behaviour, 'especially in view of the good relations between the Jiangsu Government and the Victorian Government'. Jenkins told Liu that the Victorian Government shared the Chinese embarrassment and that he would advise Australian authorities of the situation. He later telephoned the Melbourne office of the Department of Foreign Affairs and Trade to report Victoria's displeasure. A Foreign Affairs official told Jenkins that he would inform 'Sydney'.

The documents revealed communication between the Foreign Affairs Office of Jiangsu Province and the Victorian Department of the Premier and Cabinet. Most importantly, they revealed that on 4 August 1987 Ni Chuanrong, Cultural Attaché in the Chinese Embassy, Canberra, met with Jenkins over lunch in Melbourne. Liu also attended, as interpreter. She was described in a subsequent letter from Jenkins to the Department of Foreign Affairs as 'very well

257

connected in Beijing as well as Nanjing'. Ni Chuanrong suggested to Jenkins that I was attempting either to secure permanent residence in Australia, or to seek political asylum, with the possible encouragement of a Melbourne academic. He repeated that the Chinese would be very embarrassed if such an application had indeed been made, and Jenkins again assured him that the Victorian Government would 'share that embarrassment'.

As I pored over the documents I was stunned to see what Jenkins had written to Foreign Affairs:

Mr Fang can hardly claim to be maltreated in his own country and certainly not to an extent which would justify risking the good relations between Governments in China and in Victoria and Australia by allowing a Lecturer in a *Teachers College* to defect.

He also wrote: 'My Minister is aware that I am reporting these details to you.' How could he so blatantly involve himself? The Secretary to the Department of the Premier and Cabinet had said, in a letter to the Immigration Department, 'I have now informed the Jiangsu Government that immigration is a federal matter and that the State has no jurisdiction over it.' And yet here was an education bureaucrat dealing directly with Foreign Affairs over an immigration matter.

As I recovered from the initial impact of discovery, I began to be fascinated by the picture that emerged from the documents. There had been a discussion among Immigration Department officials as to whether the Chinese attempts to track me down constituted evidence of impending persecution, whether I should be given the 'benefit of the doubt', etc. But all of that melted under the glare of opposition from Foreign Affairs, who had written to the Immigration Department:

We are strongly of the view that Fang's application should be refused. We would be grateful, therefore, for reasonable forewarning of any intention to grant Fang's application, so that we can brief our Minister to make our views known to Mr Young [then Federal Minister for Immigration].

By now my solicitors had the scent of blood. They encouraged me, and gave me unlimited access to their time. I spent hour after hectic hour in consultation, not only with two solicitors but with a retired Federal Court judge, who almost snarled with indignation as he pored over the documents. After some weeks of preparation, they submitted twenty-eight pages of additional materials to the Immigration Review Panel. I was thrilled by the spirit and daring of their attack on Foreign Affairs and the Victorian Ministry of Education. I felt like one of those revolutionary heroes in a Cultural Revolution poster, brandishing, not Mao's 'Little Red Book', but the Fitzroy Legal Service's *Law Handbook*.

On 8 March 1989 I appeared in the County Court, Melbourne, to give evidence about my photographs of Trevor's injuries. When I was waiting in the corridor outside the courtrooms, I noticed a number of police sitting around, yawning and stretching. There were some people, like me, in a suit and tie, who looked uncomfortable and nervous. From time to time a barrister came out of the lift, wearing the costume I had so often seen in the movies. Suddenly I heard my name called – not exactly my name, but something I was sure was meant to be it.

I gave my evidence, but to my relief, and disappointment, I was not cross-examined. The judge said to me, very slowly, 'They don't seem to be interested in asking you any more questions. You may step down.'

Now that I had given evidence I was allowed to sit in

the courtroom and listen to the proceedings. It took me some time to calm down so that I could concentrate. I looked around. The judge was sitting behind a great desk on a stage. He was wearing a wig, but his was different from those worn by the barristers. His was made up of tight, fine little curls, while the barristers had rough and grubby ones, like an old ram. I could see that several people in the jury box were tired and bored. One young woman in a yellow dress was whispering to another, who was trying not to laugh. It was already the eighth day. I never dreamed that a case like this could go on for such a long time.

Next day the prosecutor began his summing-up. It took him a day and a half, during which he emphasised that credibility was the key issue in the case, and that a belief in the defendant's story required the jury to accept that several police would perjure themselves and collaborate in a conspiracy. He droned on and on from the transcript, rocking monotonously from one foot to the other, and stressing the difference between the defendant's account and that of the police. The defence barrister started his summing-up late on the afternoon of Friday, 10 March. He did not make much progress. I heard him tell Trevor's wife, Jenny, before he began, that Friday afternoon was no time to be making points with a jury – especially on the eve of a long weekend, after a week of intense heat. Nevertheless, at the close of proceedings on that Friday afternoon, I was confident that Trevor would be acquitted. I had not noticed any 'proof' – just the word of the police officers versus the word of the defendant. The injured knee could have been the result of the incident as Trevor described it, or as the police described it. Even the orthopaedic surgeon who had examined the knee, and been called as a witness by the police, conceded that the injury could have been caused by a twisting motion. And the 'Crown' had to prove guilt 'beyond reasonable doubt'. But a number of things worried me. The prosecution had presented several variations on the same charge: 'intentionally' or 'recklessly' causing 'serious injury' or 'injury'. Would a jury just opt for a compromise and convict on the less serious charge of recklessness? Would they understand that even 'recklessness', as defined by this court, required the defendant to be aware that an injury would probably occur as a result of his action? Or would they just interpret it as I once would have, as 'not being careful'? Most of all I was worried about the long weekend. Perhaps it was just my superstitious Chinese nature, but I felt very uncomfortable and anxious. The longer the delay, the more chance of some change in the elements surrounding this affair.

The following Tuesday morning the prosecutor moved to dismiss the jury on the grounds that Trevor's barrister had 'led evidence' – because during his summing-up he had commented on some aspect of the medical evidence which had not been dealt with during cross-examination. That came as a terrible shock to Trevor's friends and relatives sitting there in the courtroom. Not only had things gone very well, as far as the defence was concerned, but it was impossible to consider the stress and expense of another trial. This affair had already cost the accused $37 000 since the charges were first laid. The judge ruled against dismissal of the jury, after some considerable time, and much argument. Then he summed up for the jury.

He seemed very tentative, and his comments meandered along legal paths that I could not follow at all. To compensate, I listened to the tone of his voice as carefully as I could, and watched all his gestures and mannerisms and expressions, for clues. The way he pitched his voice worried me. It seemed to me that the points which should have counted strongly in the defendant's favour just got lost. Perhaps the prosecutor had landed a telling blow with his attempt to dismiss the jury, and the judge was treading extremely carefully. Or perhaps it was just my state of mind,

261

and the things I believed in seemed less prominent than they should have been.

After that, the jury went out to consider their verdict. The judge refused bail, and Trevor was taken into custody in the County Court cells. In spite of the judge, I was still very optimistic. Apart from my own feelings about the evidence, someone overheard the prosecutor saying that he believed the jury would acquit. Late in the afternoon the jury were recalled to see whether they were likely to reach a verdict soon. The foreman of the jury said they definitely were not. The accused was taken in handcuffs to Pentridge Remand for the night. Jenny was near collapse when she found out.

The jury stayed out all through the following morning. In the afternoon they requested that part of the transcript of the evidence be read to them again. They wanted only the part relating to the incident in the police station, in which one of the police claimed that the accused had kneed him in the corner of the right knee. The accused's evidence was that, while handcuffed, he had been punched in the stomach, had fallen face-first to the ground, had been kicked in the ribs by someone he could not see, and that someone had fallen on top of him. His evidence was that he did not know how the officer's kneecap came to be dislocated. The jury listened very attentively to the transcript, and some took notes. After the jury went out again, Trevor was granted bail on medical grounds. He had been ill for some hours in the cells below the courtroom.

Late in the afternoon the jury reassembled. There were four versions of the charge: 'intentionally causing serious injury', 'intentionally causing injury', 'recklessly causing serious injury', and 'recklessly causing injury'. The clerk of the court read each of the charges out aloud, in that order. The foreman of the jury replied 'Not guilty' to the first two. On the third charge the verdict was 'Guilty'. I heard a loud

262

noise from the dock, but when I looked behind me Trevor was standing still and silent.

Next morning the defence barrister called character witnesses to speak for the convicted man before the judge passed sentence. He told Jenny that he hoped this would keep his client out of jail. After listening to these witnesses, the judge said that, while the defendant's conduct was completely out of character, his story of assault was 'unbelievable'. He said that the case was a 'tragedy', a matter that should have been heard two years earlier in the Magistrates' Court. He seemed to think that Trevor had chosen to have the case heard in the County Court. He said something that I did not understand at the time, and I had to ask about it afterwards – 'A man who defends himself has a fool for a client.' He fined Trevor $2000. Everyone said it could have been much worse.

In June Bi Lijun and I watched the horror of the Beijing massacre on television in our bungalow. Deng Xiaoping had finally shown his bloody hand. Perhaps now foreigners would understand what it was like to be a Chinese, and not a tourist. I attended a memorial service at the Melbourne Town Hall. That night on television I saw the Australian Prime Minister grieving with a young Chinese woman, and marvelled at the fact that, while a foreign leader could shed tears for murdered youth, the Chinese leaders had only hatred and violence in their hearts.

Early in the morning of 22 September 1989 I received a phone call from America from a friend of my brother. He was ringing for my sister-in-law, who was unable to speak, to tell me that Yang Xiaoping had collapsed in his office in New York. His blood pressure was extremely high. He had been under a lot of stress: he had just finished his Doctor of Laws degree at Columbia University, taken his bar exams and started a practice – and he was soon to be a father. My sister-in-law, Chen Dandan, had been with him in New York since 1987. On 24 September I received another phone call. He was dead, aged thirty-seven. I could not say a word. I could not cry then, and I have not cried since. I still cannot accept that he is really gone. None of my family in China were able to attend his funeral, and my sister-in-law was in desperate need of help and comfort. Bi Lijun and I applied to the Immigration Department for a temporary permit to go to America. The application was immediately approved.

We flew to New York, and attended a memorial service at St Paul's Chapel, Columbia University, on 20 October. Many people spoke of their memories of Yang Xiaoping, as a student and friend and colleague. When it was my turn to speak, I recalled a movie that my brother and I had seen together in Shanghai after the Cultural Revolution. It was the first English movie we had seen, about an Englishwoman who fell in love with a French pilot during the Second World War. They married, and she became pregnant. In one scene, towards the end of his leave, as they are lying together in a meadow, he recites a poem of farewell to her. Yang Xiaoping and I struggled to help each other understand it. Perhaps we never did get it quite right, but I remember that he loved it. For his memorial service I recited it once more for him:

> *The life that I have is all that I have,*
> *The life that I have is yours,*
> *The love that I have of the life that I have*
> *Is yours, and yours, and yours.*
>
> *The sleep I shall have, the rest I shall have,*
> *Yet death will be but a pause,*
> *For the peace of my years in the long green grass*
> *Will be yours, and yours, and yours.*

Before we left, Chen Dandan gave birth to a daughter, and she asked me to choose a name for the child. I named her Helen, after Helen Keller, whom my brother had always admired.

My sister, Yang Xinhan, was given three months' leave to see Chen Dandan and Helen. We were together, perhaps for the last time – a bittersweet reunion.

Bi Lijun and I returned to Melbourne at the end of November, to find that Trevor's case had become a 'cause célèbre,' as *Time Australia* put it. There had been headlines in the *Age*, and an editorial. A journalist, Margaret Simons, had written a series of articles on the way the Internal Investigations Department handled complaints against police. In Trevor's case, the police officer investigating his complaint had been assigned to gather evidence for the prosecution. Then there were articles about how this case ended up in the County Court rather than the Magistrates' Court. Through Freedom of Information legislation, documents were obtained that contradicted police evidence about how the charges were changed. Shortly after the stories began, police served notice on Trevor that they intended to proceed with further charges arising from the night of 25 July 1986.

Late in December the Immigration Department informed me that it had not been possible for the Review Panel to reach a decision before the passing of the Migration Amendment Legislation Act 1989. As a result, the review of my case would not be continued. The whole case was to be considered afresh under new legislation. I was now certain that all our progress, all our 'freedom of information', had been a waste of time. The bureaucrats had just found a new way of dealing with us. The most we had gained was time. I was desperate, and I think I must have been on the verge of madness. I thought seriously of going on a hunger strike. Bi Lijun was at her wit's end. We were both too exhausted to argue, or plan, or hope, for much longer.

In January I went to see Peter Milton, the Federal Member for La Trobe. He wrote to the Immigration Minister, Senator Robert Ray, advising him of his concern at the apparent interference of the Victorian Ministry of Education and the Department of Foreign Affairs and Trade. On 26 January 1990 I was at the Hays' place. I heard the phone ring, and shortly afterwards Trevor came to tell me that my solicitor wanted to speak to me.

My solicitor said, 'The decision has been made to grant permanent residence to you and your wife. Welcome to Australia!' That day was Australia Day. In the evening we went out to a Lebanese restaurant with Jean, Ted, Trevor and Jenny. We must have seemed very happy because the waiter asked if we were celebrating a special occasion.

In March Trevor appeared in court again. There was a further hearing, of six days, this time in the Magistrates' Court. At the conclusion, the magistrate said he was not at all impressed with the defendant as a witness, but he was impressed by the candour of the police. He said that the defendant had exaggerated his injuries in order to run down the police and that his story of assault was unbelievable. I suppose I had allowed myself to believe that the tide had turned since Bi Lijun and I had permanent residence, and I had not prepared myself for the worst, as I had always done in the past. But I had not expected an attack from this direction. I had seen the medical evidence, and had read the doctors' reports, and had read the transcript from the County Court over and over again. Trevor had simply repeated what his doctor had written, using precisely the same words. The magistrate went on. I heard him say, in a strangely low, almost hushed tone, that he was quite satisfied that the defendant was a flagrant liar. My head began to swim, and I felt as I had done in the 1960s, when it was *I* who was being abused and denounced. Trevor was convicted of two further charges of assaulting police and fined again.

I remember that Mao often spoke of the East Wind and the West Wind. He thought the East Wind of China's socialist leadership would prevail in the world. I believed, or hoped, that a gentle Western breeze of human rights would also be felt in China some day. It was perhaps a naive faith in the West Wind that sustained me during desperate times, but, unfortunately for me, too many Westerners appeared to have an even more naive faith in the East Wind. Finally, worldwide television audiences witnessed the Imperial Bodyguard at work in Beijing, and it was not so easy for bureaucrats to pretend that people like myself were exaggerating the terrors of life in China. But soon it was being said that there was no real proof of the massacre, or that it had been greatly exaggerated. Evidence always has its weaknesses it seems, and it is always easy enough for the powerful to question the credibility of this witness, or the motive of that victim, or even the reliability of films and documents. I see now that 'credibility' is not just the power to make people believe, but power itself.

The debased have triumphed over the upright in China. That is the way it has been since June 1989, although the matter of guilt and innocence is as plain as blood in the streets.

As for the West, what have I learnt of democracy and justice? What can I say to those who are still dreaming in China, as I once did? I still believe the differences between China and the West are reality, not just dreams. But my nights are still troubled. Not so long ago I had a nightmare, in which Red Guards paraded me through the streets of Shanghai, wearing a huge wooden collar like criminals wore in feudal times. I was kicked to my knees in front of a screaming mob, and made to confess my crimes. But my crimes were confessed in English, and I had to bawl out that

I was a 'prohibited non-citizen' and a 'flagrant liar'. So what can I say to those brave and idealistic compatriots who look to the 'Blue Ocean' to liberate them from the 'Yellow River'? I still share their vision, but I know that both the East Wind and the West Wind can tear savagely at the truth and make it seem the flimsiest of shelters for those who accuse the State. For me at least the wind has passed, and perhaps now that it is still, my song will be heard.

The Umbrella Tree   Rose Zwi

16 June 1976, Soweto – the date and place that gave a name to an era.

On that morning 20,000 schoolchildren marched in peaceful protest against a decree that Afrikaans, regarded by blacks as the language of the oppressor, be used for instruction in black schools. This Revolt of the Children was the spark that set off the conflagration in black townships throughout the country, already seething in discontent over the misery and degradation imposed on their lives by Apartheid.

The Umbrella Tree is the story of both black and white resistance to Apartheid and the point at which they meet, briefly, in the shade of an umbrella tree in a rural 'homeland' in South Africa.

Manly Girls   Elisabeth Wynhausen

Elisabeth Wynhausen was four when her family arrived from Holland intent on fitting in. In this exuberant and engaging memoir, she propels herself from one comic debacle to the next, pausing now and again to marvel over the customs and the cooking of the locals.

Manly Girls catapults through two decades at a time of Australia's most frantic development. By chance, the author and the country emerge from adolescence together.

West Block   Sara Dowse

Sara Dowse has drawn on her life in the public sector to write a novel about the hidden world of Canberra's mandarins, their tensions and relationships in the hot-house world of politics.

Furious Agreement Edited by Michael Dugan

To celebrate the fiftieth year of its founding, the Australian Institute of Management invited forty Australians distinguished in the fields of business, the arts and humanities, politics and the sciences to consider what they saw as the vital issues for our future over the next fifty years. The result is a provocative and stimulating collection of essays notable as much for its differences of opinion as its furious agreement about the need for change.

Stirring the Possum James McClelland

From his days as a young Trotskyist in the 1940s – secretly in love with an enemy Stalinist – to his role in the 1980s as commissioner in an inquiry into the Maralinga nuclear tests, Jim McClelland has been known as a stirrer.

In his autobiography he offers us a perspective on Australian politics that spans 50 years. His critical assessment of public figures and events is both humorous and acerbic; his account of a distinguished and varied career reflects his energy, his sharp mind and his unfailing capacity to 'liven things up'.

Millenium Helen Daniel

Australia is entering a decade which is not only the last of the century but the last of the millennium. Here is a collection of pieces written by 41 leading Australians expressing their thoughts about the future of our society.

High Banks, Heavy Logs Nikom Rayawa

In the clear morning sunlight Kham Ngai urges his elephant down to the river, where he attaches chains to the dragging harness.

Set on the lush, green banks of the Yom River in central Thailand, *High Banks, Heavy Logs* is the lyrical, compelling story of a woodcarver from a community whose traditions are vanishing along with the forests that once surrounded them.

Winner of the South East Asian Writer's Award.

Avenue of Eternal Peace Nicolas Jose

After forty years of communist rule, the ancient civilisation of China, newly exposed to western influences, is in a state of vigorous contradiction. Enter Wally Frith, a leading cancer specialist, who travels from the gritty frozen north to the tranquil lakes and mountains of the south, looking for information.

As he fights through the maze of bureaucracy and subterfuge, Wally falls in with people whose lives reflect the diversity of contemporary Peking: a model, shady traders, a basketballer, students, a dissident artist and a band of eccentric westerners.

Awakenings Pramoedya Ananta Toer
(combining *This Earth of Mankind* and *Child of All Nations*)
Footsteps
House of Glass

These epic novels are banned in his own country, Indonesia, but Pramoedya Ananta Toer's writing reaches far beyond politics, to achieve a vivid historical picture of the richly varied culture of the Dutch East Indies, and a deep understanding of a people's painful emergence from colonial domination. The novels are translated by Max Lane.